BEING IN THE WORLD

*The publication of this volume was made possible
by funds generously provided by the Basilian Fathers
of the University of St. Michael's College.*

BEING
in
THE WORLD

**A QUOTABLE
MARITAIN READER**

MARIO O. D'SOUZA, C.S.B

with

JONATHAN R. SEILING

University of Notre Dame Press
Notre Dame, Indiana

Copyright © 2014 by University of Notre Dame
Notre Dame, Indiana 46556
www.undpress.nd.edu
All Rights Reserved

Manufactured in the United States of America

Library of Congress Cataloging-in-Publication Data

Maritain, Jacques, 1882–1973, author.
[Works. Selections. English]
Being in the world : a quotable Maritain reader /
[edited by] Mario O. D'Souza, C.S.B with Jonathan R. Seiling.
pages   cm
Includes bibliographical references and index.
ISBN 0-268-00899-X (pbk. : alk. paper)
1. Maritain, Jacques, 1882–1973—Quotations.
I. D'Souza, Mario O., 1956– editor.
II. Seiling, Jonathan R., editor.   III. Title.
B2430.M32E5   2014
194—dc23

2014028629

∞ *The paper in this book meets the guidelines for permanence and durability of the Committee on Production Guidelines for Book Longevity of the Council on Library Resources.*

Dedicated to my brother Melvyn:

With love, admiration, and the warmth of memories.

Requiescat in pace

CONTENTS

Acknowledgments ix
List of Abbreviations xiii

Introduction 1
Mario O. D'Souza, C.S.B

ONE	Aristotle	15
TWO	Art and the Artist	18
THREE	Being	32
FOUR	The Christian Life	40
FIVE	Christian Philosophy	49
SIX	The Church	55
SEVEN	Culture and Civilization	61
EIGHT	Democracy and Democratic Society	69
NINE	Descartes and Cartesian Philosophy	73
TEN	Philosophy of Education	81
ELEVEN	Evil	96
TWELVE	Ethics	106
THIRTEEN	Faith	113

FOURTEEN	Freedom	117
FIFTEEN	God	126
SIXTEEN	History	135
SEVENTEEN	Humanism	144
EIGHTEEN	Intellect and Intelligence	147
NINETEEN	Knowing and Knowledge	158
TWENTY	Man	163
TWENTY-ONE	Marx and Marxism	172
TWENTY-TWO	Metaphysics and Metaphysicians	176
TWENTY-THREE	Moral Philosophy	184
TWENTY-FOUR	Mystery and Mysticism	195
TWENTY-FIVE	Natural Law and Human Rights	198
TWENTY-SIX	The Person	203
TWENTY-SEVEN	The Person and the Individual	211
TWENTY-EIGHT	Personality	216
TWENTY-NINE	Philosophers	223
THIRTY	Philosophy	230
THIRTY-ONE	Poetry and the Poet	236
THIRTY-TWO	Politics, Society, and the State	241
THIRTY-THREE	Prayer and Contemplation	252
THIRTY-FOUR	Reason and Reasoning	262
THIRTY-FIVE	Science	266
THIRTY-SIX	Theology and the Theologian	273
THIRTY-SEVEN	St. Thomas and Thomism	279
THIRTY-EIGHT	Truth	286
THIRTY-NINE	Varia	290
FORTY	Wisdom	293

Bibliography of Maritain Sources   298
Index   302

ACKNOWLEDGMENTS

This work began while I was on a sabbatical in 1996–1997, after having served on the General Council of my religious congregation; I was preparing to return to my teaching position at the Faculty of Theology in the University of St. Michael's College. During that sabbatical leave, I reread fifty-five of Maritain's works (including two collections) in English, and I took over sixteen hundred pages of notes, partly because most of his works lack a subject index but mainly because the depth of sophistication of his thought and the variety of its application require detailed notes. I rediscovered the poignancy and beauty of his writings, and in so doing I also identified passages that could easily become part of a quotable Maritain, a collection that might interest many others besides myself. I approached Charles Van Hof at the University of Notre Dame Press, who immediately expressed enthusiasm for this project and encouraged me to pursue it. I wish to thank him for this. The manuscript subsequently moved to the desk of Stephen Little, also of the University of Notre Dame Press, and, in addition to being equally encouraging and supportive, he moved the project quickly along the path to completion. I am enormously grateful to him. I have no doubt that this work would not be realized were it not for his unfailing help, ready encouragement, peaceful demeanor, and gentle advice. Over the years, Harv Humphrey, the acting director of the University of Notre Dame Press, has also supported me with his encouragement, advice, and professionalism. I thank him as well, most sincerely.

Jonathan R. Seiling has assisted me as an associate editor at the final stages, checking quotations, editing and expanding the manuscript into new chapters, creating an index, and attending to other details. I am enormously grateful to Jonathan for his help, advice, assistance, meticulous work, and kind and patient disposition. I thank Fr. Donald Finlay, C.S.B., sometime chief librarian of the John M. Kelly Library, University of St. Michael's College, and the library of the Pontifical Institute of Mediaeval Studies, and Andrew West, formerly head of cataloguing, of the John M. Kelly Library, University of St. Michael's College, both of whom helped me build my Maritain collection.

My religious congregation, The Congregation of St. Basil—also known as the Basilian Fathers—made possible the original sabbatical, thus enabling me to devote time to this work. Maritain taught many Basilians when he held faculty positions at St. Michael's College and the Pontifical Institute of Mediaeval Studies, both in Toronto. And although I neither knew nor was taught by Maritain, those Basilians who were his students have never failed to speak of their debt to him for the intellectual and spiritual framework he gave them. They would undoubtedly echo those beautiful words of Pope Paul VI in 1973 on the occasion of Maritain's death, describing him publicly as a "master of the art of thinking, of living, and of praying." In thanking the Basilian Fathers, I particularly thank the then Basilian Superior General, The Very Reverend Kenneth J. Decker, C.S.B., who granted me permission for a sabbatical. I would also like to thank my local religious community, the Basilian Fathers of the University of St. Michael's College. I have known this house since 1984, when I began my doctoral studies on Jacques Maritain's philosophy of education at the University of Toronto. I am particularly indebted to Fr. James K. McConica, C.S.B., sometime president and vice-chancellor of the University of St. Michael's College, who encouraged me to study Maritain. Fr. Andrew Leung, C.S.B., patiently helped me with many computer queries. Without his assistance I would still be roaming, baffled and confused, in that electronic jungle. I thank Anne Anderson, C.S.J., president and vice-chancellor of the University of St. Michael's College, for her encouragement and support. Fr. Neil Hibberd, C.S.B., has been generous with his time in reading the introduction and has made helpful suggestions. I am very grateful to him.

Finally, I wish to express my immense gratitude to John P. O'Callaghan and Alice Osberger at the Jacques Maritain Center of the University of Notre Dame for their encouragement and for the Maritain Center's permission to reproduce the English language quotations of Maritain's works found in this reader.

My sister-in-law, Cynthia D'Souza, and my nieces, Melanie and Michelle, have been an inspiration to me as they have drawn comfort and strength from our Catholic faith. My one regret, as is theirs, is that my younger brother Melvyn did not live to see this book brought to print. I had told him that I would be dedicating it to him. His strong Catholic faith was a source of great comfort to us, and his devotion to the Mother of God was an inspiration. I know, however, that he rejoices from a much more enduring home. Given his faith, I thought of this comforting and faith-filled quotation from Maritain as I presided at his funeral mass:

> There is something which scandalizes me: it is the manner in which Christians speak of their deceased. They call them the dead—they have not been capable of renewing the miserable human vocabulary on a point which nevertheless concerns the essential data of their faith. The dead! One attends masses for the dead! One goes to the cemetery with flowers for the dead, one prays for the dead! As if they weren't billions of times more living than we! As if the fundamental truth stated in the Preface of the Burial Mass: *vita mutatur, non tollitur*—life is changed, it is not taken away—was itself a dead truth, incapable of fecundating and of transforming the common routine of our manner of conceiving and of speaking. (*NB*, 266)

ABBREVIATIONS

The following abbreviations are used for works by Jacques Maritain or coauthored by Jacques and Raïssa Maritain. The full publication information for all Maritain sources quoted or cited in this reader is given in the bibliography.

AF	*Art and Faith*
AG	*Approaches to God*
AN	*Antisemitism*
AP	*Art and Poetry*
AS	*Art and Scholasticism and the Frontiers of Poetry*
BP	*An Introduction to the Basic Problems of Moral Philosophy*
BPT	*Bergsonian Philosophy and Thomism*
CC	*On the Church of Christ*
CD	*Christianity and Democracy*
CI	*Creative Intuition in Art and Poetry*
CP	*An Essay on Christian Philosophy*
CR	*Challenges and Renewals*
CW	*The Collected Works of Jacques Maritain* (series)
DD	*The Dream of Descartes*
DK	*Distinguish to Unite or The Degrees of Knowledge*
EC	*Education at the Crossroads*
EE	*Existence and the Existent*

EM	The Education of Man
FC	France My Country
FMW	Freedom in the Modern World
GE	God and the Permission of Evil
GJ	The Grace and Humanity of Jesus
IH	Integral Humanism
IL	An Introduction to Logic
IP	An Introduction to Philosophy
LC	Liturgy and Contemplation
LI	A Letter on Independence
LT	The Living Thoughts of Saint Paul
MP	Moral Philosophy
MS	Man and the State
NB	Notebooks
NC	The Things that Are Not Caesar's
PE	St. Thomas and the Problem of Evil
PG	The Person and the Common Good
PH	On the Philosophy of History
PI	Prayer and Intelligence
PM	A Preface to Metaphysics
PN	On the Philosophy of Nature
PP	Social and Political Philosophy
RA	The Responsibility of the Artist
RC	Religion and Culture
RM	The Rights of Man and Natural Law
RON	Reflections on America
RR	The Range of Reason
RT	Ransoming the Time
SA	The Sin of the Angel
SO	The Situation of Poetry
SP	Scholasticism and Politics
SW	Science and Wisdom
TA	St. Thomas Aquinas
TC	Twilight of Civilization
TP	The Peasant of the Garonne
TR	Three Reformers
TS	Theonas: Conversations of a Sage
UA	Untrammeled Approaches
UP	On the Use of Philosophy

INTRODUCTION

Mario O. D'Souza, C.S.B.

I first began reading the works of Jacques Maritain during my undergraduate years while studying philosophy at University College, Dublin. I remember our professor of general metaphysics, the then Fr. Desmond Connell, later the cardinal archbishop of Dublin, encouraging us to read Maritain, adding that he was sure that Maritain was a saint. I soon discovered the intellectual rigor of Maritain's thought. Preparatory and rudimentary as Maritain's book *An Introduction to Philosophy* may seem from its title, it was hardly a work for an undergraduate to grapple with. I am reminded of another "introductory" work that is equally demanding and, although written in a different way and with a different audience in mind, equally rewarding. Like Maritain's *Introduction to Philosophy*, it can overwhelm the neophyte expecting a rudimentary work for beginners. I refer to *Introduction to Christianity* by Fr. Joseph Ratzinger, later Pope Benedict XVI.

Maritain's *Introduction to Philosophy* presupposes more than a cursory knowledge of the history of philosophy. I was taught philosophy historically, as I believe it should be taught to undergraduates, and I have learned over the years that Maritain's philosophical corpus is as much a sustained commentary on the history of philosophy as it is a commentary on the integral life of the human person in interaction with the wealth of the created and uncreated orders. Maritain's engagement with the history of philosophy leads him to state: "The answers which philosophers have given to the problem of human nature correspond strictly with the position they adopt towards the problem of abstraction."[1] Maritain's name remains closely associated with that of St. Thomas Aquinas, but his knowledge of the history of philosophy enables him to comment upon, critique, and, when necessary, incorporate the thought of philosophers ranging from the Pre-Socratics to Edmund Husserl. Maritain commands this vast historical field with articulate intellectual precision, and he does not shrink from taking on philosophical giants such as Descartes, Kant, Hegel, and Bergson. And although his disagreement with three great Western thinkers was particularly strong and polemical in his work *The Three Reformers: Luther—Descartes—Rousseau*, most of his works show a much more measured and charitable tone. Nevertheless, Maritain does not shy away from stating his disagreements clearly and unequivocally.

It is also worth noting the enormous project that Maritain undertook as a philosopher. His own philosophical edifice is both imposing and capacious, containing within it the many ways of encountering the world. He developed a systematic and synthetic corpus on the human engagement with the created and uncreated orders, ranging from metaphysics and political philosophy to the philosophy of nature and aesthetics. Maritain recognized the legitimate place and role of science, both as a specialized form of knowledge and as an essential means of revealing and responding to the given of the world. However, he vigorously opposed interacting or responding to the world in exclusively empirical and measurable terms, for in this he saw the reduction and diminution of human personhood itself, which, in turn, would lead to the diminution of society and of the common good. For, as he reminds the reader, in ultimate terms, the common good is much more than the visible patrimony of a state; it is much more than bricks and mortar, essential though they are. In holding that the common good is something "ethically good," he maintained that "the common good is not only a system of advantages and utilities but also a rectitude of life, an end, good in itself or, as the Ancients expressed it, a *bonum honestum*. . . . Only on condition that it is according to justice and moral goodness is the common good what it is, namely, the good of a people and a city, rather than a mob of gangsters and murderers."[2]

For Maritain, human values—goodness, truth, beauty, the progression of society, the pursuit of the common good, the transcendence of religious faith and belief—were all forms and examples of responding to the invitation of being in the world. Reducing such human responses and engagement to the empirical and measurable alone would be to confine human experience to a dark and lonesome prison, where the dynamic and life-giving light of the intellect and reason were shut out, leaving one to languish, bereft of any source, means, or hope of freedom. Maritain would undoubtedly have agreed with Bernard Lonergan, another philosopher in the Thomist tradition, in condemning the "infantile solution that the real is what is given in immediate experience," and that "knowing . . . is a matter of taking a good look; objectivity is a matter of seeing of what is there to be seen; reality is whatever is given in immediate experience."[3] Like Lonergan, Maritain believed that meaning, values, and the quest for goodness, truth, and beauty could not be contained by what was given in immediate and sensible experience alone. Of course, he affirmed, like his master St. Thomas Aquinas, that knowledge begins in and through the senses, but human knowledge is more than just *sense knowledge.*

It is also important to acknowledge and recall the great philosophic project that Maritain undertook as he celebrated and contributed to the revival of Thomism. Although Thomism had dominated the Catholic intellectual tradition since the time of St. Thomas Aquinas, the modern Thomistic revival began with papal support in the encyclical *Aeterni Patris—On the Restoration of Christian Philosophy*, promulgated by Pope Leo XII on 4 August 1879. From the time of its proclamation to the close of the Second Vatican Council in 1965, Thomistic philosophy occupied a primordial place of leadership and synthesis, both in the faith life of the Catholic Church and within the Catholic academy. In the years following the close of the Second Vatican Council, however, theology rather than philosophy assumed the role of intellectual leadership in Catholic thought. While it is well beyond the scope of these introductory remarks to pursue the reasons for this change and how it manifests itself, suffice it to say that, given the change in the intellectual climate, a comprehensive philosophical enterprise similar to Maritain's would be both unthinkable and impossible today. Furthermore, differences among Thomistic philosophers in interpreting St. Thomas have led to distinct philosophical schools of Thomism. In addition, the rise of the social and empirical sciences and the various specialized fields and forms of knowledge, as well as the understanding of culture empirically and the importance and role of hermeneutics, has added to this complexity. And although contemporary Catholic theology is rich in its ability to engage men and women in the synthesis between faith and culture and between faith and life, as well as attending to the many other doctrinal, moral, ecclesial, scriptural, and pastoral dimensions of faith, it is clear that it does not see itself as having, or as being able to provide, the broad intellectual foundations of the kind that Maritain's philosophical thought attempted to provide across so many different aspects of human knowledge.

In fairness to contemporary theology, the world today envisages the intellectual order and the bodies of knowledge in quite a different way than Maritain's world did. It would seem that today, at least in the Catholic academy, the attempt to encapsulate that order in a single system or discipline not only is not viable but is also seen as a rejection of a true engagement with the many and varied dimensions that men and women find themselves in today, morally, politically, culturally, socially, and intellectually. An excellent summary of some of these questions, in the context of Thomism in relation to Catholic philosophy, is found in John Haldane's 1998 Aquinas Lecture.[4]

Nonetheless, what Maritain was able to cover and deal with is breathtaking. His thought and writings were very much concerned with the history and events of his time. When reading Maritain, one never notices any nostalgic harkening to the past to comfort an intellectual sentimentality, and, as a student of Maritain, I am not suggesting or yearning for such a sentimental harkening. I am simply saying that his intellectual synthesis—made possible by his broad knowledge of the various elements of philosophy and the philosophic *habitus*, and because his age and time were intellectually receptive to comprehensive syntheses—provided a bulwark against the atrocities of his age, particularly atrocities against human dignity, whether historical, cultural, political, social, or ideological. Against these he fought valiantly and bravely, armed with Christian charity and hope. He taught us that philosophers in each age must attend to their time and place in interaction with the history of ideas and must apply those ideas to their time and place. His was not a nostalgic Thomism; it was a Thomism for his time and in relation to the events and trends of his day. It was a living, breathing Thomism.

There is no doubt that Jacques Maritain is a demanding philosopher, but the demand he puts on the reader reaps rich philosophical rewards. He is relentless in his search for truth: "nothing is superior to truth."[5] His works have broadened and widened our understanding of what it means to live in the world and to live fully in the Christian sense. He reminds us that we are called to complete through our wills what is sketched out in our nature.[6] And, although he lived in the world as a staunch Roman Catholic, his philosophical *habitus*, grounded upon the primacy of being, the search for truth, and the unflinching quest to ensure the dignity and nobility of the human person, enabled him to be devoted to the many issues that we too encounter today in the context of politics and of religious, cultural, and moral pluralism. His devotion to the dignity of the human person—with the evils of Nazism, racism, fascism, and other totalitarian regimes fresh in his mind—spans cultural divides and theological differences, for it is rooted in the intellect, in reason, and in the will. It rests on four universal principles: intelligence and will, and knowledge and love.[7] As Maritain says in *The Rights of Man and Natural Law*, "I am taking it for granted that you admit that there is a human nature, and that this human nature is the same in all men. I am taking it for granted that you also admit that man is a being gifted with intelligence, and who, as such, acts with an understanding of what he is doing, and therefore with a power to determine for himself the ends which he pursues."[8]

Reading Maritain is a contemplative experience; indeed, one of the fruits is that one begins to gradually experience all that contributes to one's personal and inner metaphysical unity, as well as to better understand those forces that lead to personal fragmentation, resulting in alienation. Since Maritain's death in 1973, the world has recorded material, technological, and scientific advancements and discoveries of a breathtaking nature and at an unmatched pace. And yet, amid this wealth, today's world and our encounter of being in the world seem increasingly reduced to the material and the tangible. Human society appears increasingly weighed down by a world encountered as sheer materiality. Despite all the calls to ensure human dignity, a world encountered in exclusively material terms strikes first at the internal unity of each person. This was a theme very dear to Maritain and one that grounded his thought. His concern for human unity, the personal, metaphysical unity of each person, is a beacon of light, and it is precisely this concern that makes his thought so rewarding, enriching, and perennial, and thus so applicable to our age: "If his [St. Thomas Aquinas's] spirit and his doctrine tend to create unity in man, it is always by virtue of the same secret—which is to understand all things in the light and the generosity of being."[9]

Maritain is too sophisticated and rigorous a thinker to be bound by the often lazy and imprisoning categories of optimist or pessimist, conservative or liberal, conventional or progressive. He is a realist who believes in God, and the combination results in a metaphysical and philosophical response that shines with a gentle care and love. An example of that care and love is his profound respect for, and dependence upon, the various analogical modes of knowing and understanding. It is because his philosophy is grounded on the primacy of being and truth that he relies on the place and role of analogy in human knowledge and understanding, a dependence that blossoms in the depth and the diversity of his thought: "This analogical character, an example of which is called the analogy of strict proportionality, is inscribed in the very nature of the concept of being. It is analogous from the outset, not a univocal concept afterwards employed analogously. It is essentially analogous, polyvalent. In itself it is but a simple unity of proportionality, that is, it is purely and simply manifold and one in a particular respect."[10]

Maritain's philosophical pillars include the primacy of being, the search for and acquisition of truth, the dignity of the human person, internal and spiritual freedom, the revelation of God in the natural and supernatural orders, the primacy of the common good, the abstractive nature of the intellect, the crucial role of analogy in human knowing and understanding, and the hierarchies of knowledge, to name just a few. Accordingly, he does more than weave these themes throughout his work. Rather, they secure his philosophy, and his ready reference to them prevents his thought from becoming either artificially specialized or intellectually prideful. His works possess a warmth and humanity, all aiming toward human unity culminating in an integral humanism. These pillars and their towering shadows are evident across his philosophical corpus.

All this is by way of saying that the reader should not expect an exhaustive treatment of any given topic in any one of Maritain's works. To know the depth and rich application of Maritain's thought, one must read as many of his works as possible. My own area of study is the philosophy of education, but I soon discovered, when writing my doctoral thesis on Maritain's distinction between the person and the individual and its implications for education, that I needed to read nearly all the works quoted in this volume. His political philosophy, particularly in *The Person and the Common Good* and *Man and the State*, draws important distinctions concerning the person and the individual, the nature of society, and all that makes up the common good. His work *Art and Scholasticism and the Frontiers of Poetry* presents crucial distinctions between art and science and art and prudence, with implications for his educational theory. A familiarity with his work *Integral Humanism* is essential to understanding what he meant by an integral education; and his *Freedom in the Modern World* and *Distinguish to Unite or The Degrees of Knowledge* have substantial implications for education as nurturing internal freedom and the role of abstraction in knowledge. In short, Maritain's thought is not confined by the modern obsession with specialization. His thought and writings are expansive, and necessarily so, since human understanding, to be human and integral, must also be expansive. It must refuse to be contained within the boundaries of narrow-minded specializations, which are often overly influenced by, and end up being imprisoned by, what is sensory, measurable, and empirical.

Maritain's thought has formed and disciplined my own work in the philosophy of education; his distinction between a habit and a *habitus*[11] has been a shining beacon for me. I have learned that there is great wisdom in attaching an applied field, such as the philosophy of education, to the thought of a profound philosopher, and Jacques Maritain has been that kind of philosopher for me. Today, the field of education, Catholic or otherwise, is in great need of epistemological and metaphysical principles. Mesmerized by technical innovations and material progress, we appear to have forgotten that institutional education that cannot attest to philosophically coherent principles, such as the purpose and end of education, the nature of the student as a person, the curriculum and the internal unity of the student, the hierarchies of knowledge and values, the unity of the intellect, the role of analogy in education, and the importance of the abstractive nature of the intellect, is not an education worthy of a human person. Not only will it fail to be an integral education, it will also fail in being an education of the *whole person*, a term that seems to trip off the tongues of many who are charged with the responsibility of education but who lack attention to what is entailed in so great a responsibility. Maritain's philosophy of education, grounded on the primacy of being and the dignity of the human intellect, provides our age with just those philosophical principles that it so desperately needs; the fact that this need often goes unrecognized only compounds the urgency. A vision of education founded on secure philosophical principles is a particular way of being in the world. Maritain's philosophy, and not merely his philosophy of education, clears the ground for understanding *our being in the world*.

I have long admired the lyrical beauty of Maritain's writings; many passages have moved me deeply and have led me to prayer. Many are included among the quotations in this reader. The length of the selected quotations varies greatly: some are a single line, others run into paragraphs. In all of them, however, there is a distinctly stand-alone quality, which is remarkable, given the sophistication and the complexity of Maritain's thought. The quotations have been divided into forty chapters under different topical headings, but some quotations could easily have been placed under different or even several headings—again, suggesting the universality of Maritain's thought.

This reader is not an introduction to Maritain's thought. As indicated above, the quotations stand independently of each other. Some require no special knowledge of philosophy or the history of philosophy, but others fit within a wider philosophical context. Those who are already familiar with Maritain's writings, at least to some degree, will have an advantage in using this reader, certainly; but I also believe that many quotations speak directly to the Christian life in its broad dimensions, a life driven by the quest for truth, goodness, and beauty. The quotations in this book demonstrate how Maritain, too, was driven by and remained faithful to such a quest.

However, for those who have not read Maritain and might wish to turn to secondary sources as guides to his philosophical thought—I hope, as a result of being inspired by the quotations in this book—I suggest a short list of fifteen works. Three works on Thomism and Maritain's role in its revival are Gerald A. McCool's *From Unity to Pluralism: The Internal Evolution of Thomism*; *The Future of Thomism*, edited by Deal W. Hudson and Dennis Wm. Moran; and *The Vocation of the Catholic Philosopher: From Maritain to John Paul II*, edited by John P. Hittinger.[12] A beautiful, poetic, and faith-filled work that presents the life and works of Jacques and his wife Raïssa Maritain according to the different hours of the Catholic Church's liturgical office is Ralph McInerny's *The Very Rich Hours of Jacques Maritain: A Spiritual Life*, a truly contemplative read.[13] Of the innumerable works on Maritain's political and social philosophy, two are of special note, one older and one more recent: Norah W. Michener's *Maritain on the Nature of Man in a Christian Democracy* and James V. Schall's *Jacques Maritain: The Philosopher in Society*.[14] A very fine overall introduction to the philosophy of Maritain is Charles A. Fecher's *The Philosophy of Jacques Maritain*.[15] Another commendable introductory work, a collection of essays by notable Maritain scholars, is *Jacques Maritain: The Man and His Achievement*, edited by Joseph W. Evans, a former director of the Jacques Maritain Center at the University of Notre Dame and also a contributor.[16] A very short, classic, introductory work is *Jacques Maritain* by Gerald B. Phelan, former director of the institute later named the Pontifical Institute of Mediaeval Studies, in Toronto, was written when Maritain was in his fifties, and it reflects on his contributions as a philosopher thus far.[17] Another concise introduction, described on its back cover in 2003 as "the most complete introduction to Maritain yet to be published," is Jude P. Dougherty's *Jacques Maritain: An Intellectual Profile*.[18] For those interested in understanding Maritain in the context of his time as well as learning more about what influenced him intellectually, I recommend Bernard E. Doering's *Jacques Maritain and the French Catholic Intellectuals*.[19] A useful work on Maritain's philosophy of education is Jean-Louis Allard's *Education for Freedom: The Philosophy of Education of Jacques Maritain.*[20] Maritain wrote a number of important and influential works on aesthetics, and one fine commentary is John G. Trapani's *Poetry, Beauty and Contemplation: The Complete Aesthetics of Jacques Maritain.*[21] Some of the other collections mentioned above also contain important essays on Maritain's aesthetics, as well as on other philosophical themes. Maritain depended upon and honored the various ways of knowing, and one collection of essays particularly devoted to this theme is *Jacques Maritain and the Many Ways of Knowing*, edited by Douglas A. Ollivant.[22] And finally, a critically acclaimed and recent detailed biography, in its English translation, is Jean-Luc Barré's *Jacques and Raïssa Maritain: Beggars for Heaven.*[23]

A complementary resource that may be helpful for some readers (particularly those with Italian and French proficiency) is Piero Viotto's *Jacques Maritain Dizionario delle Opere.*[24] Viotto provides a summary of sixty-five published works of Maritain, along with full bibliographic information on editions and translations. A short index of thirty-seven major themes ("Indice tematico per grandi problemi") lists many topics that overlap with the forty chapters of the present reader. A detailed index of key terms ("Indice per argomenti") refers back to Viotto's summaries, in which one can locate pertinent texts in the original publications. A few noteworthy topics in this index, such as that of connaturality, are not covered by quotations in the present volume. The index of proper names is a valuable resource for locating additional works by Maritain that refer to a specific person. In addition to Viotto's *Dizionario*, at least three other helpful bibliographies may be consulted (see note).[25] Finally, the collected works of Jacques and Raïssa Maritain are available in the sixteen volumes of the French series *Oeuvres Complètes.*[26]

Let me add a few more points about the nature and the structure of this book. First, its principal aim is to provide a book of quotations as a ready reference for those who are familiar with Maritain's thought and writings. However, as already suggested above, I believe it is accessible to a wider audience. For those not familiar with Maritain's thought or writings, the quotations in this book should give them a fairly strong understanding of the unity of his thought and of how he understood the role of a Catholic philosopher.

Second, there were various ways that this book could have been structured. Chapters and quotations could have been organized under broader umbrella categories, such as political and social philosophy, metaphysics and philosophy, aesthetics, philosophy of education, God and the moral life, culture and civilization, science and reason, and so forth. I chose the sheer simplicity of an alphabetical listing of forty topics because I believed that it offered the greatest freedom in the selection of quotations. Furthermore, grouping chapters under broader categories would have required some elaboration as to the reasons for that ordering. And while it is quite true that some of Maritain's themes take primacy over others, for example, the concepts of being, the person, types of knowing, the spiritual nature of the intellect, and so on, this primacy is already known to those readers familiar with Maritain, to whom this book is primarily directed. On the other hand, the alphabetical listing, I believe, makes the book more accessible to those unfamiliar with Maritain's writings, yet interested in the topics according to which the chapters are divided.

Third, earlier in this introduction I referred to Maritain's philosophical pillars. Providing a thematic commentary is not my intention here because I want each quotation to speak for itself. Fecher's work *The Philosophy of Jacques Maritain*, mentioned above, is the best introduction to Maritain's philosophy, both thematically and in terms of the progressive structure of his thought. I heartily recommend that book for those interested in looking further into Maritain's philosophical themes.

Fourth, the chapters that could be described as Maritain's philosophical anthropology, that is, the chapters entitled "Humanism," "Man," "The Person," "The Person and the Individual," and "Personality," deserve special comment. The theme of humanism is devoted to Maritain's concerns in his work *Integral Humanism*, but as this theme is developed and traced in other works, particularly his political and social philosophy. The theme "man" is broader and more general, whereas "the person" is what emerges as a result of moral, intellectual, social, political, aesthetic, cultural, religious, and other influences and responsibilities. The themes of personality and individuality attend to the unity and distinction that contribute to human unity: personality is the spiritual dimension and individuality the material dimension, but both are vital for human unity. The distinctions that arise from the theme of personality show that, for Maritain, this category is much wider than an exclusively psychological one.

Last, this reader is by no means an exhaustive record of the most memorable quotations—far from it. Furthermore, during my reading of Maritain, I often came across beautiful lines of philosophical rhapsody interspersed in the text that could not, however, be included here. Providing them in a meaningful way would have required presenting large sections of the surrounding text; it would also have required editorial clarification, thus violating my conviction that a work such as this should see as little of the editor's silhouette as possible.

The quotations have been reproduced almost exactly as found in the original publications, preserving the original spelling, punctuation, italics, and so on, with only a few minor exceptions. Regional English spelling differences, reflecting the place of publication, are preserved. In a few cases there were spelling errors in the original, which have been corrected. In only one case was there a translation error, which has been corrected with an explanatory footnote provided. If the original text referred back to a prior section or idea, this reference has been replaced with ellipsis points for omission, to improve the flow of the quotation. Much care has been taken to ensure that such editorial changes do not alter the meaning of the text. Ellipsis points are not used at the beginning or end of a quotation, even if the quote begins mid-sentence or cuts the original short. When a quoted sentence begins after the first word of the original sentence, its initial letter has been capitalized.

No quotation appears more than once, even though several quotes speak to more than one topic. For that reason, after consulting a chapter on a given topic, the reader is strongly advised to turn to the index at the back to locate additional chapters with passages on that topic. For example, several important quotes dealing with Descartes are in chapters other than the one entitled "Descartes." However, considerable deliberation went into the ideal placement of each quote in the attempt to ensure that each chapter contains the most essential quotes pertaining to the stated topic.

The parenthetical citations following each quotation consist of an abbreviation for the English source edition, identified in full in the bibliography, and the page numbers in that edition. In three cases—*Freedom in the Modern World*, *Distinguish to Unite or The Degrees of Knowledge*, and *Integral Humanism*, two sets of page numbers are provided parenthetically: the pages in the earlier edition, using the abbreviation of the title; and the pages in the later edition in the series Collected Works, using the abbreviation CW with the series volume number. For these three works, there are minor differences between the earlier translation and the CW version; the anthology quotations follow the CW version. Of the fifty-four works quoted, three are jointly authored by Jacques and Raïssa Maritain: *Liturgy and Contemplation*; *Prayer and Intelligence*; and *The Situation of Poetry*.

Notes

1. Maritain, *An Introduction to Philosophy*, 131. For full details of the works of Maritain cited here, see the bibliography.
2. Maritain, *The Person and the Common Good*, 53.
3. Bernard Lonergan, "The Origins of Christian Realism," in *A Second Collection*, ed. William Ryan and Bernard Tyrrell (London: Darton, Longman & Todd, 1974), 241.
4. John Haldane, "Thomism and the Future of Catholic Philosophy: 1998 Aquinas Lecture," *New Blackfriars* 80, no. 938 (April 1999): 158–69.
5. Maritain, *The Peasant of the Garonne*, 71.
6. See Maritain, *Scholasticism and Politics*, 52.
7. See Maritain, *Education at the Crossroads*, 7–8.
8. Maritain, *The Rights of Man and Natural Law*, 60.
9. Maritain, *Existence and the Existent*, 143.
10. Maritain, *A Preface to Metaphysics*, 64.
11. See Maritain, *Art and Scholasticism and the Frontiers of Poetry*, 11.
12. Gerald A. McCool, S.J., *From Unity to Pluralism: The Internal Evolution of Thomism* (New York: Fordham University Press, 1989; repr. 1992); Deal W. Hudson and Dennis Wm. Moran, eds., *The Future of Thomism* (Mishawaka, IN: American Maritain Association, 1992); John P. Hittinger, ed., *The Vocation of the Catholic Philosopher: From Maritain to John Paul II* (Washington, DC: American Maritain Association, 2010).
13. Ralph McInerny, *The Very Rich Hours of Jacques Maritain: A Spiritual Life* (Notre Dame, IN: University of Notre Dame Press, 2003).
14. Norah W. Michener, *Maritain on the Nature of Man in a Christian Democracy* (Hull, Canada: Éditions L'Éclair, 1955); James V. Schall, *Jacques Maritain: The Philosopher in Society* (Lanham, MD: Rowman & Littlefield Publishers, 1998).

15. Charles A. Fecher, *The Philosophy of Jacques Maritain* (New York: Greenwood Press, 1969).

16. Joseph W. Evans, ed., *Jacques Maritain: The Man and His Achievement* (New York: Sheed & Ward, 1963).

17. Gerald B. Phelan, *Jacques Maritain* (New York: Sheed & Ward, 1937).

18. Jude P. Dougherty, *Jacques Maritain: An Intellectual Profile* (Washington, DC: Catholic University of America Press, 2003).

19. Bernard E. Doering, *Jacques Maritain and the French Catholic Intellectuals* (Notre Dame, IN: University of Notre Dame Press, 1983).

20. Jean-Louis Allard, *Education for Freedom: The Philosophy of Education of Jacques Maritain* (Notre Dame, IN: University of Notre Dame Press; Ottawa, Canada: University of Ottawa Press, 1982).

21. John G. Trapani, Jr., *Poetry, Beauty and Contemplation: The Complete Aesthetics of Jacques Maritain* (Washington, DC: Catholic University of America Press, 2011).

22. Douglas A. Ollivant, ed., *Jacques Maritain and the Many Ways of Knowing* (Washington, DC: American Maritain Association, 2002).

23. Jean-Luc Barré, *Jacques and Raïssa Maritain: Beggars for Heaven* (Notre Dame, IN: University of Notre Dame Press, 2005).

24. Piero Viotto, *Jacques Maritain Dizionario delle Opere* (Rome: Città Nuova, 2003).

25. D. Gallagher and I. Gallagher, eds., *The Achievement of Jacques and Raïssa Maritain: A Bibliography, 1906–1961* (New York: Doubleday & Co., 1962); J. L. Allard and P. Germaine eds., *Répertoire bibliographique sur la vie et l'oeuvre de Jacques et Raïssa Maritain* (Ottawa, Canada: University of Ottawa Press, 1994); D. Gallagher et al., "Bibliographie sur Jacques et Raïssa Maritain," *Notes et Documents* 49/50 (May–December 1997): 1–82.

26. *Jacques and Raïssa Maritain: Oeuvres Complètes*, ed. J.-M. Allion et al., 16 vols. (Fribourg, Switzerland: Éditions Universitaires/Paris: Éditions Saint-Paul, c1982–c2000).

CHAPTER ONE

ARISTOTLE

1. Aristotle is a pure philosopher: he establishes the theory of what we call 'pure nature.' But the state of pure nature, as a fact and in the concrete, has never existed for man, who is always found either in the state of grace—that is super-nature—or in the state of *fallen* nature. In so far as man is concerned, many of the problems that Aristotle left and had to leave unsolved, find their solution—just as many of the principles that he formulated find their true value—only in a higher order, of whose existence he had not the least suspicion. The true supermen are the saints: true contemplation is not that of Aristotle, for it presupposes grace and the love of God. (*TS*, pp. 24–25)

2. In epistemology Aristotle showed that physics, mathematics, and metaphysics, or the first philosophy, are indeed three distinct sciences, but that they are distinguished by their subject-matter, not by the faculty employed, which in all alike is reason. But his most important achievement in this sphere was to prove, by the marvellous analysis of *abstraction* which dominates his entire philosophy, that our ideas are not innate memories of prenatal experience, but derived from the senses by an activity of the mind. (*IP*, p. 64)

3. Aristotle's mind was at once extremely practical and extremely metaphysical. A rigorous logician, but also a keen-sighted realist, he gladly respected the demands of the actual, and found room in his speculation for every variety of being without violating or distorting the facts at any point, displaying an intellectual vigour and freedom to be surpassed only by the crystalline lucidity and angelic force of St. Thomas Aquinas. But this vast wealth is arranged in the light of principles, mastered, classified, measured, and dominated by the intellect. It is the masterpiece of wisdom, a wisdom which is still wholly human, but nevertheless, from its lofty throne, embraces with a single glance the totality of things.

Aristotle, however, was a profound rather than a comprehensive thinker. He took little care to display the proportions and wide perspectives of his philosophy; his primary object was to apprehend by an absolutely reliable method and with a faultless precision what in every nature accessible to human knowledge is most characteristic, most intimate—in short, most truly itself. Therefore he not only organised human knowledge, and laid the solid foundations of logic, biology, psychology, natural history, metaphysics, ethics, and politics, but also cut and polished a host of precious definitions and conclusions sparkling with the fires of reality.

It can therefore be affirmed without hesitation that among philosophers Aristotle holds a position altogether apart: genius, gifts, and achievement—all are unique. It is the law of nature that the sublime is difficult to achieve and that what is difficult is rare. But when a task is of extraordinary difficulty both in itself and in the conditions it requires, we may expect that there will be but one workman capable of its accomplishment. Moreover, a well-built edifice is usually built not on the plans of several architects, but on the plan of a single one. If, therefore, the edifice of human wisdom or philosophy is to be adequately constructed, the foundations must be laid once for all by a single thinker. On these foundations thousands of builders will be able to build in turn, for the growth of knowledge represents the labour of generations and will never be complete. But there can be but one master-builder. (*IP*, pp. 66–67)

4. Aristotle could philosophize without ordering metaphysics to a higher science (though he really had the idea of a higher contemplation, which he placed at the peak of metaphysics, and where man participates in the life of the gods), he could do so because in the first place he was living under the régime of the Gentiles, outside of the Mosaic revelation, before the Christian revelation; and because he found himself in absolutely unique conditions, exactly at the culminating point of Greek civilization and intellectuality, and because he profited by that Grecian success which could never again be found with the help of nature alone. Descartes could not philosophize in that way because he was living under the régime of the Gospel, and because Christian riches are heavy, much heavier to carry than the light crowns of pagans. By a merciless and blessed necessity, which springs from the depths of our natural weakness and of the demands of divine love, the Christian cannot neglect the comfortings from above and the order they demand, without collapsing everywhere. (***DD*, pp. 87–88**)

5. Aristotelian ethics is *par excellence* the natural (purely natural) ethics and the philosophical (purely philosophical) ethics. And in what concerns the real direction of human conduct it runs aground in inefficacy. (***MP*, p. 51**)

6. The great truth which the Greeks discovered (and which their philosophers conceptualized in very divers spiritual ways) is the superiority of contemplation, as such, to action. As Aristotle puts it, life according to the intellect is better than a merely human life.

But the error follows. What did that assertion mean to them practically? It meant that mankind lives for the sake of a few intellectuals. There is a category of specialists—the philosophers—who lead a superhuman life; then in a lower category, destined to serve them, come those who lead the ordinary human life, the civil or political one; they in turn are served by those who lead a sub-human life, the life of work—that is, the slaves. The high truth of the superiority of contemplative life was bound up with the contempt of work and the plague of slavery. (***SP*, p. 137**)

CHAPTER TWO

ART AND THE ARTIST

1. Through the *habitus* or virtue of art superelevating his mind from within, the artist is a ruler who *uses* rules according to his ends; it is as senseless to conceive of him as the slave of the rules as to consider the worker the slave of his tools. Properly speaking, he possesses them and is not possessed by them: he is not *held* by them, it is he who *holds*—through them—matter and the real; and sometimes, in those superior moments where the working of genius resembles in art the miracles of God in nature, he will act, not against the rules, but outside of and above them, in conformity with a higher rule and a more hidden order. (**AS, p. 39**)

2. Morality has nothing to say when it comes to the good of the work, or to Beauty. Art has nothing to say when it comes to the good of human life. Yet human life is in need of that very Beauty and intellectual creativity, where art has the last word; and art exercises itself in the midst of that very human life, those human needs and human ends, where morality has the last word. In other words it is true that Art and Morality are two autonomous worlds, each sovereign in its own sphere, but they cannot ignore or disregard one another, for man belongs in these two worlds, both as intellectual maker and as moral agent, doer of actions which engage his own destiny. And be-

cause an artist is a man before being an artist, the autonomous world of morality is simply superior to (and more inclusive than) the autonomous world of art. There is no law against the law on which the destiny of man depends. In other words Art is indirectly and extrinsically subordinate to morality. (*RA,* **p. 41**)

3. Because it exists in man and because its good is not the good of man, art is subject in its exercise to an extrinsic control, imposed in the name of a higher end which is the very beatitude of the living being in whom it resides. (*AS,* **p. 71**)

4. The motto *Art for Art's sake* simply disregards the world of morality, and the values and rights of human life. *Art for Art's sake* does not mean art for the work, which is the right formula. It means an absurdity, that is, a supposed necessity for the artist to be only an artist, not a man, and for art to cut itself off from its own supplies, and from all the food, fuel and energy it receives from human life. (*RA,* **p. 48**)

5. Art, as such, does not consist in imitating, but in making, in composing or constructing, in accordance with the laws of the very object to be posited in being (ship, house, carpet, colored canvas or hewn block). This exigency of its generic concept takes precedence over everything else; and to make the representation of the real its essential end is to destroy it. (*AS,* **p. 53**)

6. The imitative arts aim neither at copying the appearances of nature, nor at depicting the "ideal," but at making an object beautiful by manifesting a *form* with the help of sensible signs. (*AS,* **p. 59**)

7. Art, then, remains fundamentally inventive and creative. It is the faculty of producing, not of course *ex nihilo,* but from a pre-existing matter, a new creature, an original being, capable of stirring in turn a human soul. This new creature is the fruit of a spiritual marriage which joins the activity of the artist to the passivity of a given matter.

Hence in the artist the feeling of his peculiar dignity. He is as it were an associate of God in the making of beautiful works; by developing the powers placed in him by the Creator—for "every perfect gift is from above, coming down from the Father of lights"—and by making use of created matter, he creates, so to speak, at second remove....

Artistic creation does not copy God's creation, it continues it. And just as the trace and the image of God appear in His creatures, so the human stamp is imprinted on the work of art—the full stamp, sensitive and spiritual, not only that of the hands, but of the whole soul. Before the work of art passes from art into the matter, by a transitive action, the very conception of the art has had to emerge from within the soul, by an immanent and vital action, like the emergence of the mental word. (**AS, p. 60**)

8. Art is not an abstract entity without flesh and bones, a separate Platonic Idea supposedly come down on earth and acting among us as the Angel of Making or a metaphysical Dragon let loose; Art is a virtue of the practical intellect, and the intellect itself does not stand alone, but is a power of Man. When the intellect thinks, it is not the intellect which thinks: it is man, a particular man, who thinks through his intellect. When Art operates, it is man, a particular man, who operates through his Art....

It is nonsense to believe that the genuineness or the purity of a work of art depends upon a rupture with, a moving away from the living forces which animate and move the human being—it is nonsense to believe that this purity of the work depends on a wall of separation built up between art and desire or love. The purity of the work depends upon the strength of the inner dynamism which generates the work, that is, the strength of the virtue of art.

No wall of separation isolates the virtue of art from the inner universe of man's desire and love. (**RA, pp. 49–50**)

9. Art as such, for instance, transcends, like the spirit, every frontier of space or time, every historical or national boundary. Like science and philosophy, it is universal of itself.

But art does not reside in an angelic mind: it resides in a soul which animates a living body, and which, by the natural necessity in which it finds itself of learning, and progressing little by little and with the assistance of others, makes the rational animal a naturally social animal. Art is therefore basically dependent upon everything which the human community, spiritual tradition and history transmit to the body and mind of man. By its human subject and its human roots, art belongs to a time and a country. (***RA,* p. 58**)

10. Art, like knowledge, is appendent to values which are independent of the interests, even the noblest interests, of human life, for they are values of the intellectual order. Poets do not come on the stage after dinner, to afford ladies and gentlemen previously satiated with terrestrial food the intoxication of pleasures which are of no consequence. But neither are they waiters who provide them with the bread of existentialist nausea, Marxist dialectics or traditional morality, the beef of political realism or idealism and the ice-cream of philanthropy. They provide mankind with a spiritual food, which is intuitive experience, revelation and beauty: for man, as I said in my youth, is an animal who lives on transcendentals. (***RA,* p. 73**)

11. One of the vicious trends which outrage our modern industrial civilization is a kind of asceticism at the service of the useful, a kind of unholy mortification for the sake of no superior life. Men are still capable of excitation and relaxation, but almost deprived of any pleasure and rest of the soul — a life which would seem insane even to the great materialists of antiquity. They flog themselves, they renounce the sweetness of the world and all the ornaments of the terrestrial abode, *omnem ornatum saeculi,* with the single incentive of working, working, working, and acquiring technological empire over matter. Their daily life lacks nothing so much as the delectations of the intelligence-permeated sense; and even the churches in which they pray are not uncommonly masterworks in ugliness. Then, since we cannot live without delectation, they have no other resource left but those arts and pleasures which satisfy "the brute curiosity of an *animal's* stare" — all the better as they produce stupefaction and obliviousness, as a substitute for Epicurean ataraxy. No wonder that other kinds of drugs, from alcohol or marijuana to the cult of carnal Venus, occupy a growing place in the process of compensation.

This dehumanizing process can be overcome. Art in this connection has an outstanding mission. It is the most natural power of healing and agent of spiritualization needed by the human community. (***CI,* pp. 190–91**)

12. The highest moral virtues can never make up for the lack or mediocrity of the virtue of art. But it is clear that laziness, cowardice or self-complacency, which are moral vices, are a bad soil for the exercise of artistic activity. The moral constitution of the human subject has some kind of indirect impact on his art. (***RA*, p. 92**)

13. In contradistinction to Prudence, which is also a perfection of the Practical Intellect, Art is concerned with the good of the work, not with the good of man. The Ancients took pleasure in laying stress on this difference, in their thorough-going comparison between Art and Prudence. If a craftsman contrives a good piece of woodwork or jewelry, the fact of his being spiteful or debauched is immaterial, just as it is immaterial for a geometer to be a jealous or wicked man, if his demonstrations provide us with geometrical truth. As Thomas Aquinas put it, Art, in this respect, resembles the virtues of the Speculative Intellect: it causes man to act in a right way, not with regard to the use of man's own free will, and to the rightness of the human will, but with regard to the rightness of a particular operating power. The good that Art pursues is not the good of the human will, but the good of the very artifact. Thus, art does not require, as a necessary precondition, that the will or appetite should be straight and undeviating with respect to its own nature and its own—human or moral—ends and dynamism, or in the line of human destiny. Oscar Wilde was but a good Thomist when he wrote: "The fact of a man being a poisoner is nothing against his prose." (***RA*, pp. 23–24**)

14. For an artist to spoil his work and sin against his art is forbidden by his artistic conscience. But what about his moral conscience? Is not his moral conscience also involved? My answer is yes. Not only his artistic conscience, but his moral conscience also, his conscience as a man is here on the alert. For moral conscience deals with all the acts of a man; moral conscience envelops, so to speak, all the more particularized kinds of conscience—not moral in themselves, but artistic, medical, scientific, etc.—of which I just spoke. There are no precepts in natural law or in the Decalogue dealing with painting and poetry, prescribing a particular style and forbidding another. But there is a primary principle in moral matters, which states that it is always bad, and always forbidden, to act against one's own conscience. The artist who, yielding to ill-advised moral exhortations, decides to betray his own singular truth as an artist, and his artistic conscience, breaks within himself one of the springs, the sacred springs, of human conscience, and to that extent wounds moral conscience itself. (***RA,* p. 37**)

15. The artist as an artist has ends which deal with his work and the good of his work, not with human life. The artist as a man has ends which deal with his own life, and the good of his own life, not with his work. If he took the end of his art, or the good of his artifact, for his own supreme good and ultimate end, he would be but an idolater. Art in its own domain is sovereign like wisdom; through its object it is subordinate neither to wisdom nor to prudence nor to any other virtue. But by the subject in which it exists, by man and in man it is subordinate—extrinsically subordinate—to the good of the human subject. As used by man's free will art enters a sphere which is not its own, but the sphere of moral standards and values, and in which there is no good against the good of human life. Whereas Art is supreme with respect to the work, Prudence—that is, moral wisdom, the virtue of right practical decision—Prudence is supreme with respect to man. (***RA,* pp. 39–40**)

16. If the perfection of human life consisted in some stoic athleticism of moral virtue, and in a man-made righteousness achieved to the point of impeccability, all of us, and especially the Artist and the Poet, would be in a rather sad predicament in this regard, and we would have to despair of the possibility of a single wise man, as the late Stoics did. But if the perfection of human life consists in a ceaselessly increasing love, despite our mistakes and weaknesses, between the Uncreated Self and the created self, there is some hope and some mercy for all of us, and especially for the Artist and the Poet.

The fact remains that the Prudent Man and the Artist have difficulty in understanding one another. But the Contemplative and the Artist, the one bound to wisdom, the other to beauty, are naturally close. They also have the same brand of enemies. The Contemplative, who looks at the highest cause on which every being and activity depend, knows the place and the value of art, and understands the Artist. The Artist in his turn divines the grandeur of the Contemplative, and feels congenial with him. When his path crosses the Contemplative's, he will recognize love and beauty. (***RA,* pp. 42–43**)

17. We maintain that the exercise of art or work is the formal reason of individual appropriation; but only because it presupposes the rational nature and personality of the artist or workman.

In the case of the bee, for instance, or of the beaver there is no exercise of art or of work in the strict sense (since there is no *reason* making); neither is there any individual ownership. (***FMW*, p. 198; CW 11, p. 103**)

18. Through the *factible*—the exercise of art or work—the proprietorship that the person has over himself is thus extended to the ownership of things.

How does this come about? Through those internal qualities which the Schoolmen call *habitus,* stable dispositions that perfect the subject, especially in the field of action.

The "artistic" work (we use the word 'artistic' equivocally) of the bee proceeds from its specific nature; but the artistic and productive work of man is the outcome of personal activity and of the *habitus* of each. The very word '*habitus*' is significant: one *has* what the other has not.

This is why the work of art or the thing to be made, *the factibile* which proceeds from the *habitus,* requires the personal power of management and use *(potestas procurandi et dispensandi)* of which St. Thomas speaks. It requires that things, materials, and means of work be possessed by man as a personal right, in lasting and permanent possession that befits an agent who has foresight and intelligence and whose judgment and action are taken with eyes wide open to the future. In short the material that is to be wrought needs to be the property of him who works on it, of the person who operates on it—a rational being which is individual and which has an individual perfection. (***FMW*, pp. 199–200; CW 11, p. 104**)

19. Beauty is essentially an object of *intelligence,* for that which *knows* in the full sense of the word is intelligence, which alone is open to the infinity of being. The natural place of beauty is the intelligible world, it is from there that it descends. But it also, in a way, falls under the grasp of the senses, in so far as in man they serve the intellect and can themselves take delight in knowing. . . . The part played by the senses in the perception of beauty is even rendered enormous in us, and well-nigh indispensable, by the very fact that our intelligence is not intuitive, as is the intelligence of the angel; it sees, to be sure, but on condition of abstracting and discoursing; only sense knowledge possesses perfectly in man the intuitiveness required for the perception of the beautiful. Thus man can doubtless enjoy purely intelligible beauty, but the beautiful that is *connatural* to man is the beautiful that delights the intellect through the senses and through their intuition. Such is also the beautiful that is proper to our art, which shapes a sensible matter in order to delight the spirit. It would thus like to believe that paradise is not lost. It has the savor of the terrestrial paradise, because it restores, for a moment, the peace and the simultaneous delight of the intellect and the senses.

If beauty delights the intellect, it is because it is essentially a certain excellence or perfection in the proportion of things to the intellect. (*AS,* **pp. 23–24**)

20. Art in general tends to make a work. But certain arts tend to make a *beautiful* work, and in this they differ essentially from all the others. The work to which all the other arts tend is itself ordered to the service of man, and is therefore a simple means; and it is entirely enclosed in a determined material genus. The work to which the fine arts tend is ordered to beauty; as beautiful, it is an end, an absolute, it suffices of itself; and if, as work-to-be-made, it is material and enclosed in a genus, as beautiful it belongs to the kingdom of the spirit and plunges deep into the transcendence and the infinity of being.

The fine arts thus stand out in the *genus* art as man stands out in the *genus* animal. And like man himself they are like a horizon where matter and spirit meet. They have a spiritual soul. Hence they possess many distinctive properties. Their contact with the beautiful modifies in them certain characteristics of art in general, notably . . . with respect to the rules of art; on the other hand, this contact discloses and carries to a sort of excess other generic characteristics of the virtue of art, above all its intellectual character and its resemblance to the speculative virtues. (*AS,* **p. 33**)

21. Beauty, like being, has an infinite amplitude. But the work as such, realized in matter, exists in a certain genus, *in aliquo genere.* And it is impossible for a genus to exhaust a transcendental. Outside the artistic genre to which this work belongs, there is always an infinity of ways of being a *beautiful* work. (*AS,* **p. 44**)

22. Love presupposes intellect; without it love can do nothing, and, in tending to the beautiful, love tends to what can delight the intellect. (*AS*, **p. 47**)

23. To say with the Schoolmen that beauty is *the splendor of the form on the proportioned parts of matter,* is to say that it is a flashing of intelligence on a matter intelligibly arranged. The intelligence delights in the beautiful because in the beautiful it finds itself again and recognizes itself, and makes contact with its own light. This is so true that those—such as Saint Francis of Assisi—perceive and savor more the beauty of things, who know that things come forth from an intelligence, and who relate them to their author.

Every sensible beauty implies, it is true, a certain delight of the eye itself or of the ear or the imagination: but there is beauty only if the intelligence also takes delight in some way. A beautiful color "washes the eye," just as a strong scent dilates the nostril; but of these two "forms" or qualities color only is said to be *beautiful,* because, being received, unlike the perfume, in a sense power capable of disinterested knowledge, it can be, even through its purely sensible brilliance, an object of delight for the intellect. Moreover, the higher the level of man's culture, the more spiritual becomes the brilliance of the form that delights him. (*AS*, **p. 25**)

24. The beautiful is essentially delightful. This is why, of its very nature and precisely as beautiful, it stirs desire and produces love, where as the true as such only illumines. (*AS*, **p. 26**)

25. In the eyes of God all that exists is beautiful, to the very extent to which it participates in being. For the beauty that God beholds is transcendental beauty, which permeates every existent, to one degree or another.

This is not the beauty that the senses perceive, and here we are obliged to introduce a new idea, the idea of aesthetic beauty, as contradistinguished to transcendental beauty. For when it comes to aesthetic beauty, we have to do with a province of beauty in which senses and sense perception play an essential part, and in which, as a result, not all things are beautiful. (*CI,* **pp. 163–64**)

26. The Angels, perfect natures, cannot turn aside naturally from nature; it is at the supernatural stage that their evil begins; the devil has a supernatural hatred of nature. He uses art to teach it to us. (*AP,* **p. 42**)

27. Where if not in musical creation could be found a better image of the creation of a world? Like the cantata or the symphony, the world was constructed in time (in a time that began with it), and is being preserved all the length of its successive duration by the thought from which it receives existence. There is nothing closer to the abyss of the created than the movement of that which passes, the flux, rhythmed and ordered, of the impermanent blossoming of a sensory joy that yields and fades away. Like the world and like motion, song has its countenance only in a memory.... And no more than the flow of time is music in itself limited and closed. Why should the song stop? Why should a musical work ever finish? ... As the time of the world shall one day emerge into the instant of eternity, so music should cease only by emerging into a silence *of another order*, filled with a substantial voice, where the soul for a moment tastes that time no longer is. (*AP,* **p. 82**)

28. Music no doubt has this peculiarity that, signifying with its rhythms and its sounds the very movements of the soul—*cantare amantis est*—it produces, in producing emotion, precisely what it signifies. But this production is not what it aims at, any more than a representation or a description of the emotions is. The emotions which it makes present to the soul by sounds and by rhythms, are the *matter* through which it must give us the felt joy of a spiritual form, of a transcendent order, of the radiance of being. Thus music, like tragedy, purifies the passions, by developing them within the limits and in the order of beauty, by harmonizing them with the intellect, in a harmony that fallen nature experiences nowhere else. (*AS,* **p. 62**)

29. But am I God, then, to make a divine work and to form without being formed? Am I asked to create out of nothing? If my work is a kind of concept or word that my creative intuition fashions for itself outside of me out of the dust, what then will it express?

In proportion as the artist approaches his pure type and realizes his most fundamental law, it is indeed himself and his own essence and his own intelligence of himself that he expresses in his work; here is the hidden substance of his creative intuition. (*AP,* **pp. 87–88**)

30. Words are not pure signs ("formal signs") as concepts are. They strike the ear before speaking to the mind, and they signify ideas only by first calling up sense images. They have their own proper realm, their own resonances and associations, and it is only on condition that we master them by constant effort that we may come to use them well.

The psychological mechanism of oral expression is more complex than it would seem at first glance. Since the object of language is to lead the hearer actively to form within him the ideas which are in the mind of the speaker, the latter can succeed in his task only by re-forming in his own mind, beginning with the images which will supply him with words, the same ideas that he bids the hearer to form in his mind. Therefore the word is naturally ordained as to its end, not to an *image* which would be simply "plastered" on to the idea, but to form and manifest the *idea* itself, starting from images which merely serve as matter. The art of oral expression consists in disposing this sensible matter by means of words so as exactly to reveal the idea—which is an entirely spiritual thing. This is by no means easy to do. It has been said that perhaps the most striking and unusual poetic "images" originate in the difficulties that man experiences in telling himself and really making himself *see* even the most ordinary things by the help of the imagery of speech, difficulties which constantly constrain the poets to renew this imagery. (***IL*, pp. 46–47**)

31. The substance of man is obscure to himself; it is only by receiving and suffering things, by awakening to the world, that our substance awakens to itself. The poet can only express his own substance in a work if things resound in him, and if, in him, at the same awakening, they and he emerge together from sleep. All that he discerns and divines in things is thus inseparable from himself and his emotion, and it is actually as a part of himself that he discerns and divines it, and in order to grasp obscurely his own being through a knowledge the end of which is to create. His intuition, the creative intuition or emotion, is an obscure grasping of himself and things together in a knowledge by union of connaturality, which only takes shape, bears fruit and finds expression in the work, and which, in all its vital weight, seeks to create and produce. This is a very different knowledge from what is generally called knowledge; a knowledge which cannot be expressed in notions and judgments, but which is experience rather than knowledge, and creative experience, because it wants to be expressed, and it can only be expressed in a work. This knowledge is not previous or presupposed to creative activity, but integrated in it, consubstantial with the movement toward the work, and this is precisely what I call poetic knowledge.

Poetic knowledge is the intrinsic moment of contemplation from which creation emanates. From it springs the melody that every work of art implies, and which is a meaning that animates a form. For art cannot be satisfied with the object, enclosed in a given category, to which it tends as merely *productive* activity. As *intellectual* activity, art tends in a certain way—I mean a creative way—to Being, which transcends all categories. It is therefore necessary that the object that the artist is shaping, whether it be a vase of clay or a fishing boat, be significant of something other than itself; this object must be a sign as well as an object; a meaning must animate it, and make it say more than it is. (**RR, p. 18**)

32. Nature is all the more beautiful as it is laden with emotion. Emotion is essential in the perception of beauty. But what sort of emotion? It is not the emotion which I called a while ago brute or merely subjective. It is another kind of emotion—one with knowledge. . . . Such emotion transcends mere subjectivity, and draws the mind toward things known and toward knowing more. (**CI, p. 8**)

33. Let us look at the deer and bison painted on the walls of the prehistoric caves, with the admirable and infallible élan of virgin imagination. They are the prime achievements of human art and poetic intuition. By the virtue of Sign, they make present to us an aspect of the animal shape and life, and the world of hunting. And they make present to us the spirit of those unknown men who drew them, they tell us that their makers were men, they reveal a creative Self endowed with immortal intelligence, pursuing deliberately willed ends, and capable of sensing beauty. (**CI, p. 34**)

34. With regard to the natural development of its potentialities, art does not begin with freedom and beauty for beauty's sake. It begins by making instruments for human life, canoes, vases, arrows, necklaces, or wall paintings destined to subject, through magical or non-magical signs, the human environment to the mastery of man. Art must never forget its origins. Man is *homo faber* and *homo poeta* together. But in the historical evolution of mankind the *homo faber* carries on his shoulders the *homo poeta*. (**CI, p. 45**)

35. Art is a virtue of the practical intellect—that particular virtue of the practical intellect which deals with the creation of objects to be made....

Art is intellectual by essence, as the odor of the rose pertains to the rose, or spark to fire. Art, or the proper virtue of working reason, is—in the realm of making—an intrinsic perfection of the intellect. Not in Phidias and Praxiteles only, but in the village carpenter and blacksmith as well, the Doctors of the Middle Ages acknowledged an intrinsic development of reason, a nobility of the intellect. The virtue of the craftsman was not, in their eyes, strength of muscle or nimbleness of fingers. It was a virtue of the intellect, and endowed the humblest artisan with a certain perfection of the spirit. (*CI,* p. 49)

36. Since art is a virtue of the intellect, it demands to communicate with the entire universe of the intellect. Hence it is that the normal climate of art is intelligence and knowledge: its normal soil, the civilized heritage of a consistent and integrated system of beliefs and values; its normal horizon, the infinity of human experience enlightened by the passionate insights of anguish or the intellectual virtues of a contemplative mind. The worshiping of ignorance and rudeness is for an artist but a sign of inner weakness. Yet, the fact remains that all the treasures of the earth are profitable to art only if it is strong enough to master them and make them a *means* for its own operation, an aliment for its own spark. And not all poets have the strength of a Dante. (*CI,* pp. 64–65)

37. The world of the painter is the world of the eye before being and while being the world of the intellect. (*CI,* p. 129)

38. Nature is essentially of concern to the artist only because it is a derivation of the divine art in things, *ratio artis divinae indita rebus.* The artist, whether he knows it or not, consults God in looking at things. (*AS,* p. 61)

39. Christian art is defined by the one in whom it exists and by the spirit from which it issues: one says "Christian art" or the "art of a Christian" as one says the "art of the bee" or the "art of man." It is the art of redeemed humanity. It is planted in the Christian soul, by the side of the running waters, under the sky of the theological virtues, amidst the breezes of the seven gifts of the Spirit. It is natural that it should bear Christian fruit.

Everything belongs to it, the sacred as well as the profane. It is at home wherever the ingenuity and the joy of man extend. Symphony or ballet, film or novel, landscape or still-life, puppet-show libretto or opera, it can just as well appear in any of these as in the stained-glass windows and statues of churches. (*AS,* **p. 65**)

40. Christianity does not make art *easy*. It deprives it of many facile means, it bars its course at many places, but in order to raise its level. At the same time that Christianity creates these salutary difficulties, it superelevates art from within, reveals to it a hidden beauty which is more delicious than light, and gives it what the artist has need of most—simplicity, the peace of awe and of love, the innocence which renders matter docile to men and fraternal. (*AS,* **p. 69**)

41. Art, first of all, is of the intellectual order, its action consists in imprinting an idea in some matter: it is therefore in the intelligence of the *artifex* that it resides, or, as is said, this intelligence is the subject in which it inheres. It is a certain *quality* of this intelligence. (*AS,* **p. 10**)

CHAPTER THREE

BEING

1. It is absurd to seek a cause for God's being, it is legitimate and necessary to seek a cause for the world's being. Out of these two problems is made a single pseudo-problem: why is there being?

In fact, being which is being according to its whole self and in which essence and existence are one, cannot have any cause. On the other hand, being which is participated and in which essence and existence are distinct, absolutely needs to have a cause; and this cause, far from being posited "at the bottom of everything" like a principle in logic, exists necessarily above everything like a boundless plentitude of perfect life whose being transcends infinitely the beings of things and is designated by the same word *being* only in virtue of an *analogy*. If from the outset there is confusion between God's Being, whose richness transcends all thought, and the being common to all things, which is the most general and consequently the poorest of entities, we have an *a priori* positing of pantheism. One is then obliged to choose between Spinozism and Bergsonism. (***BPT*, p. 87**)

2. What, for the philosophy of Saint Thomas and for any sane metaphysics, is the real object of intellectual knowledge, what is it the aim of intelligence to attain and possess?—It is *being*. Intelligence is satisfied only when it has seized the constitutive being, the essence of what it wants to know. (***BPT*, p. 127**)

3. As to Thomist philosophy, it is not the philosophy of time, but the philosophy of being. And it is in terms of being, the formal object of the intelligence, that it knows the distinction and the unity of the soul and the body. (***BPT*, p. 239**)

4. The mind knows that its first duty is not to sin against the light. It must subject to the most careful verification its conceptual equipment, but it cannot prevent itself from rushing toward being. No matter what the price. It is required of the mind not to fall into error, but first of all, it is required of the mind that it *see*. (***BPT*, p. 309**)

5. Being is, indeed, the proper object of the intellect; it is embowelled in all its concepts; and it is to being, wrapped up in the data of the senses, that our understanding is first of all carried. (***DK*, p. 67; *CW* 7, p. 71**)

6. For if the universe of being as being, set free by the mind when it delivers its objects from all materiality, does not fall under the senses, intelligible necessities, on the other hand, are discovered there in the most perfect manner. Thus, the knowledge ordered to such a universe of intelligibility is most certain in itself even though we find it difficult to acknowledge it. For we are an ungrateful and mediocre race which only asks to fail in the highest in what it is capable of, and which, of itself, even when higher gifts have strengthened its eyes, will always prefer the dark. (***DK*, p. 67; *CW* 7, p. 72**)

7. It is extremely remarkable that being, the first object attained by our mind in things—which cannot deceive us since being the first, it cannot involve any construction effected by the mind nor, therefore, the possibility of faulty composition—bears within itself the sign that beings of another order than the sensible are thinkable and possible. (***DK*, p. 214; *CW* 7, p. 228**)

8. The formal object of the intellect is being. What it apprehends of its very nature is what things are independently of us.

From the two truths just enunciated, *the intellect is a truthful faculty,* and *being is the necessary and immediate object of the intellect,* there arises as a corollary a fundamental truth.

By *intelligible* we mean *knowable by the intellect.* But to affirm that being is the necessary and immediate object of the intellect, and that the intellect attains true knowledge, amounts to saying that being, as such, is an object of which the intellect possesses true knowledge; that is to say, that it is intelligible. And to say that being as such is intelligible is to say that intelligibility accompanies being, so that everything is intelligible in exact proportion to its being. We therefore conclude—

... Being as such is intelligible. Everything is intelligible in exact proportion to its being. (***IP,* p. 140**)

9. What is the first truth which the intellect grasps as soon as it has formed the notion of being? It is sufficient to consider the notion to see at once that what is, is (principle of *identity*), or again that what is, cannot not be at the same time and in the same relation (principle of *non-contradiction*). That is to say, that everything is what it is, that it is not what it is not, and that it is everything that it is. (***IP,* p. 181**)

10. Thus knowledge is immersed in existence. Existence—the existence of material realities—is given us at first by sense; sense attains the object as existing; that is to say, in the real and existing influence by which it acts upon our sensorial organs. This is why the pattern of all true knowledge is the intuition of the thing that I see, and that sheds its light upon me. Sense attains existence in act without itself knowing that it is existence. Sense delivers existence to the intellect; it gives the intellect an intelligible treasure which sense does not know to be intelligible, and which the intellect, for its part, knows and calls by its name, which is *being.* (***EE,* p. 11**)

11. Being superabounds everywhere; it scatters its gifts and fruits in profusion. This is the action in which all beings here below communicate with one another and in which, thanks to the divine influx that traverses them, they are at every instant—in this world of contingent existence and of unforeseeable future contingents—either better or worse than themselves and than the mere fact of their existence at a given moment. By this action they exchange their secrets, influence one another for good or ill, and contribute to or betray in one another the fecundity of being, the while they are carried along despite themselves in the torrent of divine governance from which nothing can escape. (*EE,* pp. 42–43)

12. The fact is that Saint Thomas—and this is the most immediate benefit he confers—brings the intellect back to its object, orientates it toward its end, restores it to its nature. He tells it that it is made for being. How could it possibly not give ear? It is as if one told the eye that it is made to see, or wings that they are made to fly. It finds itself again in recovering its object; it orders itself entirely to being; in accordance with the sovereign inclination that things have for their first principle, it tends, above all, towards Subsistent Being Itself.

Simplicity of gaze is at the same time restored to it; artificial obstacles no longer obtrude to make it hesitate before the natural evidence of first principles; it re-establishes the community of philosophy and common sense. (*TA,* pp. 102–3)

13. The proper object of understanding is being. And being is a mystery, either because it is too pregnant with intelligibility, too pure for our intellect which is the case with spiritual things, or because its nature presents a more or less impenetrable barrier to understanding, a barrier due to the element of non-being in it, which is the case with becoming, potency and above all matter.

The mystery we conclude is a fullness of being with which the intellect enters into a vital union and into which it plunges without exhausting it. Could it do so it would be God, *ipsum Esse subsistens* and the author of being. The Supreme "mystery" is the supernatural mystery which is the object of faith and theology. It is concerned with the Godhead Itself, the interior life of God, to which our intellect cannot rise by its unaided natural powers. But philosophy and science also are concerned with mystery, another mystery, the mystery of nature and the mystery of being. A philosophy unaware of mystery would not be a philosophy. (*PM,* pp. 4–5)

14. The object of metaphysics—and we now pass to an altogether different level, an entirely different phase in the process of human intellection—is, according to the Thomists, being as such, *ens in quantum ens,* being not clothed or embodied in the sensible quiddity, the essence or nature of sensible things, but on the contrary *abstractum,* being disengaged and isolated, at least so far as being can be taken in abstraction from more particularized objects. It is being disengaged and isolated from the sensible quiddity, being viewed as such and set apart in its pure intelligible values.

Metaphysics therefore at the summit of natural knowledge, where it becomes fully wisdom, brings to light in its pure values and uncovers what is enveloped and veiled in the most primitive intellectual knowledge. You can see how dangerous it would be to confuse these two phases, these two states and to imagine, that, as so many modern philosophers believe, that for the Thomist the metaphysical habitus is specified by being, as it is primarily attained by our intellect. (***PM,*** **pp. 18–19**)

15. You will also see why the intuition of the principle of identity, every being is what it is, being is being, can possess such value for the metaphysician, can become the object of his enraptured contemplation. Common sense — and therefore the man in the street — makes use of the principle without scrutinising it. "A cat is a cat" says common sense — what more could it say? — so that, if the philosopher comes on the scene and enunciates the principle of identity in front of common sense, the latter will not *see* it, but will merely have the impression that an insignificant commonplace has been affirmed, in fact a tautology. The philosopher, on the other hand, when he enunciates the principle of identity enunciates it as an expression of the metaphysical intuition of being, and thus sees in it the first fundamental law of reality itself, a law which astounds him because it proclaims *ex abrupto,* the primal mystery of being, its combination of subsistence and abundance, a law which is exemplified by objects in an infinite number of different modes, and applied with an infinite variety. It is not as the result of a logistic process that the metaphysician perceives and employs the principle of identity, so that it compels him to reduce everything to a pure identity, that is to say to obliterate all the diversities and varieties of being. For it is with its mode of analogical realisation that he apprehends the principle. When he apprehends being as such, being according to its pure intelligible nature, he apprehends the essentially analogous value of the concept of being which is implicitly manifold and is realised in diverse objects in such fashion as to admit differences of essence between them, complete and vast differences. The principle of identity secures the multiplicity and variety of objects. Far from reducing all things to identity, it is . . . the guardian of universal multiplicity, the axiom of being's irreducible diversities. If each being is what it is, it is not what other beings are. (*PM*, pp. 56–58)

16. It is on the chance occasion when some individual reality is grasped in its singularity by the external sense—a tree, a bird, the calm ocean, a humble little hill, or the glance of a loved one, or a smile, or the gesture of a hand which passes in the instant, and will never return—or on the occasion when, at some privileged moment, my consciousness seizes upon the act of existing of that secret and hidden reality, but eminently mine, which is myself . . . it is . . . on the occasion of some individual reality grasped in its pure singularity that such an intellectual intuition of being is produced. But at the same time and by the same process (for in seeing that this rose *is*, I recognize at the same time that outside my mind there *are* as well, each one in its own particular way, a multitude of other things), it is being itself that is revealed to the intelligence, in the mystery of its limitless horizon, and of the irreducible diversity with which it posits before us each single existent. This is why it is precisely by the intuition of being, as *formally* given to the intellect, that the latter perceives the analogy of *esse* in the fullness of its meaning. What I want to say is that at this point the intellect perceives not only that the concept of being in itself is intrinsically varied (analogy of proper proportionality), just like the concept of all the transcendentals, but also that the analogy of being is *the reason and the key* of the analogy of the transcendentals and that this analogy crosses the boundaries of the infinite: If each one of the diverse existents is good in its own way or one in its own way, it is *because* each one *exists*, or is posited for its own sake and in its own way, outside the mind, and after all is said and done, precisely because there is a self-subsistant *Esse*—known to us analogically even though infinitely above our grasp—in which and with which all the other transcendentals, also raised to pure act, must be absolutely identified. (*UA*, pp. 225–26)

17. A philosopher is not a philosopher if he is not a metaphysician. And it is the intuition of being—even when it is distorted by the error of a system, as in Plato or Spinoza—that makes the metaphysician. I mean the intuition of being in its pure and all-pervasive properties, in its typical and primordial intelligible density; the intuition of being secundum quod est ens. Being, seen in this light, is neither the vague being of common sense, nor the particularised being of the sciences and of the philosophy of nature, nor the derealised being of logic, nor the pseudo-being of dialectics mistaken for philosophy. It is being disengaged for its own sake, in the values and resources appertaining to its own intelligibility and reality; which is to say, in that richness, that analogical and transcendental amplitude which is inviscerated in the imperfect and multiple unity of its concept and which allows it to cover the infinitude of its analogates and causes it to overflow or superabound in transcendental values and in dynamic values of propensity through which the idea of being transgresses itself. (**EE, pp. 19–20**)

18. Substance *as such* is a pure intelligible, it is nothing in itself of what makes things visible and sensible, mutable and divisible. But through it the thing has primary being, and through it all the accidents are maintained in being. Far from being an empty medium, a frame for phenomena, it is the primary ontological root of all and sundry in its permanent actuality, in its essential unity, in its irreducible reality, in its specific and individual originality, so far from being empty and inert that it is the source of all the faculties, of all the operations, of all the activity and the causality of the subject.

This division into substance and accident is a consequence of the very condition of the created being. Created things cannot fill their whole being right away, and they comprise various degrees in being itself. They cannot have immediately and totally completed all the perfection they possess simply because they have their nature; hence their metaphysical composition, hence the fact that they have potency and act, substance and accident: distinctions which suppose another still more profound distinction and which derive in a word from the fact that in God alone essence and existence are one: His nature or divinity is the same thing as His act of being, whereas in the creature *this* and *exist* are necessarily distinct, since it is not Being by itself. (***BPT,* p. 241**)

19. The moment one touches a transcendental, one touches being itself, a likeness of God, an absolute, that which ennobles and delights our life; one enters into the domain of the spirit. It is remarkable that men really communicate with one another only by passing through being or one of its properties. Only in this way do they escape from the individuality in which matter encloses them. If they remain in the world of their sense needs and of their sentimental egos, in vain do they tell their stories to one another, they do not understand each other. They observe each other without seeing each other, each one of them infinitely alone, even though work or sense pleasures bind them together. But let one touch the good and Love, like the saints, the true, like an Aristotle, the beautiful, like a Dante or a Bach or a Giotto, then contact is made, souls communicate. Men are really united only by the spirit; light alone brings them together, *intellectualia et rationalia omnia congregans, et indestructibilia faciens.* (**AS, pp. 32–33**)

20. Greek reason was able to become aware of that glory of the mind which is Knowing, and of the authentic relation between the mind and the extra-mental being of things. In an impulse arrested too soon, and for a fleeting, unforgettable moment, it had the sense of being; it was able to see that the human intellect, in identifying itself immaterially, *intentionaliter*, with the being of things, truly reaches that which exists outside our minds, beginning with the world of matter to which, through our senses, we are naturally adapted. (***TP,* p. 18**)

21. This analogical character, an example of what is called the analogy of strict proportionality, is inscribed in the very nature of the concept of being. It is analogous from the outset, not a univocal concept afterwards employed analogously. It is essentially analogous, polyvalent. In itself it is but a simple unity of proportionality, that is, it is purely and simply manifold and one in a particular respect. (***PM,* p. 64**)

CHAPTER FOUR

THE CHRISTIAN LIFE

1. Christian heroism has not the same sources as other heroisms; it proceeds from the heart of a God scourged and ridiculed, crucified outside the gates of the city. (***FMW,* p. 145; CW 11, p. 76**)

2. The hour at which Christ is nailed to the Cross is not a convenient time at which to ask Him to change water into wine or to multiply loaves and fishes. In that hour something is being enacted that is greater than miracles. The Resurrection will take place; but after the expiration of three days.

If only He will come down from the Cross, that we may see and believe: *ut videamus et credamus.* If only the Church will leave the Cross and ravish our eyes with her beauty and majesty, then shall we believe in her God. Foolish they who reverse the order of things and make the Faith vain by wishing to see before believing; they range themselves on the side of woe. For they have been declared blessed who believe before they see and that they may see: *Beati qui non viderunt et crediderunt.* (***FMW,* p. 146; CW 11, p. 76**)

3. If Faith is able to move mountains, is it powerless to shift the mighty from their seats? If Christians, who life by faith in their private lives, lay aside their faith when they approach the things of political and social life, they must be content to be towed like slaves in the wake of history. (*FMW,* **p. 152; CW 11, p. 79**)

4. The Christian knows that the work of the spirit though often thwarted and often obscure makes constant progress in time; and as one failure follows on another, one secret gain is yet added to another, and time goes forward to the Resurrection, and the history of the world always moves towards the Eternal Jerusalem. (*FMW,* **pp. 156–57; CW 11, pp. 81–82**)

5. It is in the hour of Sorrows of the Messiah that His Kingdom will come, in a way that shall be invisible to the eyes of flesh and to the fallen spirits.

It is moreover to be observed that one who uses only material means is disarmed when a stronger than he deprives him of his weapons. But the Christian is never disarmed. He expands or contracts his field of action according to the turns and changes of human history. He is in the world yet not of the world. No one can deprive him of the first and most important of the means he uses, for these means are of the spiritual order and make use of time without being consumed by it. (*FMW,* **p. 191; CW 11, p. 99**)

6. It is because the Christian conception of life is based upon so concrete, broad, and fruitful a certainty of the equality and community in nature between men that it, at the same time, insists so forcefully on the orderings and hierarchies which spring and should spring from the very heart of this essential community, and on the particular inequalities which they necessarily involve. For in the world of man as in the world of creation, there can be no concourse or communication, no life or movement without differentiation, no differentiation without inequalities. (*RT,* **p. 20**)

7. There is a certain apex of perfection and of supreme achievement, an acme of nature and of natural law to which the régime of grace inaugurated by the New Law is happily suited to carry nature, and to which nature left to itself could not succeed in attaining. Here is one of the essential aspects under which it is true to say that Christianity lifts up within their own order the things of culture and of the commonwealth. Thus there is a Christian honour, natural Christian virtues, a Christian law; thus there is, at work in history, and countered by powerful adverse forces, a Christian leaven which tends to cause human society to pass on into conditions of higher civilization. That Christians should consent to let this inner energy, which it is their task to maintain, waste itself—here is a great loss for nature and for humanity. (***RT,* p. 194**)

8. Catholicism orders our whole life to Truth itself and to subsisting Beauty. It puts into us—above the moral virtues and the intellectual virtues—the theological virtues, and through them gives us peace. *Et ego si exaltatus fuero, omnia traham ad meipsum.* Christ Crucified draws to Him all that is in man; all things are reconciled, but at the height of His heart.

Here is a religion whose moral exigencies are more elevated than those of any other, since the heroism of sanctity can alone fully satisfy them, and which at the same time loves and protects the intelligence more than any other. I say that this is a sign of the divinity of this religion. A superhuman virtue is necessary to assure among men the free play of art and science under the rule of the divine law and the primacy of Charity, and thus to achieve the higher reconciliation of the *moral* and the *intellectual.* (***AS,* pp. 98–99**)

9. Christian sainthood is not a restricted resort. (***RA,* p. 107**)

10. Love created everything in order to diffuse the divine beauty; it cannot be vanquished. (***AF,* pp. 81–82***)*

11. One imagines that in paradise innocence was to ignore good and evil. Purity consists then in behaving as if evil did not exist. I say that is a lie—the purity of the human being is to recognize the law not of the plant, but of man. In paradise all was not permitted; innocence was not to do good or evil without constraint, but to do only good without suffering conflict. The desire for the knowledge of good and evil was the desire to become, like a god, the rule for good and evil, and also to scrutinize what the taste of evil contains of knowledge.

Since that time there is no purity save under another tree, where God extended his arms to die. (***AP,* p. 44**)

12. To live dangerously. The only way that is free of bravado and deception is to live as a Christian; to steal nothing from love and yet to subtract nothing from the law.

It is easy to practice the law without loving, and easy to love while scorning the law. But he who practices the law without loving does not practice the law, because the first commandment is love. And he who loves while scorning the law does not love, because the law is the first will of Him Who loves us, and Whom we love. The Christian gives up his life every day, he embraces both the law and love; which, joined together, form the cross. (*AP,* pp. 45–46)

13. "Psychic" or natural man receives through the senses all that comes to him from without; it is through them that his ideas come to him, by means of the activity of the intellect. Reason, which transcends the senses, labors however in their work-yard. Philosophy, even the best, remains tributary to their materials.

That is why mystical language knows only two terms: life according to the senses and life according to the spirit; those who sleep in their senses and those who wake in the Holy Spirit. Because there are for us only two fountain-heads: the senses and the Spirit of God.

Man has a spiritual soul, but which informs a body. If it be a question of passing to a life wholly spiritual, his reason does not suffice; his tentatives toward angelism always fail. His only authentic spirituality is bound to grace and to the Holy Spirit. (*AP,* pp. 47–48)

14. Dostoievsky met Christ at hard labor, and did not turn away. *Time Jesum transeuntem et non amplius revertentem.*

One day Dostoievsky had his eyes opened on the spiritual world by a touch of the Gospel and he remained forever troubled by it, because the intuitions of his heart did not find on the side of his intelligence the pure certitudes that should have stabilized them. Misguided by his time (and by Jean-Jacques Rousseau) he never believed that reason can justify that distinction between good and evil to which he submitted his thought. He does not seem, either, to have become aware of the essentially supernatural certitude of that faith in the Redeemer to which his soul was appendant.

His misfortune is to have created a sort of schism between love and wisdom, not to have understood that the former is exhaled by the latter. (*AP*, pp. 53–54)

15. And if we were good Christians . . . we would know that it is not we who possess the great truth, but it which possesses us; it does not belong to us, we belong to it. It loves, it preserves, it avenges, it illuminates and vivifies all truth. A Catholic ought to find singular delight, the pleasure of an angel, in rendering to his good enemies, to those friends of his, his enemies, a full and overflowing measure of justice, in recognizing in them all the good and all the true, all the signs of light enough which his God Who makes the rain to fall on the just and the unjust manifests in all of us His generosity and His sovereign dominion. (*AP*, p. 74)

16. In the ethical order, the academicism of virtue, which asks of the human being to make himself into the *copy* of an ideal, changes moral life into a cemetery of lies; in the end the ideal will have duped the conscience, and made of every act an hypocrisy. . . . To imitate the Saints is not to copy an *ideal*, and it is not to *copy* the Saints. It is after their example—and by allowing as they did Another to conduct you where you do not wish to go, and love to configurate you from within into the Form that transcends all form—to imitate the Saints is to become, precisely, an *original*, not a copy; to imitate the Saints is, like them, to become inimitable. (*AP*, p. 79)

17. The perfection of human life does not consist in a stoic athleticism of virtue or in a humanly calculated application of holy recipes, but rather in a ceaselessly increasing love, despite our mistakes and weaknesses, between the Uncreated Self and the created Self. (*RR*, pp. 101–2)

18. What is required of those who believe in God is a witness of God; and what the world demands and expects of the Christian is first and foremost to see the love of truth and brotherly love made genuinely present in and through man's personal life—to see a gleam of the Gospel shining in the one place where the crucial test and crucial proof are to be found, namely the obscure context of relations from person to person. (*RR*, p. 115)

19. Shall we look for the deepest impulse toward that monstrosity—Christians who are anti-Semites? They are seeking an alibi for their innermost sense of guilt, for the death of Christ of which they want to clear themselves: but if Christ did not die for their sins, then they flee from the mercy of Christ! In reality they want *not to be redeemed.* Here is the most secret and vicious root by virtue of which anti-Semitism dechristianizes Christians, and leads them to paganism. (***RR*, p. 132**)

20. Each time one rereads the Gospel, one sees a new reflection of its demands and its freedom, as terrible and sweet as God Himself. Happy is he who loses himself forever in that forest of light, who is ensnared by the Absolute whose rays penetrate everything human. The greater our experience, the more inadequate we feel in the practice of the evangelical teachings, yet at the same time the more we are impressed with their mysterious truth, the more deeply we desire it. That is what may be called the descent of the Gospel within us. When we meditate upon the theological truths, it is we who do the meditating upon theological truths, but when we meditate upon the Gospels, it is the Gospels which are speaking to us; we need only give heed. And no doubt, when we are thus walking with Matthew, Mark, Luke and John, the One Whom the Gospel tells of draws near us, to make our mind a little more alert. *Mane nobiscum, Domine, quoniam advesperascit.* Abide with us, Oh, Lord, for the evening comes.

It seems to me that if a new Christendom is to come into being, it will be an age when men will read and meditate upon the Gospel more than ever before. (***RR*, pp. 216–17**)

21. Suffering, agony, death, are never an end in *themselves.* But *as redemptive, as instruments of love and of gift-of-self in the victory over sin, as exhausting on the absolutely Innocent all the suffering in which the sins of men fructify*—that which is to satisfy in full the justice of God most holy, and to deliver the world from its sin by taking upon Himself the sin of the world—they are an end, the primary end itself for which the Word became flesh and became as one of us.

The Passion of Good Friday is no doubt ordered to the glory of Easter, pledge of the glory of all the elect, and of the final transfiguration of the world. But it is not a mere means, it is an end, an intermediary end. And of itself this victory over sin, over the offense or the evil of God of which the free nihilation of the creature is the cause, is something greater than the victory over death. If, in the couple Passion-Resurrection, Easter appears as a supreme accomplishment, it is because, inseparable from Good Friday, Easter, far from effacing the latter, presupposes it and contains it, by causing the scandal of God nailed to wood to emerge into the exaltation of God risen and of the creature saved; the joy of Easter, insofar as joy of the victory over death, is a dazzling crown of pure silver on the bloody gold of Good Friday. (*GJ*, p. 15)

22. The Christians who think that the Kingdom of God comes in noise and din, and who would like to cause to pass to the front rank of its equipment the resources of modern publicity and of the *mass media of communication* (without suspecting that all these means tend by nature to serve the illusory more than the true) would no doubt do well to reread a little the Gospel. (*GJ*, p. 125)

23. The Cross is so repugnant to our nature, it is so difficult for men to admit the Cross, it is such a reversal of values, that there has been required a very long time, and that there will be required as a long time as the world will endure, in order for the Christian conscience to enter more—and finally to enter fully—into the depths of this mystery.

And likewise, our whole life is not too much for each of us in order to arrive at the end to *regard truly* the Cross of Jesus. Even if our theological faith is without defect and if we do not fall into any doctrinal error, we refuse for a long time to open our eyes on the horror and the dereliction signified by the Cross. We try to find excuses. (*GJ*, p. 34)

24. The Gospel tells us that we are *in* the world and not *of* the world. This is to tell us that the effort we make in the world will remain incomplete in the world, but that we must nevertheless make it with all the more hope, in the assurance that it is completed elsewhere, and that the little good we are able to manage here below, and ever so much more still our sufferings and our very infirmities, are turned to good account by Him Whom we love. (*TA*, p. 158)

25. What is normal for the Christian is to go straight to paradise, to meet our Lord. Not only the reprobate in hell, but even the soul who passes through purgatory as well, whatever question there may be about number or frequency, both represent *abnormal* cases, the first because it supposes revolt against God, the second because it indicates that the soul has not let the redemptive work come to completion within it here below. (*UA*, p. 393)

26. There is something which scandalizes me: it is the manner in which Christians speak of their deceased. They call them the dead—they have not been capable of renewing the miserable human vocabulary on a point which nevertheless concerns the essential data of their faith. The dead! One attends masses for the dead! One goes to the cemetery with flowers for the dead, one prays for the dead! As if they weren't billions of times more living than we! As if the fundamental truth stated in the Preface of the Burial Mass: *vita mutatur, non tollitur*—life is changed, it is not taken away—was itself a dead truth, incapable of fecundating and of transforming the common routine of our manner of conceiving and of speaking. (*NB*, p. 266)

27. As for its moral characterisation from the Catholic viewpoint, antisemitism, if it spreads among those calling themselves disciples of Jesus Christ, seems to be a pathological phenomenon, which indicates a deterioration of Christian conscience when it becomes incapable of accepting its own historic responsibilities and of remaining existentially faithful to the high exigencies of Christian truth. Then, instead of recognising the trials and shocks of history as the visitations of God, and instead of shouldering those burdens of justice and charity demanded by that great fact, it turns aside to substitute phantoms relating to an entire race, phantoms which derive a certain consistency from various real or fancied pretexts; and in giving free rein to feelings of hate which it believes justified by religion, it seeks for itself a sort of alibi.

It is no little matter, however, for a Christian to hate or to despise or to wish to treat degradingly the race from which sprung his God and the Immaculate Mother of his God. That is why the bitter zeal of antisemitism always turns in the end into a bitter zeal against Christianity itself....

We forget, or rather we do not wish to know, that as a man Our Lord was a Jew, the epitome *par excellence* of the Jewish nature, the Lion of

Judah; that His Mother was a Jewess, the flower of the Jewish race; that the apostles were Jews, among with all the prophets; finally, that our whole liturgy is based on Jewish books. How, then, can we express the enormity of the outrage and the blasphemy involved in vilifying the Jewish race? (**AN, pp. 27–28**)

28. In reality, the justice of the gospel and the life of Christ within us want the whole of us, they want to take possession of everything, to impregnate all that which we are and all that which we do, in the secular as well as in the sacred. Action is an epiphany of being. If grace takes hold of us and remakes us in the depth of our being, it is so that our whole action should feel its effects and be illuminated by it. (**IH, p. 293; CW 11, p. 338**)

29. He [St. John of the Cross] tirelessly repeats that the excellence of the love of God, into whom the soul must be transformed, is the measure of the stripping which the senses must undergo. Even the imperfect spirituality of profane wisdom demands a certain measure of this sort of stripping; is it surprising that a divine spiritualization should require a still more radical stripping of the senses? (**DK, p. 359; CW 7, p. 382**)

30. For Christian conscience ... there do not exist two categories in humanity, *homo faber* whose task it is to work, and *homo sapiens* whose task is the contemplation of truth. The same man is both *faber* and *sapiens,* and wisdom calls us all to the freedom of the children of God. (**SP, p. 141**)

CHAPTER FIVE

CHRISTIAN PHILOSOPHY

1. As soon as it no longer is a question of philosophy considered in itself but of the manner in which men philosophize, and of the divers philosophies which the concrete course of history has brought into existence, the consideration of the *essence* of philosophy no longer suffices; that of its *state* must be undertaken.

From this viewpoint of the state, or the conditions of exercise, it is manifest that before philosophy can attain its full, normal development in the mind it will exact of the individual many emendations and purifications, a disciplining not only of the reason but of the heart as well. To philosophize man must put his whole soul into play, in much the same manner that to run he must use his heart and lungs.

And here we encounter what in my opinion is the crucial point of the discussion, a point, moreover, at which dissent among Christians and non-Christians becomes unavoidable. One does not have to be a Christian to be convinced that our nature is weak (although the Christian's knowledge that nature is wounded makes him more keenly aware of these matters), or that the mere fact that wisdom is an arduous attainment is enough to account for the very high incidence of error in this area. But the Christian believes that grace changes man's state by elevating his nature to the supernatural plane and by divulging to him things which unaided reason would be unable to grasp. He also believes that if reason is to attain without admixture of error the highest truths that are naturally within its ken it requires assistance, either from within in the form of inner strengthening or from without in the form of an offering of objective data; and he believes that such assistance has in fact become so much an established part of things under the New Law that it has ushered in a new regimen for human intelligence. (*CP*, pp. 17–18)

2. To be a prince or merely his minister is not an alternative which affects a man's nature, but it considerably alters his state. In one sense, the advent of Christianity did dethrone philosophic wisdom and raise theological wisdom and the wisdom of the Holy Spirit above it. Once philosophy acknowledges this new arrangement, its condition in the human mind is thoroughly changed. I think that every great philosophy harbors a mystical yearning, which in fact is quite capable of throwing it out of joint. In a Christian regime, philosophy understands that even if it can and ought to sharpen this desire, it is not up to philosophy itself to consummate it. Philosophy, then, is wholly orientated toward a higher wisdom, and thus it is made able to achieve some degree of self-detachment and be relieved by some of its ponderousness. (*CP*, pp. 27–28)

3. Let us bear in mind that if we are to grasp Christian thought in its integrity we must take into account not only philosophy (even Christian) but also, and inseparably, theology and the wisdom of the contemplatives. Today as a consequence of the breakdown of Christian unity, philosophy has fallen heir to all kinds of tasks, preoccupations, and troubles which in former times were part and parcel of the other two forms of wisdom. (An example of this is seen in the idea of the Kingdom of God, which the philosophers turned into the Realm of Minds and finally into Mankind in the sense of a Herder or an Auguste Comte.) As philosophy became inwardly less Christian it grew fat on the left-overs of Christian consciousness. This accounts for the paradox of a philosophy like that of Descartes, or even of Hegel, appearing more deeply tinged with Christianity and less strictly philosophic than the formally Aristotelian (but inspirationally supra-Aristotelian) philosophy of St. Thomas Aquinas. (*CP*, p. 32)

4. [Christian philosophy] may be described as Christian, not on account of its essence, indeed, but only on account of its state or conditions of existence. This is the case in the domain of speculative philosophy. Or it may be described as Christian on account of the use which it makes, within its very texture, of truths of another order established in theology by reason of the existential state of its very subject (human conduct). This is the case in the domain of moral philosophy.... St. Thomas, without explicitly dealing with it, took an extremely clear position on it. He affirmed this position not only by his principles but by his action—by fighting and suffering; for his whole battle was to gain recognition for Aristotle and to overthrow Averroës, which is to say, to gain recognition of the essential autonomy of philosophy and at the same time to link it vitally, in its human exercise, with the higher illumination of theological wisdom and the wisdom of the saints. "If today there are Thomist writers who are shocked by the very idea of a Christian philosophy, this simply proves that one can repeat a master's formula without knowing of what spirit one is, and that Thomism, like every other great doctrine, can be dissected like a corpse by professors of anatomy instead of being thought by philosophers." (*EE,* **pp. 140–41**)

5. By nature, religion and philosophy are made to give one another mutual aid and support. It happens, through the fault of the human subject, that the one can harm the other and vitiate its development. There is nothing quite so dangerous for a philosopher and a philosophy as the religious exploitation sometimes too eagerly undertaken as a result of a mistaken and imprudent zeal. (*BPT,* **p. 18**)

6. As for us, we know that intelligence is what, as they say, makes our specific difference, what makes us *men;* and that it is by the intellect that we possess our good, the *truth.* In it therefore we defend both our very nature, our humanity, and our beatitude, the joy of the truth.

This is what Christian philosophy proclaims. This is why there is no conciliation possible between Christian philosophy and any thought set up against the intellect. (*BPT,* **p. 145**)

7. Philosophy, however, though distinct from Christianity, is in interrelation with it, and must deal with matters pertaining to religion, if it is to understand and analyze concretely the problems of human life and human conduct. Not after the fashion of any necessary requirement, but after the fashion of a concrete and existential suitability, the natural manifestation of the eternal Word, in which philosophy is rooted, in a certain sense invokes the supernatural manifestation of the Incarnate Word, in which faith is rooted. (*RT*, p. 197)

8. I am aware that there are other forms of philosophical existentialism, and that there is, in particular, a Christian existentialism which challenges atheistic existentialism with a perspicacity all the keener and a pugnacity all the more lively for the fact that theirs is a family quarrel. In the order of a genuine phenomenology (where moral and psychological analysis is really an approach to ontological problems and where the very purity of an unprejudiced investigation allows philosophy to plumb human experience and to isolate its real meanings and values) this Christian existentialism is past master, and it contributes very valuable discoveries. Nevertheless, I do not believe that it can ever develop into a metaphysic properly so called, any more than any other philosophy which refuses to admit the intellectual intuition of being. It cannot father a metaphysics that is comprehensive, articulated, founded upon reason, and capable of exercising the functions of wisdom as well as of knowledge. For the same reason I do not believe that in the evolution of philosophical thought, it will ever succeed in becoming more than a side issue, nor will it successfully resist the historic impetus which at the present time gives to atheistic existentialism (and will in the future give to new systems issuing in like fashion out of the central positions of the long tradition that goes back to Descartes) an ephemeral but vast power over men's minds. To arrest that trend the springs would have to be purified all the way back to their original source. It would be necessary to overcome acquired habits and critical negligence accumulated in the course of three centuries, and to break with the errors common to existentialist irrationalism, idealism, empirical nominalism, and classical rationalism. (*EE*, pp. 129–30)

9. A strange and thrilling conflict this, between Descartes and Aristotle! Descartes is a sincere Christian, and a true philosopher, and, encouraged by the Reverend Cardinal de Bérulle, he wishes to give us a Christian philosophy of such a kind, as Malebranche is soon to say, that we shall not be obliged to go to pagans like Plato and Aristotle to seek philosophical truth.

But is being a true philosopher and a sincere Christian enough to build up a Christian philosophy? Or does that rather call both for achievements which result from superior wisdom and light, and for foundations which, depending in themselves upon natural reason alone, are not necessarily guaranteed by the sincerity of the philosopher's faith, and can be more insecure in him than in a pagan, in spite of the most brilliant apologetic? Could it not be that this miscreant of an Aristotle, so bitterly envied by Descartes—that this Greek, much more of a realist and much less an idealist than certain Christians, may alone have succeeded—not certainly in building up a Christian philosophy—but in giving birth to the principles of reason which the Angel of the School will come to use, carrying them to a much higher degree of purity, in order to give to Christian philosophy its real and proper form? Could that not be, perhaps, because Aristotle followed most faithfully the line of nature, and doubtless also because it pleased God, in order better to establish the universality of His domain as well as the fairness of His conduct, to prepare in pagan ground, cut off from the influence of revealed faith, the work of natural reason which was to become the preferred instrument of the sacred doctrine? (**DD, pp. 88–89**)

10. Christian philosophy is a philosophy of being; more than that, a philosophy of the superabundance of being; and in this it stands incomparably higher than other great philosophies of being.... Christian philosophy, better than the Greek, has seen that it is natural that immanent activity should superabound, since it is super-existing. Purely transitive activity is egoistic.... Immanent activity is 'generous', because, striving to be achieved in love, it strives to achieve the good of other men, disinterestedly, gratuitously, as a gift. Christian theology is a theology of divine generosity, of that superabundance of divine being which is manifested in God Himself, as only revelation can tell us, in the plurality of Persons, and which is also manifested, as we could have discovered by reason alone, by the fact that God is Love, and that He is the Creator. And God, whose essence is his own beatitude and his own eternal contemplation, God who creates, gives, has

never ceased to give, He gives Himself through Incarnation, He gives Himself through the Holy Ghost's mission. It is not for Himself, St. Thomas says, it is for us that God has made everything to His glory. When contemplation superabounds in efficacious love and in action, it corresponds within us to that divine superabundance communicative of its own good. (*SP,* pp. 145–46)

CHAPTER SIX

THE CHURCH

1. It is no accident that some of the greatest saints in the Christian Calendar were non-conformist deviants in their time; but they still grasp the future with their conceptions. (*RON,* **p. 198**)

2. It is sometimes said that psychoanalysis is a substitute for, the 'ersatz' of, the confessional, as that is practised—especially in the Catholic Church. This seems to me completely inaccurate. On the one hand, it would be an illusion to think that confession exercises a curative power on neuroses and psychoses. Its aim and object are not therapeutic. Moreover, the memories which the penitent imparts to his confessor, belong by definition to the sphere of the conscious or of the pre-conscious, and depend upon voluntary evocation. If the penitent scrutinizes himself and strains his will to go further, he risks suffering from being over-scrupulous: he does not enter the world of the unconscious. Far from uncovering the roots of his neurosis or of his frenzy, a neurotic who goes to confession overwhelms his confessor with the deliverances of his neurosis.

On the other hand, confession is in itself an act of reason and of will, in which the two personalities facing each other are as much as possible closed to each other. It is characteristic of the relations between confessor and penitent, that the penitent unveils the secret of his heart to the priest as to the instrument of God; while the confessor subordinates all his personality to his ministry. (*SP,* pp. 123–24)

3. Though the law of progress tends to dominate in history wherever the effort of the mind is able to succeed—especially in the order of knowledge and in the order of industrial technique—yet the law of human things is for the most part the law not of progress, but of alteration—the law of generation and corruption.

There is one human thing, it is true, that is an exception—the Church, which must grow and be made perfect to the fullness of the age of Christ, and which will know no decline. But that is precisely because it is not only human but divine, and it is animated by an omnipotent "form" which if it tolerates the imperfections of matter is never dominated by matter. In every other human society there follows decrepitude after growth, the alternation of lower forms and higher forms, the equilibrium of good and evil striking their balance in a variety of modes. But observe that the Church is not a foreign body isolated in the midst of humanity, but on the contrary the divinely formed organism into which the human race is called to enter that it may share in the Divine life. (*TS,* p. 113)

4. A superior agent is not confined or shut up within itself. It radiates. It stimulates the inner forces and energies of other agents—even autonomous in their own peculiar spheres—whose place is less high in the scale of being. Superiority implies a penetrating and vivifying influence. The very token of the superiority of the Church is the moral power with which she vitally influences, penetrates, and quickens, as a spiritual leaven, temporal existence and the inner energies of nature, so as to carry them to a higher and more perfect level in their own order—in that very order of the world and of the life of civilization, within which the body politic is supremely autonomous, and yet inferior with regard to the spiritual order and the things that are of the eternal life. This is exactly what the absolutist or the totalitarian States (as well as, in the intellectual realm, rationalist philosophy) most stubbornly refuse to admit, even when they claim to respect freedom of religion (by shutting up religion in its own heavenly sphere, and forbidding it any in-

fluence on earthly life, as if it were possible to forbid heaven to send rain on the earth or shine upon it). (*MS,* **pp. 164–65**)

5. The universal supplications of Good Friday are heard above the din and clamour of the age . . . as though the Church were gathering all her love together in preparation for some divine work before the great anguish. (*NC,* **p. 87**)

6. The soul and the life of the Church are grace and charity, which are realities invisible in themselves. There where grace and charity are, there there is the life of the Church, and there there passes the blood of Christ. There where grace and charity are not, there there is not either the life of the Church, and there there does not pass either the Blood of Christ. (*CC,* **p. 11**)

7. Like Christ, the Church is of God, not of the world. And we have to choose to be friends of the world or friends of God. Because the world is not only created nature as God made it, but this very nature insofar as crowned with the triple diadem of the evil desires of human Liberty—Pride at being supremely self-sufficient; Intoxication with knowledge, not for the sake of truth but for power and possession; Intoxication in being overcome and torn by pleasure. (*TP,* **p. 34**)

8. There are believers, however, whose faith consists merely in accepting what the Church teaches them, while leaving the responsibility to the Church, and without risking themselves in this adventure. If they inquire as to what the Church holds to be the truth, it is in order to be advised as to the properly authenticated formulas which they are asked to accept, not in order to learn the realities which are given them to know. God said certain things to His Church; in turn the Church said them to me; it is the priests' business, not mine; I subscribe to what I am told, and the less I think about it the happier I am. I have a deaf and merely mechanical faith (or, as Frenchmen say, *la foi du charbonnier*), and I am proud of it. A faith of this kind if it were put to the extreme would be no longer a matter of knowledge at all, but merely one of obedience, as Spinoza saw it. And in that conception of faith I do not believe because of the testimony of the Prime Truth teaching me from within, by means of the truths universally presented by the Church. I believe because of the testimony of the Church *as a separate agent*, because of the testimony of the apostles taken apart from the testimony of the Prime Truth which they heard, but which means nothing to me; I believe because of the testimony of men. But then where is the theological virtue of faith? Here again the way in which intelligence functions within faith leads, practically speaking, to emptying faith of its content. Here again we have to do with an intellect which in its general way of functioning has given up seeing, and thus warps the conditions of exercise required by faith. For faith, which believes, and does not see, dwells—dependent on the will moved by grace—in the intellect, the law of which is to see. From this it follows that it is essential for faith not to be quiet, to suffer a tension, an anxiety, a movement, which beatific vision alone shall end. *Credo ut intelligam.* Essentially faith is an élan toward vision. That is why it wants to flower here below in contemplation, to come to be *fides oculata* through love and gifts of the Spirit to enter into the very experience of that which it knows through riddles and "in a glass, darkly." Actually faith's eyes are never closed. It opens its eyes in the sacred night and if it does not see, it is because the light which fills this night is too pure for sight which is not yet one with God. (***RR*, pp. 209–10**)

9. God has his adversaries, not in the metaphysical but in the moral order. Yet his adversaries are always at His service. He is served by the martyrs, and by the executioners who made them martyrs. Everything that happens in the history of the world serves in one way or another the progress of the Church and, in a more or less obscure way, some kind of progress of the world. This line of thought is apt to enlarge our horizon in a notable way. (***FMW*, p. 87; CW 11, p. 47**)

10. The history of the Church is already the history of the kingdom of God begun in time, of the "crucified kingdom," which at the end will be revealed; whereas the history of the secular world will come to its final term only by the means of a substantial "mutation," which is designated as the conflagration of the world, and which will engender it to the kingdom. (***IH*, p. 102; CW 11, p. 216**)

11. I hold that while awaiting the "beyond-of-history" in which the kingdom of God will be accomplished in the glory of full manifestation, the Church is already the kingdom of God in the order called *spiritual* and in the state of pilgrimage and crucifixion; and that the world, itself, the order called *temporal,* this world enclosed in history, is a divided and ambiguous domain—at once of God, of man, and of "the Prince of this world."

The Church is holy, the world is not holy; but the world is saved in hope, and the blood of Christ, the vivifying principle of the redemption, acts already within it; a divine and hidden work is being pursued in history, and in each age of civilization, under each "historic sky," the Christian must work for a proportionate realization (while awaiting the definitive realization of the Gospel, which is for beyond time), for a realization of the Gospel exigencies and of Christian practical wisdom in the socio-temporal order—a realization which is itself thwarted, in fact, and more or less masked and deformed by sin: but that is another matter.

Since men taken collectively live most often "in the senses," and not according to reason, the work of which I am speaking (when Christians themselves do not fail to do it—otherwise, it is adverse forces which undertake it, under the sign of destruction) is, according to the ordinary course of things, all the more combated and all the more betrayed the more it succeeds in passing into existence: hence a necessity of recommencement, of renewal of effort at the lowest point, obliging history to surmount itself perpetually—"from fall to fall"—until it comes to its goal. (***IH,*** **p. 126; CW 11, pp. 231–32**)

12. It is true that death is but a second birth, and that our life on earth is a kind of uterine life, in the obscure womb of the griefs and dreams and passing images of this enigmatic world. "Life is changed, life is not taken away." That is why, in the liturgy of the Catholic Church, the feasts of the saints are celebrated on the anniversary of their death, that is, of their real and definite birth. But this is so only because the soul of man is an individual substance, existing by and unto itself as a perfectly defined unit; because it is destined to objective immortality, genuine personal immortality, not in time and history, but in eternity. (***RR,*** **p. 54**)

13. Descartes' error ... was to belittle and to misunderstand the nature of theology among the sciences, as it was to belittle and misunderstand the role of the Church in the intellectual government of humanity.

It is true enough that, as theology is able in fact to exist *in us* only by making use of human wisdom, a theological system which makes use of a mistaken philosophy will itself be mistaken; but Descartes did not see that theology, being a science *in itself* superior to and independent of our systems of human wisdom, must judge according to its light and choose for its service the philosophic system which in its hands will be the best instrument of truth, and which for that reason will itself be true. Nor did he see that the Church, not being a simple human administration of the spiritual, nor merely the archivist of the Lord, but being rather His Bride attended by His Spirit, has not as its role the sole function of preserving the deposit of revealed truth but rather to make the light of this truth shine forth in human intelligence. It is therefore scarcely credible that she should have had to wait for the philosophy of Descartes in order to be able to set up the true theology; hardly credible either that Scholastic theology, the theology the Church affirms as being fully her own, where her whole tradition reaches its highest point, should be an erroneous theology. (For in Descartes' time the Church had already taken St. Thomas for her *doctor communis*.) Nay more, in virtue of her essential mission constituted guardian of the natural order and of the health of reason, as well as of the supernatural order and truth, the philosophic tradition itself which she had assumed could not without temerity be held as null and void. (**DD, pp. 84–85**)

CHAPTER SEVEN

CULTURE AND CIVILIZATION

1. Culture or civilization is the expansion of the properly human life, including not only whatever material development may be necessary and sufficient to enable us to lead an upright life on this earth, but also and above all moral development, that development of speculative activities and of practical (artistic and ethical) activities which is properly worthy of being called a human development. It appears thus that culture is natural in the same sense as the labor of reason and virtue, of which it is the fruit and earthly fulfillment. It answers the fundamental desire of human nature, but it is the work of the spirit and liberty adding their effort to the effort of nature. Because this development is not only material, but also and principally moral, it goes without saying that the religious element plays a principal part in it—civilization developing thus between two poles: the economic pole on the side of the most urgent human necessities of the ethico-biological order, the religious pole on the side of the most urgent human necessities as regards the life of the soul. (*IH,* **pp. 95–96; CW 11, p. 212**)

2. In the eyes of the Christian, culture and civilization, being ordered to a terrestrial end, must be referred and subordinated to the eternal life which is the end of religion, and must procure the terrestrial good and the development

of the diverse natural activities of man according to an efficacious attention to the eternal interests of the person and in such a manner as to facilitate the access of the latter to his supernatural ultimate end: all of which thus superelevates civilization in its own proper order. But it remains that culture and civilization have a specifying object—the earthly and perishable good of our life here below—whose proper order is the natural order (superelevated as I have said). In themselves and by their own end, they are engaged in time and in the vicissitudes of time. Moreover, it can be said that none of them has clean hands. The order of culture or civilization appears then as the order of the things of time, as the *temporal* order.

Whereas the order of faith and the gifts of grace, being concerned with an eternal life which is a participation in the intimate life of God, constitutes by opposition an order to which the name *spiritual* most rightly belongs and which, as such, transcends the temporal sphere....

Thus, the distinction between the temporal and the spiritual appears as a distinction essentially Christian. (***IH*, pp. 97–98; CW 11, pp. 213–14**)

3. The truly and fully natural man is not nature's man, the uncultivated soil, but the virtuous man, the human soil cultivated by undeviating reason, man formed by the inner culture of the intellectual and moral virtues. He alone has consistency, a personality....

But nature acquires a countenance in our case only when it is perfected by the mind, man acquires his truth only when he is fashioned from within by reason and virtue (I mean undeviating reason whose supremacy in our life is guaranteed only by the supernatural gifts; I mean true virtue which is entirely deserving of the name only if it is vivified by charity). (***RC*, p. 7**)

4. Culture consists in knowing, but it does not consist only in knowing: it consists even more in *having known*, and in the forgetting of a great many things because we know them too well and because they have passed down from memory into the very marrow of our bones. Culture implies the possessing of the means of liberty, but first it implies being inwardly free....
The richest and most beautiful of cultures is nothing if moral development does not keep pace with scientific and artistic development, if man is not

conscious of the reasons he has for living, and the reasons he has for dying. (*EM*, pp. 154–55)

5. By virtue of the Charity which is its essential source and principle, Christian spirituality overflows into things outside; it diffuses its own excellence. It acts upon the world, on culture, on the temporal and political order of human life. More than ever in the days to come Christianity will seek to impregnate culture and to save even the temporal life of mankind; less than ever will it be at peace with the world. (*FMW*, pp. 109–10; CW 11, p. 59)

6. The modern world sprang out of a great aspiration of the heart of man for the blessing of worldly goods, which is the source of capitalism and mercantilism and industrialism in the economic order, as it is the source of naturalism and rationalism in philosophy. (*FMW*, p. 117; CW 11, p. 63)

7. The only authentic civilization is one where man has released the idea of knowledge in its objective purity, and kept and developed within himself the sense of truth. If civilization, which is profoundly shaken today, is to be reborn, one of the basic conditions for this rebirth must be, in the realm of human communications, that the function of language, which has been perverted by the procedures of the totalitarian states, be returned to its true nature, and, in the realm of the inner life of the spirit, that knowledge likewise be returned to its true nature; knowledge must cease being ordained to power or being confused with it; the intellect must recognize, at all degrees of the scale of knowing—whether we consider the most simple factual truths of daily experience, or truths by which science formulates, in terms of observation, the laws of phenomena, or truths by which philosophy grasps, in terms of intelligible perception, the structures of being and the universal principles of existence—the intellect must recognize in the whole expanse and diversity of its domain the *sacred* nature of truth. (*RR*, p. 16)

8. With regard to culture, atheism is a mirror of the state to which the human being has been reduced. For since man is the image of God, it is but natural that he thinks of God according to the state in which that image presents itself at a given moment of culture. Absolute atheism means that the personality of man is definitely endangered; and that all the masks, the words, the shams, the facades, the palliatives, the plasters and cosmetics with which human conscience tries to deceive itself and to give us the appearance of men are henceforth useless and will be cast away. Picasso's art, in its present character, is the true art of atheism; I mean of that thorough defacement of contemporary man, which is mirrored in atheism. We are no more persons than the distorted, imbecile faces of those ferocious females are true human faces. (***RR*, p. 99**)

9. Civilization has its origin at once in the exigencies of our rational nature and in freedom, in the sense of freedom of choice or free will, thanks to which the constitution of the political community—commenced, prepared and dictated by nature—is completed as a human achievement of reason and virtue. And, through the *dynamism of freedom*, civilization, taking thus its point of departure in nature and liberty, tends toward freedom in the sense of *freedom of autonomy*—the expansion and growing realization of human nature. It tends towards a *terminal freedom*, which is terminal only from a certain point of view and in a certain order of things (since it concerns but an infra-valent or intermediary end), which ... can be described as follows. Civilized life tends to grant the human person—that is, the concrete person of each member of the multitude—an increasingly larger measure of independence from the external and internal constraints of Nature; an independence growing according to the very tendencies and the intimate law of human nature itself, as human and endowed with reason; and assured by the economic guarantees of labour and property, by political rights, by civil virtues, and the culture of the mind. In this way, certain conditions and certain means are prepared, and certain beginnings of spiritual freedom, of the freedom *purely and simply terminal*, whose conquest and achievement transcend the proper order of nature and the civil community. (***SP*, p. 109**)

10. The life of civilization, even when responding to natural inclination and primordial instinct, is not a simple physical fact: it is a work of reason and of virtue. And what are the virtues directly concerned with this life? They are the natural virtues which are grouped around the four cardinal virtues of prudence, justice, fortitude and temperance. (***SP*, p. 179**)

11. It is possible to conceive in the abstract a civilization which unites all men in the purely natural unity of a temporal life, conducted in accordance with pure reason. This, however, is a fiction because humanity is not in a state of pure nature; it is in the state of a nature which has fallen and been redeemed. As a matter of fact, civilizations vary as much as languages, and are often opposed to each other. Can we hope that one day there will exist here below a civilization which is really universal? By this I certainly do not mean a uniform civilization, but one which would allow for inward variety and internal dissimilarities in accord with the historical, national and cultural heritage, and the vocations proper to different human groups; for such a variety responds to the natural necessity of exchange and metabolism and also of the activating tension between these groups. If one day there is to exist here below a truly universal civilization, that is to say, one founded—no matter how strong its internal differences—on first common principles, and recognizing in an organic and actual manner the same common good, it will have risen higher, in its own order, by the influence of the energies whose source is the grace of Christ. (*SP,* **pp. 181–82**)

12. The man of common humanity has a right to the "pursuit of happiness"—a slogan which, if well-understood, denotes a series of implications: it denotes the pursuit of the primary conditions and primary possessions which are the prerequisites of a free life and whose denial, endured by so many multitudes, is a cruel wound in the flesh of humanity; it denotes the pursuit of the superior possessions of culture and the mind, the pursuit of liberation from want, from fear and from servitude; it denotes the pursuit of that freedom and that human plenitude bound up with the mastery of self which, in the imperfect order of temporal life, is the highest goal of civilization and which, in a superior order, asks to be perfectly realized by means of the spiritual transformation of the human being and which man can attain only by great love and the incessant gift of self. (***CD,* p. 94**)

13. Modern civilization is a wornout garment. One cannot sew new pieces on it. It requires a total, and, I may say, substantial recasting, a transvaluation of cultural principles: since it is a question of arriving at a vital primacy of quality over quantity, of work over money, of the human over the technological, of wisdom over science, of the common service of human persons over the individual covetousness of unlimited enrichment or the State's covetousness of unlimited power. (*IH,* p. 207; *CW* 11, p. 283)

14. For the Christian, what constitutes the bond and the unity of those who must work for a temporal renovation of the world is, first of all—to whatever class, or race or nation they may belong—a community of thought, of love and of will, the passion of a common task to be accomplished, and it is here a community not material-biological like that of race, or material-sociological like that of class, but truly human. The idea of class, the idea of the proletariat is here transcended. (*IH,* p. 236; *CW* 11, p. 300)

15. If bad philosophy is a plague of society, what a blessing good philosophy must be for it! Let us not forget, moreover, that if Hegel was the father of the world of today insofar as it denies the superiority of the human person and the transcendence of God, and kneels before history, St. Augustine was the father of Christian Western civilization, in which the world of today, despite all threats and failures, still participates. (*UP,* p. 4)

16. What determines the unity of a culture is first and above all a common philosophical structure, a certain metaphysical and moral attitude, a common scale of values—in short, a common idea of the universe, of man and of life, of which the social, linguistic, and juridical structures are, so to speak, the embodiment.

This metaphysical unity has long been broken—not completely destroyed, certainly, but broken and as it were effaced in the West. What constitutes the drama of Western culture is that its common metaphysical basis is reduced to an absolutely insufficient minimum, so that it holds together now primarily through matter, and matter is incapable of keeping anything together. (*TA,* p. 69)

17. I have a notion that the widespread infatuation that today prevails for action, technique, organization, inquiries, committees, mass movements, and the new possibilities that sociology and psychology are discovering—all things that are far from being contemptible, but which, if one confided only in them, would lead to a strange naturalism in the service (so one hopes) of the supernatural—will some day give rise to a great deal of strong disappointments. (*TP,* p. 233)

18. One of the gravest lessons afforded us by the experience of life is that, in fact, in the practical conduct of most people, all those things which in themselves are good and very good—science, technical progress, culture, etc., and even the knowledge of moral laws, and religious faith itself, faith in the living God (which of itself demands the love of charity)—all these things, *without love and good will,* serve to make men all the more evil and the more unhappy.... without love and charity, man turns the best in him into an evil that is yet greater. (*PP*, pp. 342–43)

19. Man is not merely an animal of nature, like a skylark or a bear. He is also an animal of culture, whose race can subsist only within the development of society and civilization, he is a *historical* animal: hence the multiplicity of cultural or ethico-historical patterns into which man is diversified; hence, too, the essential importance of education. Due to the very fact that he is endowed with a knowing power which is unlimited and which nonetheless only advances step by step, man cannot progress in his own specific life, both intellectually and morally, without being helped by collective experience previously accumulated and preserved, and by a regular transmission of acquired knowledge. In order to reach self-determination, for which he is made, he needs discipline and tradition, which will both weigh heavily on him and strengthen him so as to enable him to struggle against them—which will enrich that very tradition—and the enriched tradition will make possible new struggles, and so forth. (*EC,* p. 2)

20. Christian wisdom does not suggest that we return to the Middle Ages: it would have us move further forward. Besides, the civilization of the Middle Ages, however magnificent and splendid it may have been, more splendid still, no doubt, in the refined memories of history than in the reality of experience, was very far removed from the full realisation of the Christian idea of civilization. (*RC,* p. 23)

21. The world is perishing of dead weight. It will recover its youth only through poverty of the spirit. To seek to save the things of the spirit by going in the first place to try and discover, in order to serve it, the most powerful means in the order of matter, is an illusion which is all too common. You might as well tie the wings of a dove to a steam hammer. (*RC,* p. 48)

22. What makes the modern world so terribly tempting is that it puts forward, it vulgarizes so, rich temporal means which are so crushing and oppressive; it uses them with so much ostentation and such power as to induce the belief that they are the principal means. They are a principal means for matter, not a principal means for the spirit. (*RC,* p. 49)

CHAPTER EIGHT

DEMOCRACY AND DEMOCRATIC SOCIETY

1. Democracy is a paradox and a challenge hurled at nature, at that thankless and wounded human nature whose original aspirations and reserves of grandeur it evokes. (*CD,* p. 65)

2. I am convinced that a democratic society is not necessarily an unarmed society, which the enemies of liberty can calmly lead to the slaughterhouse in the name of liberty. Precisely because it is a commonwealth of free men, it must defend itself with particular energy against those who, out of principle, refuse to accept, and who even work to destroy the foundations of common life in such a regime, the foundations which are liberty and cooperation and mutual civic respect. What here distinguishes a society of free men from a despotic society is that this restriction of the destructive liberties take place, in a society of free men, only with the institutional guarantees of justice and law. (*RM,* pp. 90–91)

3. Is not the tragedy of our age to be found in the fact that modern democracies have lost all confidence in themselves? Their vital principle is justice, and they do not want to run the risks of justice. They do not want, it seems, to run any risks whatsoever. They invoke justice, but they pursue purely utilitarian politics, and they pursue them inefficiently and clumsily....

Modern democracies suffer from a philosophy of life which undermines and annihilates their vital principle from within. If they must refind the sense of justice, and of risk, and of heroism, it is under condition of rejecting their materialist philosophy, and of viewing in full light a personalist conception of life and of society. (*SP,* p. 70)

4. The scientific spirit is of invaluable help for culture in so far as it develops in human minds, in a general way, respect and love for truth and the habits of intellectual accuracy. (This is why, let us observe parenthetically, the scientific spirit of the thirteenth-century Schoolmen played so basic a part in the rise of Western culture.) Yet neither culture nor democracy lives on science alone. Science, especially modern science, deals with the means, especially with the material means, of human life. Wisdom, which deals with the ends, is also— and above all—necessary. And the fact remains that democratic faith— implying as it does faith in justice, in freedom, in brotherly love, in the dignity of the human person, in his rights as well as in his responsibilities, in that power of binding men in conscience which appertains to just laws, in the deep-rooted aspirations which call for political and social coming of age of the people—cannot be justified, nurtured, strengthened, and enriched without philosophical or religious convictions—"whether theological, metaphysical, or naturalistic"—which deal with the very substance and meaning of human life. (*RR,* p. 169)

5. The internal contradiction of the delusive democracies ... is to want to build up a work of justice and of law, of respect for the human person, and of civic friendship; and, at the same time, to refuse in this work all traces of transcendence of the supreme foundation of justice and personality; in short, to wish to be surpassingly human, and also practically atheistic. (*SP,* p. 79)

6. Faith in the dignity of the human personality, in brotherly love, in justice, and in the over-worldly worth of the human soul as outweighing the whole material universe—faith, in a word, in the conception of Man and his Destiny which the Gospel has deposited at the very centre of human history—this faith is the only genuine principle by which the democratic ideal may truly live. Any democracy which, by its very nature as a political entity, lets this faith be corrupted, lays itself open to that extent to disruption. (*FC*, pp. 14–15)

7. Civic friendship, which is a profane image of brotherly love, is ... not an original state, granted ready-made; it is something to be conquered ceaselessly and at the price of great difficulties. It is a work of virtue and of sacrifice, and in this sense it is that we behold therein the heroic ideal of such a democracy. (*SP*, p. 87)

8. But the important thing for the political life of the world and for the solution of the crisis of civilization is by no means to pretend that Christianity is linked to democracy and that Christian faith compels every believer to be a democrat; it is to affirm that democracy is linked to Christianity and that the democratic impulse has arisen in human history as a temporal manifestation of the inspiration of the Gospel. The question does not deal here with Christianity as a religious creed and road to eternal life, but rather with Christianity as leaven in the social and political life of nations and as bearer of the temporal hope of mankind; it does not deal with Christianity as a treasure of divine truth sustained and propagated by the Church, but with Christianity as historical energy at work in the world. It is not in the heights of theology, it is in the depths of the secular conscience and secular existence that Christianity works in this fashion, while sometimes even assuming heretical forms or forms of revolt where it seems to be denying itself, as though the broken bits of the key to paradise, falling into our destitute lives and combining with the metals of the earth, were more effective in activating the history of this world than the pure essence of the celestial metal. (*CD*, pp. 37–38)

9. Even under mixed and aberrant forms, and even in the Rousseauist tendency to naturize (and denaturize) the Gospel, is it not the Christian leaven that is still seen fermenting in the bosom of human history, while the unhappy adventure of the individualist democracy is unfolding itself? Under purer forms, and tending this time ... to evangelize nature, is it not always, and more truly, the Christian leaven that is at work in history, preparing in it a personalist democracy? (*SP*, p. 69)

10. Democracy of the individual and humanism of the individual arise from an anthropocentric inspiration. Materialism, atheism, dictatorship, are their fatalities. By saying to men, you are gods by your own essence and will, they have debased men. Practically they have left to men no other internal weight than flat egoism and longing for material possessions. (*SP,* **p. 67**)

11. As regards ... the internal dynamism of human life, modern man looked for happiness—without any final end to be aimed at, or any rational pattern to which to adhere; the most natural concept and motive power, that of happiness, was thus warped by the loss of the concept and the sense of purpose or finality (for finality is but one with desirability, and desirability but one with happiness). Happiness became the movement itself toward happiness, a movement at once limitless and increasingly lower, more and more stagnant. And modern man looked for democracy—without any heroic task of justice to be performed and without brotherly love from which to get inspiration. The most significant political improvement of modern times, the concept of, and the devotion to, the rights of the human person and the rights of the people, was thus warped by the same loss of the concept and the sense of purpose or finality, and by the repudiation of the evangelical ferment acting in human history; democracy tended to become an embodiment of the sovereign will of the people in the machinery of a bureaucratic state more and more irresponsible and more and more asleep. (***RR,* pp. 187–88**)

CHAPTER NINE

DESCARTES AND CARTESIAN PHILOSOPHY

1. But thought that is involuntarily ambiguous, therefore ambiguous in its essential mode of thought, is but the more insidious. Descartes' thought is cloaked in a double prestige . . . that of science and of apologetics, of geometry and of spirituality. His thought quite sincerely takes the part of religion against theists and libertines, and presents itself as Christian, and as such will be received; and yet its fundamental principles will develop into a sheer enmity of reason against faith. By intention, Descartes' philosophy is realistic, and by its theory of knowledge as by its *angelism,* it introduces into modern philosophy the germ of the most intense idealism. It is turned toward physical reality, which it wishes to submit to knowledge more perfectly than anyone has ever before dreamed of doing—and in isolating metaphysics from experience as in making the physical world the domain of mechanicism, it prepares the fatal separation in modern times of metaphysics from science. In the practical realm it is rooted in submission to the established order—and in the realm of intellectual speculation it brings about the triumph, willy-nilly, of the very principle of individualism. (***DD,*** **pp. 44–45**)

2. May we be allowed at this point to dwell upon a curious way in which Cartesian philosophy proceeds: as Mr. Gilson has remarked, it breaks the superior conciliations in which the great antinomies of the real were resolved by Scholasticism into two contrasting pieces which it affirms separately and which it cannot reunite; and from there on at almost every point this philosophy places side by side a thesis and an antithesis equally extreme, one of which serves to mask the other. It declares, for example, that the idea of God is the clearest and most distinct of all our ideas, and claims to grasp the existence of God in His idea alone—and thus it inclines toward ontologism; but it also states that the infinite absolutely cannot be an object of knowledge, and that it is presumptuous to seek in things the mark of their ordination by the intelligence of God—and thus it inclines toward agnosticism. (***DD*, p. 45**)

3. Descartes' religion seems like a simple insurance taken against the risks of the beyond, which should leave him free here below to conduct his life, his philosophy and his pleasures as his reason alone dictates. All that in no way prevents that faith from being sincere. But it is the sign that this sincere faith has been seriously immobilized, in a water-tight compartment. Thanks to a happy and sagacious division of labor which the Gospel had not foreseen, one can serve two masters at the same time, drawing nothing but profit from the one without losing any of the benefits promised by the other. (***DD*, pp. 67–68**)

4. Descartes thought to safeguard faith by isolating it from intelligence, by making a discrimination at once simple, radical, expeditious and particularly adapted to his personal convenience, between the *clear*, object of science and the *obscure*, which can be object of revelation (for our finite understanding cannot impose its limits upon the Creator). He thought to safeguard faith by making both the human domain of science and the divine dominion of revelation appendant to the incomprehensible and infinite omnipotence of the God Who can neither err nor cause to err. But he kept them two absolutely disconnected domains having no contact one with the other, in such a way as to put the divine realm *wholly and completely* out of reach of our understanding.

He did not perceive that he was succeeding only too well with his enterprise. He has so much respect for revealed datum that he does not dare even to apply his intelligence to it; he places the things of God so carefully beyond the reach of our mind that it can henceforth understand nothing about them; in order the better to worship God, he raises the Cross so high that it becomes invisible. It is a case of too much respect, too much fear: as though the union of reason with infused faith could only bring about disasters, and as though our understanding was *absolutely* incapable, even with grace and faith, of arriving at *some intelligence* of the depth of God. There, in its pure formal line, is the most characteristic tendency of Cartesian thought, irrespective of the attenuations and the deflections which it may have undergone at the hands of the philosopher in virtue of his subjective inclinations. . . . The separation is too perfect and the solution is only too obviously a provisional one, this friendly estrangement being bound, by the very nature of things, to turn to conflict. Henceforth between reason and mystery, between science and faith, the antinomy is inevitable. (**DD, pp. 79–80**)

5. It is often said that Descartes is first of all a physicist and a scientist: that is true as far as his predilections are concerned, true also with regard to his most genuine claims to glory and to his most inspired activity. But Descartes is not a "positivist" scientist such as we see about us nowadays; he remains substantially a metaphysician—and that is why he has done so much harm to metaphysics, which can be hurt only by its own. Descartes is a metaphysician unfaithful to metaphysics, who turns aside voluntarily toward the plains, toward the vast, flat country watered by the river Mathematics; a metaphysician who does not like metaphysical truth, who finds this too-white manna tasteless, and who makes his way, followed by countless people, toward the savory onions of the physical world. (**DD, p. 92**)

6. The most deep-seated characteristic of the Cartesian reform is more than anything else, in my opinion, one of disjunction and rupture. St. Thomas brings together, Descartes cleaves and separates, and this in the most violently dogmatic way.

The most apparent of these cleavages, the most obvious for the public at large, the least typical for the philosopher, is the break with intellectual tradition. A classical platitude shows us Descartes confronting authority with evidence, at the birth of individualism in modern philosophy.

In reality he himself would have detested that individualism. What he wanted was to be the Aristotle of the modern era and to reign forever over the Schools. On the other hand, Cartesianism has nothing of an absolute beginning about it—it is in continuity with Scholasticism.

Yes—that is perfectly true. But Descartes' continuity with Scholasticism, with a Scholasticism itself considerably abased, is, indeed, a *material* continuity. In the order of *formal* and decisive characteristics, he breaks with it, completely reversing its movement of thought. And the fact remains that the example he gave of making a clean sweep and finding out everything by himself all over again (supposedly by himself alone) is the part of his work best retained by his successors. He has not been the Aristotle of the modern schools—not at all. But every modern philosopher is a Cartesian in the sense that he looks upon himself as starting off in the absolute, and as having the mission of bringing men a new conception of the world. (***DD*, pp. 166–67**)

7. Concerning metaphysics itself, Descartes left an insoluble contradiction as a legacy to modern thought. On the one hand, in order that the knowledge of the existence of God may be the most certain of all knowledge, the idea of God must be a clear idea in the Cartesian system, the clearest and most distinct idea of all—an intellectual intuition. Here we have modern thought launched in the direction of ontology and of pantheism. On the other hand, the infinite is in no way intelligible to us; it is vain to speculate upon it; no science of it is possible. And there we have modern thought launched toward agnosticism. Pantheism, agnosticism, it will ceaselessly swing back and forth between the two terms of this contradiction. (***DD*, pp. 175–76**)

8. Aristotle said that there is more joy in knowing divine things imperfectly and obscurely than in knowing perfectly the things proportioned to our minds. And thus the nature of our intellect is to drag itself along toward divine things. Descartes on the contrary, boasted of devoting only a very few hours a year to metaphysical thoughts. In his eyes, it is important "to have thoroughly understood once in one's life the principles of metaphysics," but "it would be very harmful to occupy one's understanding in meditating

upon them, because it would then be unable to attend to the functions of the imagination and the senses as well." Cartesian understanding does not drag itself along toward things divine, it settles comfortably in worldly things. Cartesian science is by essence a rich man's, a propertied man's science. What is, first of all, important to him is not the dignity of the object, even though it be obtained only through certainly not luxurious means—what is important to him is the perfection of the means, it is the comfort of clear ideas. (***DD*, pp. 176–77**)

9. In the moral realm one cannot throw off the supernatural order without warping at the same time the order of nature, for nature itself requires that order should be everywhere acknowledged. In the realm of wisdom it is the same, and Descartes' offense against the theological order necessarily is accompanied by an offense against the philosophical order. Turning aside from the mysterious lights which used to dominate it, philosophy which had once been Christian undergoes an upsetting of its internal order, the hierarchy proper to philosophy is subverted. . . .

In the *Principles* he [Descartes] represents philosophy or science as a tree whose roots are Metaphysics, whose trunk is Physics, and whose branches are Medicine, Mechanics and Ethics; Metaphysics does nothing then but fasten the tree of science to the soil and begin the production of the sap. The fruit—the delectable ultimate, according to the ancients—we are to demand of the practical sciences.

The Cartesian upsetting consists then in making metaphysics the first part and no longer the last, the beginning and not the end, the base and no longer the peak of philosophy—a useful organ and no longer the head; an upsetting of capital importance one might say, since it amounts to putting the head in the place of the feet. (***DD*, pp. 90–92**)

10. Cartesian idealism did not build up a theodicy, it imagined one, brilliant, incoherent and invulnerable, like great edifices in a dream. Rationalism dreams a great deal; because reason left to itself asks only to sleep the sleep of the senses. It stirs in its sleep; the flash of a human glance gleams on the side of a heap of torpor, that the mischievous genii weary with illusions. If Christian philosophy remains more awake, if in it reason comes out of the shadows of "admirable science" to adhere to the real with all its strength, it is because an ardor for being far sharper than the ardor which springs from reason's sole resources inwardly stimulates it. (***DD*, p. 160**)

11. In Descartes's case, God is the guarantor of science and of geometric reason, and the idea of God is the clearest of all ideas. Yet the divine infinite is declared to be absolutely inscrutable; we are blind to it; and so a germ of agnosticism is already present in Cartesian rationalism. God acts by a pure plenitude of efficiency, without ordering things to an end; and just as His despotic liberty could make square circles and mountains without valleys, so it rules good and evil by an act of pleasure. (***IH*, p. 33; CW 11, pp. 172–73**)

12. Such is the admirable feat of authentic realism: basing itself on the *unity* of man, an intelligent corporal substance, it distinguishes in him *two* principles, each incomplete, whose union makes up the human being. It is impossible more profoundly to distinguish the soul and the body, since this soul has a proper activity and life, independent (at least if one considers them in their intrinsic structure) of the body itself which it informs. It is impossible more closely to unite them, since they constitute one single essence and exist in one and the same existence (which is that of the soul communicated to the body). The body *is* not, it cannot be without the soul. It is not a machine once made which then receives life, and which the soul directs from the middle of the brain, like Descartes's fountain-maker, "who must be at the observation points where all the pipes of his machinery converge." For it, to be is to live; from the sole fact that it is, it is living and organic, because what causes it to be is the union of prime matter, pure ontological potency, with the soul which informs it and which, being in the body as substantial form, is entirely in all the body and in each of its parts. As to the soul, it is spiritual and subsistant, it is a substance, it can be without the body, but without the body it is an *incomplete* substance because it has in its nature not only to be able to exercise the spiritual operations of the intellect and the will, but also to inform the body substantially: so that according to its natural mode of operating, the very exercise of its spiritual operations depends *(extrinsically)* on the body and the sensitive faculties. Thus the soul alone is not man, the human person. Although it derives from the soul both its subsistence and the characteristic properties of personality (that is intelligence and the control of its acts), the human person is the complete substance, composed of spiritual soul and of body; to the point that the soul, when separate—deprived moreover of the exercise of the sensitive faculties, which *are* not without the body—cannot as an incomplete substance (incomplete *in ratione speciei*) be called a person, the very metaphysical notion of person requiring the integrity of nature. Thus it is that philosophy prepares the way for the revealed dogma of the resurrection of the body.

Here we are then, far from the ingenuous scorn of the body and the sensitive faculties professed by the spiritualists of the school of Descartes or of Plato. But at the same time all the being, the life, the actuality that man has he derives from his soul, and that soul is an immaterial substance—a doctrine which is truly the friend of truth and of peace, truly human, which honours all that God has made. (***BPT*, pp. 245–46**)

13. Cartesian dualism breaks man up into two complete substances, joined to one another no one knows how: on the one hand, the body which is only geometric extension; on the other, the soul which is only thought—an angel inhabiting a machine and directing it by means of the pineal gland. (***DD*, p. 179**)

14. The notion Descartes had of science itself indicates the strangest confusion of ideas. It is a science purely human, since it is obtained through reason alone; but instead of being an ensemble of different kinds of science, each having its own special degree of abstraction and intelligibility, its own principles and methods, and its own mode of certitude, it is a single universal science, completely one, as is the science of God, Who sees everything in its essence. Instead of resulting in the slow labor of generations, in the imperfect way of human things, which means both continued effort on the part of everyone and the magisterial authority, however precarious, of a few, it is established perfect at one stroke, by one man, just as the revelation was accomplished in its perfection by One alone, by the only Son, and as "the state of true religion" was "ordained by God alone." Instead of having as its supreme criterion the evidence of the object, and of resolving itself into real things by means of sense intuition, the source of all our knowledge, it resolves into divine truthfulness itself, like angelic knowledge, and it rests formally and above all on the authority of God the Author of clear ideas and Creator of our faculties of knowledge, just as supernatural faith has for its formal reason the authority of God the Author of revelation. Instead of being purely speculative, in so far as it studies nature, it is both speculative and practical like theology—*scientia eminenter speculatica et practica,* or rather it is first of all practical, and it will provide by itself "the sovereign good of human life," in giving us mastery of ourselves and of the world. Science as Descartes conceives it is a human science which would be at the same time divine by revelation, or better still, would be the very science of God and of the Angels. If this be so, it is no doubt by virtue of the idealism and, if I may use the word, of *the angelism* which in general characterizes Cartesian philosophy; but it is also that Knowledge always remained for Descartes the *science admirable* of the tenth of November, 1619, and that his dream was for him truly the revelation of Knowledge. (**DD, pp. 27–29**)

15. With Descartes, everything changes. . . . Philosophy is sufficient absolutely and unto itself alone in the soul; not only is its object of the natural order, but to all intents and purposes it demands that its subject as such be cut off from all supernatural life, cut off from itself as Christian. Hence is explained the absurd myth from which we are still suffering, of a man presumably in the state of pure nature in order to philosophize, who crowns himself with grace in order to merit heaven. The crown will not be long in falling away like a useless accessory. The man of nature—of fallen nature—will remain. The Cartesian revolution has been a process of secularization of wisdom. (**DD, p. 174**)

CHAPTER TEN

PHILOSOPHY OF EDUCATION

1. The educational task is both greater and more mysterious and, in a sense, humbler than many imagine. If the aim of education is the helping and guiding of man toward his own human achievement, education cannot escape the problems and entanglements of philosophy, for it supposes by its very nature a philosophy of man, and from the outset it is obliged to answer the question: "What is man?" which the philosophical sphinx is asking. (*EC,* **p. 4**)

2. [The aim of education] is to guide man in the evolving dynamism through which he shapes himself as a human person—armed with knowledge, strength of judgment, and moral virtues—while at the same time conveying to him the spiritual heritage of the nation and the civilization in which he is involved, and preserving in this way the century-old achievements of generations. The utilitarian aspect of education—which enables the youth to get a job and make a living—must surely not be disregarded, for the children of man are not made for aristocratic leisure. But this practical aim is best provided by the general human capacities developed. And the ulterior specialized training which may be required must never imperil the essential aim of education. (*EC,* **p. 10**)

3. It is clear that the primary aim [of education] is determined by human nature. The question "What is man?" is the unavoidable preamble to any philosophy of education. It has two implications: first, a philosophic or "ontological" implication, dealing with human nature in its essential being; second, a scientific or "empiriological" implication, dealing with human nature in the phenomenal characteristics that lie open to our modern sciences of observation and measurement. These two implications are in no way incompatible; they complement each other.

With respect to both the mind and the body, science, and especially empirical psychology, provides us with invaluable and ever-growing information, by which our practical approach to the child and the youth must profit. But, by itself, it can neither primarily found nor primarily guide education, for education needs primarily to know what man is—what are the constitutive principles of his being, what are his place and value in the world, what is his destiny. This has to do with the philosophical knowledge of man—including additional data which relate to his existential condition. (*EM*, p. 51)

4. Every theory of education is based on a conception of life and, consequently, is associated necessarily with a system of philosophy.... Education "follows the flux and reflux of philosophical currents." It is not an autonomous science, but dependent upon Philosophy. (*EM*, pp. 39–40)

5. If the conception of man, of human life, human culture, and human destiny is the basis of all education, we must insist that there is no really complete science of education, just as there is no really complete political science, except such as is correlated with and subordinate to the science of theology. The reason is simple. Man is not merely a natural being, an *ens naturale*, but is called to a supernatural end. He is in a state of either fallen nature or of nature restored. The existence or non-existence of original sin and the effects thereof, the *vulnera naturae*, is a question of no small importance to education. (*EM*, pp. 41–42)

6. Christian education is intent on making sense-perception, which is the very basis of man's intellectual life, more and more alert, accurate, and integrated; it appeals confidently to the deep, living power of imagination

and feeling as well as to the spiritual power of reason; it realizes that in the development of the child hand and mind must be at work together; it stresses the properly human dignity of manual activity. (*EM,* **p. 130**)

7. Christian education does not tend to make a man naturally perfect, an athletic, self-sufficient hero with all the energies and beauty of nature, impeccable and unbeatable in tennis and football as well as in moral and intellectual competitions. It tries to develop as far as possible natural energies and virtues, both intellectual and moral, and tied up with, and quickened by, infused virtues, but it counts more on grace than on nature; it sees man as tending toward the perfection of love despite any possible mistakes and missteps and through the very frailty of nature, praying not to be put to trial and sensing himself a failure, but being at the same time more and more deeply and totally in love with his God and united with Him. (*EM,* **p. 132**)

8. The curriculum in the humanities of a Christian college must deal still more than that of a secular college with the whole of human culture. The significant thing, and what causes our approach to be Christian, is the perspective and inspiration, the *light* in which all this is viewed. (*EM,* **p. 135**)

9. Thus the fact remains that the complete and integral idea of man which is the prerequisite of education can only be a philosophical and religious idea of man. I say philosophical, because this idea pertains to the nature or essence of man; I say religious, because of the existential status of this human nature in relation to God and the special gifts and trials and vocation involved. (*EC,* **p. 6**)

10. In truth, if the modern world is so concerned with education, it is not because of the fact that it has made any extraordinary discoveries in that field; it is, as Chesterton says, because modern man has lost his bearings; he knows neither where he is nor where he is going. Without doubt, this is why he is so concerned about others. (*EM,* **p. 41**)

11. It is obvious that man's education must be concerned with the social group and prepare him to play his part in it. Shaping man to lead a normal, useful, and cooperative life in the community, or guiding the development of the human person in the social sphere, awakening and strengthening both his sense of freedom and his sense of obligation and responsibility, is an essential aim. But it is not the primary, it is the secondary essential aim. The ultimate end of education concerns the human person in his personal life and spiritual progress, not in his relationship to the social environment. (*EC,* pp. 14–15)

12. [Man] is a political animal because he is a reasonable animal, because his reason seeks to develop with the help of education, through the teaching and co-operation of other men, and because society is thus required to accomplish human dignity. (*SP,* p. 55)

13. The rôle of the instincts, of the feelings, of the irrational is even greater in social and political than in individual life. It follows, therefore, that a work of education, taming the irrational to reason, and developing the moral virtues, must constantly be pursued within the political body. (*RM,* pp. 55–56)

14. As concerns the social changes in the contemporary world, teachers have neither to make the school into a stronghold of the established order nor to make it into a weapon to change society. The dilemma would not be solved if the primary aim and function of education were defined in relation to society and social work. In reality they are defined in relation to intelligence. Then the dilemma is transcended because teachers must be concerned, above all, with helping minds to become articulate, free, and autonomous. (*EM,* p. 59)

15. If we remember that the animal is a specialist, and a perfect one, all of its knowing-power being fixed upon a single task to be done, we ought to conclude that an educational program which would aim at forming specialists ever more perfect in ever more specialized fields, and unable to pass judgment on any matter that goes beyond their specialized competence, would lead indeed to a progressive animalization of the human mind and life. . . . As the life of bees consists of producing honey, the real life of man would consist in producing in a perfectly pigeonholed manner economic values and scientific discoveries, while some cheap pleasure or social enter-

tainment would occupy leisure time, and a vague religious feeling, without any content of thought and reality, would make existence a little less flat, perhaps a little more dramatic and stimulating, like a happy dream. The overwhelming cult of specialization dehumanizes man's life.

Fortunately, nowhere in the world has any educational system been set up solely on this basis. Yet there exists everywhere a trend toward such a conception of education, following a more or less conscious materialistic philosophy of life. This represents a great peril for the democracies, because the democratic ideal more than any other requires faith in and the development of spiritual energies—a field which is over and above any specialization—and because a complete division of the human mind and activities into specialized compartments would make impossible the very "government of the people, by the people, and for the people." How could the common man be capable of judging about the good of the people if he felt able to pass judgment only in the field of his own specialized vocational competence? (*EC,* p. 19)

16. To help a child of man to attain his full formation as a man: if man were that kind of queer animal capable of science and with no spirit, which is fancied by most contemporary philosophers—a bee, a beaver, or a wolf having conversations and making atom bombs—education should be concerned with training him in specialized skills, symbolic logic, and adjustment to the environment. But if man is a fleshly creature endowed with spiritual intelligence—a person called to exercise and conquer freedom—education has to train him in the *humanities*—but what does this word humanities mean? Does it mean composing Latin verses, sitting down in a cozy study lined with bookshelves to read Epictetus and Montaigne, or airing opinions on who was the author of Shakespeare's plays and what was the date of the first edition of Proust's novels? That's a pleasant ideal, but reserved, I fear, for old professors in the short stories of young novelists.

I submit that the humanities are those disciplines which make man more human, or nurture in man his nature as specifically human, because they convey to him the spiritual fruit and achievements of the labor of generations, and deal with things which are worth being known for their own sake, for the sake of truth or the sake of beauty. Such things bring to us, in one way or another, the impact of the transcendentals, and oblige us to think *really,* or at the level of universality.... Knowledge of these things helps man to advance toward liberty, fosters in him civilized life, and is by nature in tune with the mind's natural aspiration to wisdom. (*EM,* **pp. 83–84**)

17. Education is essentially education in the humanities and in the genuine ability to think. And it has to perform its task in a world which thirsts, no doubt, for the liberation of the human person, but in which powerful trends tend to make the human person and the human mind controlled by the constraints of matter, and thought controlled by action. (*EM,* **p. 100**)

18. As a matter of fact, a young man will choose his specialty for himself and progress all the more rapidly and perfectly in vocational, scientific, or technical training in proportion as his education has been liberal and universal. Youth has a right to education in the liberal arts, in order to be prepared for human work and human leisure. But such education is killed by premature specialization. (*EC,* **p. 64**)

19. Education directed toward wisdom, centered on the humanities, aiming to develop in people the capacity to think correctly and to enjoy truth and beauty, is education for freedom, or liberal education. Whatever his particular vocation may be, and whatever special training his vocation may require, every human being is entitled to receive such a properly human and humanistic education. (*EM,* **p. 69**)

20. There is no other foundation for the educational task than the eternal saying "It is truth which sets man free." It appears, by the same token, that education is fully human education only when it is liberal education, preparing the youth to exercise his power to think in a genuinely free and liberating manner—that is to say, when it equips him for truth and makes him capable of judging according to the worth of evidence, of enjoying truth and beauty for their own sake, and of advancing, when he has become a man, toward wisdom and some understanding of those things which bring to him intimations of immortality. (*EM,* **pp. 47–48**)

21. Moreover, is there anything of greater import in the education of man than that which is of the greatest import for man and human life? For man

and human life there is indeed nothing greater than intuition and love. Not every love is right, nor every intuition well directed or conceptualized, yet if either intuition or love exists in any hidden corner, life and the flame of life are there, and a bit of heaven in a promise. Yet neither intuition nor love is a matter of training and learning, they are gift and freedom. In spite of all that, education should be primarily concerned with them. (*EC,* p. 23)

22. School and college education is only part of education. It pertains only to the beginnings and the completed *preparation* of the upbringing of man, and no illusion is more harmful than to try to push back into the microcosm of school education the entire process of shaping the human being, as if the system of schools and universities were a big factory through the back door of which the young child enters like a raw material, and from the front door of which the youth in his brilliant twenties will go out as a successfully manufactured man. Our education goes on until our death. (*EC,* pp. 25–26)

23. The school and the university constitute an educational sphere of their own, which is autonomous both with regard to the family and to the state—there takes place here that great humanistic privilege which is academic liberties, but in which the educational rights of the family and the educational rights of the political community have to be respected, and in actual fact intertwine. The school is not an organ either of the family or of the civil community; its position is free, not subservient, yet subordinated to superior and more primordial rights: subordinated, I should like to say, to the family's rights as regards primarily morality, to the state's rights as regards primarily intellectual equipment. (*EM,* p. 112)

24. Education depends first and foremost on the family. For the end of the family is not only to beget offspring—promiscuity would be enough for that—but to beget them as children of man or to bring them up spiritually as well as physically. (*MS,* pp. 119–20)

25. The primary purpose of schools, colleges, universities, of education in general, is not to teach us how *to do* something, but rather first to furnish us with the means, and especially the knowledge, which enable us to learn how

to be in accordance with all the formative qualities and lasting perfections of soul and mind. (*EM*, p. 155)

26. The primary aim of education in the broadest sense of this word is to "form a man" or, rather, to help a child of man attain his full formation or his completeness as a man. The other aims (to convey the heritage of culture of a given area of civilization, to prepare for life in society and for good citizenship, and to secure the mental equipment required for implementing a particular function in the social whole, for performing family responsibilities, and for making a living) are corollaries and essential but secondary aims. (Parenthetically, it must be observed that education, in the broad sense of the word, continues during the entire lifetime of every one of us. The school system is only a *partial* and *inchoative* agency with respect to the task of education.) (*EM*, pp. 50–51)

27. Teaching is an art; the teacher is an artist. Is the teacher, then, like a sculptor, a powerful Michelangelo who belabors the marble or despotically imposes the form he has conceived on the passive clay? Such a conception was not infrequent in the education of old. It is a coarse and disastrous conception, contrary to the nature of things. For if the one who is being taught is not an angel, neither is he inanimate clay. (*EC*, p. 30)

28. The teacher exercises a real causal power on the mind of the pupil, but in the manner in which a doctor acts to heal his patient: by assisting nature and co-operating with it. Education, like medicine, is *ars cooperativa naturae*.... The *principal agent* in the educational process is not the teacher, but the student. (*EM*, p. 60)

29. Educators, however, must not expect too much from education.... St. Thomas holds that the teacher actually engenders knowledge in the soul of the pupil, and this is equally true of moral habits and of virtue; but, in so doing, he acts as an instrumental and not as an efficient cause. His duty is not to mold the child's mind arbitrarily as the potter molds the lifeless clay; rather it is his task to assist the mind, the living, spiritual being, which he is endeavoring to develop, and which in that process of development must be the principal agent. For education, like life, is, in the words of philosophy, an

immanent activity. In like manner, the teacher's task is to co-operate with God, Who is the Source of Truth and the First Cause, Whose action surpasses that of all created agencies, Who can obtain results that no human teacher can obtain, and Who is continually teaching His rational creatures by various means, at one time using force, at another, persuasion; now employing external agencies and now speaking directly to the individual soul. "The wisdom of Providence," says St. Augustine, "guards us from without and instructs us from within." (*EM,* **p. 43**)

30. All serious-minded observers agree that the split between religion and life is the root of the spiritual disorder from which we suffer today. It is preposterous to make this split begin in childhood and to perpetuate it in the educational system by cutting off religious training from the training proper to schools and colleges. Young people are aware of the fact that school and college education is in charge of furnishing their minds with each and every knowledge required by the realities of life. If religious knowledge is disconnected from this education, it is normal to deem it something separate and additional, either superfluous or merely related to private sentimentality. It is the very right of the child and the youth to be equipped through his formal education with religious knowledge as well as with any knowledge which plays in essential part in the life of man. (*EM,* **p. 77**)

31. As long as the teaching as a whole, in the high school as in college, is permeated with a general philosophy which relies only on sense experience and facts and figures, disintegrates reason and denies its proper perceptive power and the most valuable certainties of which the human intellect is capable— and the first of which is the rational knowledge of God's existence; as long as chaotic information is cultivated in the place of integrated knowledge and spiritual unity, the very soil and natural background on which religious convictions may thrive in youth will remain rough and barren. (*EM,* **p. 81**)

32. While dealing with the first steps in man's formation, education must itself be aware of the genuine hierarchy of intellectual values, be guided by such awareness in its task of preparation, preserve in the youth the natural germs of what is best in the life of the mind, and equip them with the beginnings of those disciplines of knowledge which matter most to man. It is a pity to see so many young people bewildered by highly developed and specialized, but chaotic, instruction about anything whatever in the field of particular sciences and miserably ignorant of everything that concerns God and the deepest realities in man and the world. What we are faced with, in this regard, is a kind of regular frustration—by adults and the general organization of teaching—of certain of the most vital needs and aspirations, and even of the basic rights, of intellectual nature in young persons. (***EM,*** **pp. 54–55**)

33. Education and teaching must start with experience, but in order to complete themselves with reason. (***EC,*** **p. 46**)

34. [The fourth fundamental rule of education] demands that teaching liberate intelligence instead of burdening it, in other words, that teaching result in the freeing of the mind through the mastery of reason over the things learned. (***EC,*** **p. 49**)

35. Reason which receives knowledge in a servile manner does not really know and is only depressed by a knowledge which is not its own but that of others. On the contrary, reason which receives knowledge by assimilating it vitally, that is, in a free and liberating manner, really knows, and is exalted in its very activity by this knowledge which henceforth is its own. Then it is that reason really masters the things learned. (***EC,*** **pp. 50–51**)

36. The right of the child to be educated requires that the educator shall have moral authority over him, and this authority is nothing else than the duty of the adult to the freedom of the youth. (***EC,*** **p. 33**)

37. [There] are many excellent things in modern methods and so-called progressive education, but that the idea of making the school into a paradise of freedom, untrammeled happiness and doing as you please for children is no better for their psychological and moral welfare than the old and nefarious idea of education by the rod. Modern psychology has become aware of the fact that it is a basic need of the child himself to feel both protected and guided by somebody invested with unquestionable authority—and this first of all in the family, of course, but also in the school. The frustration of such a need leaves the child in a vacuum which invites neurosis and anxiety; it is, to be sure, the worst of those frustrations which today's parents are so desperately eager to avoid. (*EM,* **p. 109**)

38. In the educational task, adult people do not have to impose coercion on children, with a kind of paternalism or rather imperialism of the grown-ups, in order to impress their own image upon the child as upon a bit of clay. But what this service requires from them is, first, love and, then, authority—I mean genuine authority, not arbitrary power—intellectual authority to teach and moral authority to be respected and listened to. For the child is entitled to expect from them what he needs: to be positively guided and to learn what he does not know. (*EM,* **p. 58**)

39. It is clear that the teacher must adapt himself to the child, but education properly so called does not begin until the child adapts himself to the teacher and to the culture, the truths and the systems of value which it is the mission of the teacher to transmit to the child. (*EM,* **p. 40**)

40. It is true that a teacher teaches a human subject, Tom or Mary, and that his authority must always be intent on encouraging the child and appealing to his or her own power of insight and understanding. But it is no less true that he teaches an object—mathematics or grammar—and has primarily to make the human subject capable of freely and eagerly submitting to the object and the requirements of the object; he has to teach his pupils the exacting ways through which they prepare for an adult life where they will be obliged to make the best of situations *not* of their choosing and to do not as they please but as they ought. (*EM,* **p. 109**)

41. Ready-made knowledge does not, as Plato believed, exist in human souls. But the vital and active principle of knowledge does exist in each of us. The inner seeing power of intelligence, which naturally and from the very start perceives through sense-experience the primary notions on which all knowledge depends, is thereby able to proceed from what it already knows to what it does not yet know.... This inner vital principle the teacher must respect above all; his art consists in imitating the ways of the intellectual nature in its own operations. (*EC,* **pp. 30–31**)

42. Beauty makes intelligibility pass unawares through sense-awareness. It is by virtue of the allure of beautiful things and deeds and ideas that the child is to be led and awakened to intellectual and moral life. (*EC,* p. 61)

43. It is all important to make clear that the word subconscious or unconscious covers two thoroughly different, though intermingled, fields. One is that field explored with special eagerness by the Freudian School, the field of the instincts, latent images, affective impulses, and sensual tendencies which should be called the unconscious of the irrational in man. The other, missed by the Freudians, is the field of the root life of those spiritual powers, the intellect and the will, the fathomless abyss of personal freedom and of the personal thirst and striving for knowing and seeing, grasping and expressing— I should call this the preconscious of the spirit in man. For reason does not consist only of its conscious logical tools and manifestations nor does the will consist only of its deliberate conscious determinations. Far beneath the apparent surface of explicit concepts and judgments, of words and expressed resolutions or movements of the will, are the sources of knowledge and poetry, of love and truly human desires, hidden in the spiritual darkness of the intimate vitality of the soul. Before being formed and expressed in concepts and judgments, intellectual knowledge is at first a beginning of insight, still unformulated, which proceeds from the impact of the illuminating activity of the intellect on the world of images and emotions and which is but a humble and trembling movement, yet invaluable, toward an intelligible content to be grasped. Parenthetically, it is with reference to this preconscious spiritual dynamism of human personality that keeping personal contact with the pupil is of such great import, not only as a better technique for making study more attractive and stimulating, but above all to give to that mysterious identity of the child's soul, which is unknown to himself, and which no techniques can reach, the comforting assurance of being in some way recognized by a human personal gaze, inexpressible either in concepts or words. (*EC,* pp. 40–41)

44. Let us never deceive or rebuke the thirst for seeing in youth's intelligence! The freeing of the intuitive power is achieved in the soul through the object grasped, the intelligible grasping toward which this power naturally tends. The germ of insight starts within a preconscious intellectual cloud, arising from experience, imagination, and a kind of spiritual feeling, but it is from the outset a tending toward an object to be grasped. And to the extent that this tendency is set free and the intellect becomes accustomed to grasping, seeing, expressing the objects toward which it tends, to that very extent its intuitive power is liberated and strengthened. Before giving a youth the rules of good style, let us tell him first never to write anything which does not seem to him really beautiful, whatever the result may be. (*EC,* **p. 44**)

45. What matters most in the life of reason is intellectual insight or intuition. There is no training or learning for that. Yet if the teacher keeps in view above all the inner center of vitality at work in the preconscious depths of the life of the intelligence, he may center the acquisition of knowledge and solid formation of the mind on the freeing of the child's and the youth's intuitive power. By what means? By moving forward along the paths of spontaneous interest and natural curiosity, by grounding the exercise of memory in intelligence, and primarily by giving courage, by listening a great deal, and by causing the youth to trust and give expression to those spontaneous poetic or noetic impulses of his own which seem to him fragile and bizarre, because they are not assured by any social sanction—and in fact any awkward gesture or rebuff or untimely advice on the part of the teacher can crush such timid sproutings and push them back into the shell of the unconscious. (*EC,* **p. 43**)

46. The most precious gift in an educator is a sort of sacred and loving attention to the child's mysterious identity, which is a hidden thing that no techniques can reach. Encouragement is as fundamentally necessary as humiliation is harmful. But what must be specially stressed is the fact that the teacher has to center the acquisition of knowledge and solid formation of the mind on the freeing of the learner's intuitive power. (*EM,* **p. 61**)

47. In asking a youth to read a book, let us get him to undertake a real spiritual adventure and meet and struggle with the internal world of a given man, instead of glancing over a collection of bits of thought and dead opinions, looked upon from without and with sheer indifference, according to the horrible custom of so many victims of what they call "being informed." (*EC,* **pp. 44–45**)

48. A universal knowledge which is not unified and integrated according to a firmly recognized hierarchy of values is not universal knowledge, but scattered and chaotic knowledge. (***EM*, p. 97**)

49. Yet what is perhaps most paradoxical is that the extra-educational sphere—that is, the entire field of human activity, particularly everyday work and pain, hard experiences in friendship and love, social customs, law (which is a "pedagogue," according to St. Paul), the common wisdom embodied in the behavior of the people, the inspiring radiance of art and poetry, the penetrating influence of religious feast and liturgy—all this extra-educational sphere exerts on man an action which is more important in the achievement of his education than education itself. (***EC*, p. 25**)

50. A democratic education is an education which helps human persons to shape themselves, judge by themselves, discipline themselves, to love and to prize the high truths which are the very root and safeguard of their dignity, to respect in themselves and in others human nature and conscience, and to conquer themselves in order to win their liberty. (***EM*, p. 158**)

51. If it is true that the internal principle, that is to say, nature—and grace too, for man is not merely a natural being—is what matters most in education, it follows that the entire art consists in inspiring, schooling and pruning, teaching and enlightening, so that in the intimacy of man's activities the weight of the egotistic tendencies diminishes, and that the weight of the aspirations proper to personality and its spiritual generosity increases. (***EC*, p. 35**)

52. Certain educators confuse person and individual; in order to grant personality the development and the freedom of expansion to which it aspires, they refuse all asceticism, they want man to yield fruit without being pruned.... The heart atrophies itself and the senses are exasperated. Or, in other cases, what is most human in man falls back into a kind of vacuity, which is covered by frivolity.

And there are other educators and rulers who misunderstand the distinction of person and individual. They mistake it for a separation. They think that we bear in ourselves two separate beings, that of the individual and that of the person. And, according to these educators: *Death to the indi-*

vidual! Long life the person! Unfortunately, when one kills the individual, one also kills the person. The *despotic* conception of the progress of the human being is not better than the *anarchic* one. The ideal of this despotic conception is first to take out our heart, with anaesthetics if possible, and next to replace it by the heart of an angel. The second operation is more difficult than the first one, and is but rarely successful. Instead of the authentic person, imprinted with the mysterious face of the Creator, there appears a mask, the austere mask of the Pharisee.

In reality, what is especially important for the education and the progress of the human being, in the moral and spiritual order (as well as in the order of organic growth), is the interior principle, that is to say, nature and grace. The right educational means are but auxiliaries; the art, a co-operating, at the service of this interior principle. And the entire art consists in cutting off and in pruning—both in the case of the person, and of the individual—so that, in the intimacy of our being, the weight of individuality should diminish, and that of real personality and of its generosity, should increase. And this, indeed, is far from easy. (*SP,* **pp. 53–54**)

CHAPTER ELEVEN

EVIL

1. The good is being, and plentitude or completion of being. When we reason in the line of good, we reason in the line of being, of that which exercises being or bears being to its accomplishment.

Evil, on the contrary, of itself or insofar as evil, is absence of being, *privation* of being or of good. It is a nothingness which corrodes being. When we reason in the line of evil, we reason in the line of non-being, for evil is in nowise being; evil is only a vacuum or a lack of being, a nothingness and a privation.

It follows, then, with absolute necessity that there will be a dissymmetry between our manner of looking at and explaining things in the perspective of good and our manner of looking at and explaining things in the perspective of evil. (*GE*, p. 9)

2. Now the paths of non-being—once one has, by a kind of inverted intuition, become conscious of it and of its formidable role in reality—are as difficult as those of being. (*GE*, p. 32)

3. Evil and error are of themselves versatile, not having roots in being. And the moment approaches perhaps when men, having put all the hope of

their heart in the glamour of matter and being dreadfully deceived, will cry out for the truth. (*IH,* p. 275; CW 11, p. 326)

4. The first cause or the *inventor* of moral evil *in the existential reality of the world* is the liberty of the creature—I mean, this liberty *in the line of non-being.* All of this implies that at the very first origin of the evil act—and, above all, of the evil election, which takes place in the depths of the heart—there is not only the *fallibility* of the creature, but an *actual failure* of the creature, a created initiative which—since it is not caused by God—can only be an initiative of non-being, of deficiency in being, of lack, what I have called a nihilation.

At the bottom the whole affair is contained in a Gospel saying: *Sine me nihil potestis facere,* it is said in Saint John, 15:5.

Well, this text can be read in two ways.

It can be read: *Without Me you can do nothing*—nothing *good.* This is the line of being or of good, where God has the first initiative.

And it can also be read: *Without Me you can do nothingness,* without me you can introduce into being that nothingness or that *non-being of the due good,* that *privation,* which is *evil.* And this even, this initiative of evil, you can have it only without Me (for with Me it is good only that you can do). Here we have the line of non-being or of evil, where created liberty has the first initiative. (*GE,* p. 33)

5. Natural good and supernatural good are intermingled, and Christ is interested in both. Natural evil and supernatural evil are also intermingled, and the fallen angel is interested in both. He is the Prince of this world. The world, however, cannot escape the government of God, the supreme ruler. And Christ and the devil contend with one another for the world, and the world is being snatched by Christ from the devil—not without losses. (*PH,* pp. 132–33)

6. The *cause* of evil of action is always a lack or a failure, a *defectus* in being or in the operative powers of the agent. The action of limping has for its cause a *defectus* of the motor system.

If it is a case now of the evil of action of free will, the *defectus* is question must itself, clearly, be voluntary and free. And yet on the other hand it must not already be an *evil* of free action, for then we would be in a vicious circle, and would be assigning, as cause of a certain effect (that is, of moral evil), this effect itself. We would be arguing in a circle.

Well, says Saint Thomas, we must posit at the origin of moral evil, as cause of it, a voluntary and free *defectus* which itself *is not yet* an evil or a *privation*, but which is a *mera negatio*, a mere withdrawal from being, a mere lack of being or of a good *which is not due*: a mere absence which I introduce voluntarily into being. (***GE*, pp. 34–35**)

7. We must hold with Saint Thomas that every creature is naturally fallible; God can no more make a creature, angel or man, *naturally impeccable* than He can make a square circle....

But the fallibility of an intelligent and free creature, of a person, is something awesome, and something which has awesome consequences. For God plays fair with beings, He deals with them according to the mode of their nature, and, if they are free beings, according to the proper, and therefore fallible, mode of their liberty; in other words, He permits that they fail.... Hence we must conclude that in fact God would not have created nature if He had not ordained it to grace and to that charity by which man becomes, under grace, freely the friend of God; and that sin is the ransom of glory. (***GE*, pp. 37–38**)

8. Human nature is what it is: we are a species naturally wretched—since evil comes to us more often than good. Therefore we must recognize not only the degrees, the inequalities, the limitations of every sort that the order of nature and justice demand: we must also recognize that abuses and defects beyond number, sins of malice and more sins of stupidity—a certain dose of injustice, in a word—will always be mixed in with the things of man. We must not make Rousseau's mistake of rejecting the conditions essential to life and human society because of the injustice which is found joined with them by accident. (***TS*, p. 143**)

9. In reality, all that I do which is good comes from God and all that I do which is evil comes from me, because God has the first initiative in the line of being and because I have the first initiative in the line of non-being.

If I do the good, it is because God has moved my will from end to end, without my having taken any initiative of nothingness which would have shattered His motion at the stage where it was shatterable. All the good that I do comes from God.

If I do evil, it is because I have myself taken a first initiative to shatter, by nihilating, the shatterable motion by which God inclined me to the good, and to introduce into my acts the nothingness which vitiates them. All the evil that I do comes from me. (***GE*, pp. 41–42**)

10. What is moral evil? It is the absence of a good which should be there, of a good which is the consonance or conformity of action with its rule, that is to say, with reason. Moral evil is a particular case of ontological evil, an evil in a given order. (***BP*, p. 50**)

11. The creature has played its part in the genesis of evil; it has posited, by nihilation, the cause of evil. But the effect of this cause—the evil of the free action—comes into existence only with the free act itself, which is a being—wounded or deprived being, but a being. And for this—for wounded being, a bad act, to come into the world—there is necessary a permission of the divine will, a permissive decree. (***GE*, p. 59**)

12. It is indeed true that . . . the Creator of the world does not provide Himself with the absolute safe spectacle of a game of marionettes which would but put into execution a program that He Himself has conceived for evil as well as for good. It is indeed true that in this view, if God wills that we engage ourselves headlong in the battle, it is because He Himself has first engaged in it the glory of His name, nay more, because He has engaged Himself in it completely, by sending us His Son, one with Him in nature.

In this view, the creature, each time that it does evil, introduces to this extent nothingness into being, and undoes for a part the work that God makes. The work of God runs risks, risks that are real because the drama is not merely portrayed, it is actually *lived*. There are abysses which open out, collapses, disasters. The gods from below that free agents are when they take the initiative of nothingness, cause evil and perversion to multiply, and invent forms of horror and of abomination which astonish the angels. . . .

But it is in all this, exactly, that the invincible wisdom and the dazzling power of the eternal purposes manifest themselves. He whose Name is above every name, the eternally Victorious is certain to win the game finally; He wins it at each instant, even when He seems to be losing it. Each time that a free creature undoes for its part the work that God makes, God remakes to that extent—for the better—this work and leads it to higher ends. Because of the presence of evil on earth, everything on earth, from the beginning to the end of time, is in perpetual recasting. However real the risks may be, much more real still is the strength of the arm which causes them to be surmounted by creation and repairs the damages incurred by the latter. However deep the abysses may be, however great the collapses and the disasters, sublimer are the heights and the goods to which created being will be transferred. And doubtless there will also be, finally, real losses—all too real—but themselves compensated by the manifestation of eternal justice in the creature when, in order to remain to itself its ultimate End, it prefers over love all the pains of Hell. And the more the gods from below cause horror and evil to multiply, the more the saints in their love, accomplishing in their flesh what is lacking to the sufferings of Christ, cause the magnificence of good to superabound. . . . And finally it is by having made good use of his liberty moved and activated from end to end by God, and by having from all eternity contributed for his part as free second cause to the very establishment of the eternal plan, that the creature saved—the one who in the end will not have said *No*—will enter into the glory that God has prepared for those who love Him, and which was His intention in creating the world, this world where evil is permitted.

It seems to me that it is only in such a perspective that one can glimpse *just a little* the *real* dimensions of the mystery of the Cross, and of the folly of the Cross, and of that other mystery before which Saint Paul knelt in adoration: "Oh, the depth of the riches of the wisdom and of the knowledge of God! How incomprehensible are his judgments, and how unsearchable his ways!" [Rom 11:33] (***GE*, pp. 85–87**)

13. It is clear that this greater good *simpliciter* cannot be merely the good of the universe or of the world of nature; for if it is a question of the sin of a *person* (and even of his suffering), it is not in the perfection of the machine of the world, it is only in the goods of grace and of glory, and the person-to-person love which unites created agents with God and among themselves there where we are fellow-citizens of the saints, that these evils can be compensated and super-compensated by a good incomparably greater in the line of good than they are in the line of evil. (*GE,* **p. 88**)

14. In casting a good action into the universe, a free agent increases the being of the universe; the universe then increases the being of that free agent so that the balance between them will remain stable. The good originated by the free agent—the moral good (that is to say the most invisible but also the most personal and important fullness of being for man)—must flow back on him like an (ontological) fulfillment of his own being. So one could say that the circuit of being is closed: the free agent is both a center of emanation and a center of attraction.

If, on the other hand, man exercises his freedom in the direction of evil, he will escape the order of the "expansion of being" as well as the order of divine intentions and regulations, but only to fall back into the order of the "revenge of being," the order of being compensating itself for evil and the fruits of evil. The deficiency and privation which man has freely produced in himself will produce in the universe a direct fructification of evil—for every evil engenders other evils and other suffering—and at the same time an indirect fructification of evil (I am thinking of the suffering and the difficulties and the anguish involved in any process of self-control), and finally this fructification of evil will flow back on the free agent himself, since he is a whole within the whole and has the real initiative—and this time the *first* initiative—for that nihilation which constitutes this evil. He is like a god here below. He is a whole, a universe unto himself, a god who has made being his own enemy; he cannot escape the deterioration of his own being. (*BP,* **p. 80**)

15. There is no way to escape: the free agent cannot escape one category of the universal order (itself linked to the particular order of morality) without being caught in another. If he escapes the order of the generosity of being by committing an evil act, he inevitably falls into the order of the revenge of being; and if he escapes the order of the revenge of being, he remains caught in the order of the abundance or generosity of being. (*BP,* **p. 81**)

16. Suppose that a friend of the Holy Family, devoid of any prophetic instinct but profoundly versed in all the divine and human sciences, knew on the one hand many things concerning the birth and the childhood of Jesus, and the beginnings of His public mission, and on the other hand all the historical context of the Judeo-Roman world of the period. This man could have been *certain* that being given the historical conjuncture and the idea that the princes of the priests had of the Messiah, as also the politics pursued by them with regard to the Romans, and being given the unbearable scandal that Jesus was for the world of the doctors and the public officials, there would be some among them to send Christ to His death, just as in a town where everyone is bilious there will certainly be a fight. That in one manner or in another Jesus would in the end be immolated—this was certain, inevitable.

But if on the contrary it is a question of the sin of a particular individual such as Judas, for example, then no man in the world, even supposing that he knew perfectly the character of Judas, and the circumstances, could be *certain* that he would betray Jesus. It is on an initiative of nothingness . . . of which created liberty, which escapes all necessitation of whatever sort, takes or does not take the first initiative, that this sin depends.

And on the side of the divine purposes it is because such an actual failure has been, in the eternal Instant, known by the 'science of vision' as taking place at a certain moment of time, that the betrayal of Judas has been permitted. This betrayal would not have taken place, the condition for its being permitted would not have been posited, if the actual failure in question, the nihilating first initiative of a certain creature had not taken place. (In this case it is another eternal plan which would have been immutably established by the divine will.) It was therefore possible, absolutely speaking, that Judas not betray his Master. (***GE*, pp. 96–97**)

17. To sum up St. Paul's teaching: the Law is holy because it is the revealed expression of the wisdom of God. But while the Law makes us know evil, it does not give us the strength to avoid evil. (***PH*, p. 83**)

18. I would also like to note . . . the import we must give to this thesis of Saint Thomas that God *has not the idea of evil;* in God there is not the idea of evil, because the ideas of God are creative or factive, and because evil is non-being. This means that God knows, indeed, evil, and knows it to perfection, but not as something *of which He would have had the idea.* Of Himself He knows evil only as *possible,* by His 'science of simple intelligence.' Evil as *real,* the evil which disfigures or deprives of a due good the free act of the created existent, God knows it by His 'science of vision' in the created existent itself, and as caused by the first initiative, the initiative of nothingness of the created existent. God is in no degree the *inventor* of the evil that the creature does, He has in no degree and in no respect the *initiative* of sin— or, like the author who forms in his mind the plot of a drama or the tangled destinies of the characters of a novel, the *pensée-mère,* the initial "notion" or the initial design of the sins, crimes and abominations which supervene. These things are required by the development of the drama or of the novel that a man imagines, but in God's work *they come from the improvisations of nothingness of created existents masters of their acts* to whom He gives a clear field because He is an "author" of an *infinite* power and wisdom, capable in His eternal Instant of shaping, forming, and ordaining everything in a single glance by taking account of all that which happens at each moment of time in created wills, and by drawing from the evils which He permits without having willed them, goods incomparably greater.

There you have the absolute innocence of God. (***GE*, pp. 112–13**)

19. Each time that a creature sins (and in each case the creature takes the first initiative, the initiative of nothingness), God is deprived of a joy ("above and beyond" according to our way of looking at things) which was due to Him by another and which that other does not give Him, and something inadmissible to God is produced in the world. But even before triumphing over what is inadmissible by a greater good which will overcompensate for it later on, God Himself, far from being subject to it, raises it above everything by His consent: In accepting such a privation (which in no way affects His being but only the creature's relation to Him), He takes it in hand and raises it up like a trophy attesting to the divinely pure grandeur of His victorious Acceptance (ours is never such except at the cost of some defeat); and this is something that adds absolutely nothing to the intrinsic perfection and glory of the divine *Esse,* and is eternally precontained in Its essential and supereminent infinity. For this is an integral part of a mysterious divine perfection which, even though it has reference to the privation of what is due to

God by creatures existing at some particular point in time, is infinitely beyond the reach of these creatures. In fact, the creature, by his free nihilation, is indeed the cause of the privation in question in whatever concerns itself but in no way in what concerns some effect that might be produced on God by that creature. The only effect produced is to make the creature itself, in his relation to God, which is real only from his side, responsible for some privation or other of what is due to God. And such privations are presupposed from all eternity by that mysterious divine perfection I am speaking about. This divine perfection is eternally present in God and, by the infinite transcendence of the Divine Being, is the unnamed exemplar, incapable of being designated by any of our concepts, toward which like blind men we raise our eyes, and which corresponds in uncreated glory to what suffering is in us. (**CW 20, pp. 257–58**)

20. The theory, or rather the confused idea, the fantasy of punishment as revenge, only raises questions and increases the problematic of sanction. If the death of the murderer were to bring the murdered man back to life, one would understand that in a way it made up for the latter's death. But this is not the case; it is only death added to death, suffering added to suffering. What joy is there in suffering, in evil added to evil? And who or what would be pleased with this addition of evil to evil; to what force would this redoubling of evil be attributed? To nature? It doesn't care in the least. To God? He takes no pleasure in evil. To the "order of things"? It doesn't feel pleasure or displeasure. (*BP,* **p. 203**)

21. There is no greater evil than to leave justice and charity without witness, I mean in the temporal order itself and with regard to the temporal good itself. (*LI,* **p. 135**)

22. The child may be the victim of a burdensome heredity involving a sensitivo-affective disequilibrium which touches its very soul—that soul which God created pure and immaculate but which at the moment of its union with the body, at the very instant of its creation, and by reason of the dispositions of the body, is affected by this disequilibrium—a disequilibrium which sometimes can go so far as to produce in it dispositions and tendencies which incline it toward evil. In fact, certain moral transgressions of the parents, and certain profound moral disorders which upset their vital equilibrium, have inevitably in them, it seems to me, destructive psychosomatic repercussions, capable of attaining the gonads themselves, which thus become bearers, not of (progressive) "acquired characteristics" but of alterations which are then transmitted.

In such a case a certain particular individual disorder, added on the disorder which affects all human nature due to original sin, then passes through the human generative act and through the embryonic development in such a way that we must admit, it seems to me, that, hidden in the tissues of the body, the first germ, not only of neurotic or psychotic disturbances but also of dangerous or perverse moral inclinations, is present from the very formation of the embryo and develops along with it in the course of its intra-uterine life, but in a latent manner because it is merely somatic. This latent development will continue in the infant, in darkness, and manifest itself only much later. These considerations should make us indulgent toward many of the unfortunate. (*UA,* **p. 109**)

23. The force of coercion and of aggression, the force that strikes, aims at the destruction of one evil by way of another evil (in the physical order) which it inflicts on the body. It follows that evil (on however small a scale) passes from one to other endlessly according to the law of transitive action. For the patient, unless he has understood and voluntarily *accepted* the hurt he has received—which happens rarely and anyhow depends on strength of soul—is stirred to react in more or less crafty ways of evil-doing. The force of voluntary suffering and of patience, the force of endurance, tends to annihilate the evil by accepting and dissolving it in love, absorbing its sorrow in the soul in the shape of resignation. There it stays, and goes no further. And thus the force that strikes and is necessary and, if it be just, stops the expansion of evil and limits and contracts but is unable to extinguish it, has in its own nature less strength and perfection than the force that endures and that, in the case where it is informed by Charity, is of its own strength capable of extinguishing as it arises the evil that free agents unnecessarily introduce into the world. It is evidently of its own nature a more effective instrument of redemption. (*FMW,* pp. 175–76; CW 11, p. 91)

CHAPTER TWELVE

ETHICS

1. Ethics, which we may consider as the rationalization of the use of Freedom, presupposes metaphysics as its necessary prerequisite. Ethics cannot be constituted unless its author is first able to answer the questions: *What is man? Why is he made? What is the end of human life?* (**FMW, p. 14; CW 11, p. 11**)

2. It has been justly observed that in matters of moral philosophy there exist two possible attitudes: one, which we may call *idealist*, being purely reflexive, refuses to distinguish between the speculative order and the practical order; it makes moral life the fundamental element, and if I may put it so, the very vitality of all thought; it moreover recognizes no other thought but human thought, which it calls Thought, with a capital T. The other attitude we might call *cosmic;* focussed upon being, it acknowledges that man is *situated* in a universe which spreads beyond him in every direction, and sees in the moral life of man a particular case in universal life, made specific within this universal life by the existence of free will.

The attitude of the ethics of Saint Thomas Aquinas is a cosmic attitude; that of Bergsonian ethics is also cosmic. And we cannot insist enough upon the importance of the renewal which modern thought thus owes to

Bergson. He has recognized the dependence of moral philosophy with regard to metaphysics and the philosophy of nature, and has linked to a philosophy of the universe the destinies of the philosophy of human action. He thus delivers us from the last surviving attraction of Kantianism, and rediscovers the great philosophic tradition of humanity.

An ethics of the cosmic type cannot possibly dispense with a system of the world; the universe of freedom presupposes the universe of nature and fulfills a wish of the latter: I must know where I am and who I am, before knowing, and in order to know, what I should do. All that is fundamentally true; on all that Bergson and Saint Thomas are at one. But it is immediately obvious that the problem now shifts ground and relates to the validity of that metaphysics and system of the world proposed for our consideration. Is the world, as Bergson believes, a creative evolution? Or is it, as Saint Thomas believes, a hierarchy of growing perfections? Is man's intellect capable of attaining being, and does it consequently possess a power of regulation over life and action so that, as Saint Thomas Aquinas puts it, reason is the proximate rule of human acts? (***RT*, pp. 91–92**)

3. It is significant that for antiquity the vocabulary of ethics and that of art remained substantially identical. The artist possesses his virtue just as the prudent man possesses his. The word "sin" is applied as readily to a grammatical or musical error as to a fault against justice or temperance. (***MP*, p. 35**)

4. Man is a metaphysical being, an animal that nourishes its life on transcendentals. There is no ethics among ants any more than among the stars; the road they are to follow is traced out for them in advance. But we men, merely because we know the sense of the word *Being* and of the word *Why*, and because into our poor head the whole heavens (and more than the heavens) can be fitted, we are lost before we take our first step. We must discover the road we follow; we must deliberate our end.

There is here, in truth, on the threshold of ethics a fact of nature, the fact of a spiritual nature. So soon as we act in the character of men, that is to say under the direction of reason, we cannot not will a last end for the sake of which all the rest is willed, and in which the infinite good . . . takes concrete shape. What is the absolute good? Where shall we find this beatitude?

It is our business to discover it; we are metaphysicians in spite of ourselves. We are obliged to make a choice of ends: it is the beginning of our moral life. (*FMW,* pp. 14–15; CW 11, p. 11)

5. Politics is a branch of Ethics, but a branch specifically distinct from the other branches of the same stem. For human life has two ultimate ends, the one subordinate to the other: an ultimate end *in a given order,* which is the terrestrial common good, or the *bonum vitae civilis;* and an *absolute* ultimate end, which is the transcendent, eternal common good. And individual ethics takes into account the subordinate ultimate end, but *directly aims* at the absolute ultimate one; whereas political ethics takes into account the absolute ultimate end, but its *direct aim* is the subordinate ultimate end, the good of the rational nature in its temporal achievement. Hence a specific difference of perspective between those two branches of Ethics. (*MS,* p. 62)

6. From the moment when ethical comportment is not a mere waking dream guided by the fear of social penalties or the concern to justify oneself in the eyes of other men; from the moment when man has truly crossed the threshold of moral life; from that moment . . . universal law is vitally interiorised, embowled, existentialised in the dynamism of the individual subject tending towards the ends which are of importance to him above all else. (*EE,* p. 57)

7. Now ethics belongs to the practical order. It is a species of knowledge, a true science, but one which has in view a practical object: *acts to be done.* For ethics therefore, the ends for which we act, which here means the ends of human life, play a part corresponding to that which first principles play in speculative science. It is not possible to have a science of numbers except by reference to the principles of mathematics. Neither is it possible to have a science of ethics except by reference to the ends of human action. . . .

It follows that although it examines and utilizes a great mass of material both of the speculative and of the experimental order the science of ethics is nonetheless not a science of simple statement or verification. As science and philosophy it seeks to know what must be done, and how it must be done so that it shall be well done. And it is also evident that the science of ethics is a science of Freedom. Though there may be a speculative science of the nature of Free Will there cannot be a speculative science of the use of Free Will. There is a practical science of the use of Free Will: it is the science of ethics.

Here the intellect penetrates into the proper domain of the will. It is scarcely surprising that St. Thomas, who is so purely intellectualist in metaphysics, should show himself more and more voluntarist in the measure in which his study concerns action as such. The typical object of ethical science is something willed (human acts) but it is according to a speculative norm that this science judges human acts and the rules of human action. For this reason, though ethics is a practical science, it is not fully capable of regulating these acts.

To enable me to know and judge with perfect and constant rectitude the individual acts that I have to do—I, an individual person, in such and such individual circumstances which have never before existed and will never exist again in precisely the same combination—no science, though it be a practical science, and no system of casuistry will ever suffice. For science is properly of universals. I need a means of knowledge and of practical judgment that is more than a science. I need the virtue of prudence: an intellectual virtue but also of the moral order seeing that it can only judge rightly if the will too is rectified; for prudence controls the exercise of my freedom immediately, not from a distance. Prudence is integrated with the other moral virtues; it presupposes that I know what justice and what temperance require not merely by way of theory but in an experimental way by the connatural knowledge that comes with the exercise of these virtues. And in this connection St. Thomas says that a knowledge of metaphysics (however necessary it may be as a basis for ethical science) is useless as a guarantee of right conduct, and that a knowledge of ethics (for all its necessity in turn) is of very little value for the purpose. (*FMW,* pp. 20–22; **CW 11, pp. 14–15**)

8. Separated from superior and authentically ethical criteria whose basis is in the metaphysical order, the moral guidance furnished by the positive sciences remains not only completely relative and conditional, it also remains irremediably fluid and arbitrary. Medicine can recommend sobriety, psychology can recommend humility and even, if need be, religious faith as detergents and lubricants for our human springs; but what answer can they give, if not by virtue of some conscious or unconscious metaphysics or anti-metaphysics, when they ask themselves, for example, whether trial marriage, euthanasia, scientifically controlled abortion, the sterilization of certain categories of a-social individuals, the elimination of aggressive instincts by the surgical or bio-chemical manipulation of the nerve centers, are to be recommended or advised against; when they ask themselves whether, when a desire becomes obsessive, it is or is not more reasonable to yield to it to avoid giving rise to a morbid fixation in the psyche; whether for a nation at war it is a crime or a duty to insure victory by using a weapon which annihilates millions of innocent people; and whether it is a sign of mental maturity or a sign of immaturity and infantile pride to risk one's life and the security of one's family and aggravate the tensions of the social milieu on the pretext of defending an innocent man or refusing to deny the truth? (**MP, p. 414**)

9. If man existed in a purely natural order, or, as the theologians put it, in a state of pure nature, God, who is man's real supreme good and ultimate end, would not be, for all that, the absolute happiness or beatitude of man, for in the purely natural order there would be no absolute happiness or beatitude for man. His happiness, even beyond the grave would be a happiness in motion, ceaselessly progressing, and never totally achieved. (**RA, p. 31**)

10. Not every act of force is virtuous. But fortitude is a cardinal virtue insofar as it inclines and steadies the will of man to meet and overcome difficulties that are in conflict with the claims of justice and with the life of reason and of truth. Fortitude being thus directed to the firm and loyal defence of right against every kind of evil, its proper object is to prepare the soul for the sake of justice to meet death. (**FMW, p. 172; CW 11, p. 89**)

11. [The] moral ideal of Christianity, and the ultimate End it proposes, finally possess that effectiveness of appeal to the human being and his thirst for happiness (now transfigured) which was lacking in the rational ethics of Aristotle, and to which Stoic and Epicurean ethics sacrificed everything, but only to be disappointed in the end. This moral ideal of Christianity is not an easy one; and if one considers only the capacities of human nature, and its infirmities, its propensity to evil, it would seem even more impossible to realize than the Stoic or Epicurean ideal. The fact is that Christianity has only raised the level of human civilizations at the price of bringing about trouble and division in them at the same time, as a result of the yes or no it requires of the heart. It has not put an end to wars. It has activated history—it has not subjugated it (God Himself does not do that). It has evangelized the earth—it has not subdued it. Not only contrary efforts and the rebellions of nature, but the action of humanity's own deficiencies upon the divine leaven itself, when the forces of man have undertaken to serve Christ with their own means, have brought it about that Christianity has increased suffering in our species, at the same time that it brought about all real moral progress and every real increase of goodness. But the evangelic has left its mark forever in the depths of humanity. Saintliness has transfigured the heart of man, not only among the saints, but among all the sinners whom a ray of it has touched. And in revealing to us that God is love and makes us His sons through grace, that the ultimate fulfillment toward which our poor life proceeds is to possess Him through vision, Christianity, without giving way to any illusions about the potentialities of nature or underestimating its dignity either, has succeeded in assuring the decisive effectiveness of the appeal to the human soul of the ultimate end which is proposed to it—and this is the crucial concern for ethics. (*MP,* p. 85)

12. Every human act is a judgment passed on the divine nature. (*NB,* p. 65)

13. If it is true, as Aristotle and Thomas Aquinas thought, that man cannot do without a certain amount of delectation, so that when he is deprived of spiritual delectations he passes over to carnal ones, how [they would] be surprised that all over the modern world the mass of humanity tamed by the general boredom of mathematized labor, should, if no superior flame is kindled, naturally become prey to the obsession of sex. (*RON,* p. 157)

14. It is generally believed that success is a thing good in itself, and which it is, from an ethical point of view, mandatory to strive for.
    In this American concept of success there is no greediness or egoism. It is, it seems to me, rather an over-simplified idea that "to succeed" is to bear fruit, and therefore to give proof of the fact that psychologically and morally you are not a failure.

This is a very old illusion, already denounced by Socrates: mistaking external success, which depends on a great many ingredients extraneous to ethical life—good connections, cleverness, good luck, ruthlessness, and so forth—for genuine "success" in the metaphysical sense, that is, for the genuinely human happy issue which is internal, and consists in having, as Socrates said a "good and beautiful soul." (***RON,* p. 133**)

CHAPTER THIRTEEN

FAITH

1. In reality, faith necessarily postulates God's descent into history in order to establish communion with human beings and undertake a personal dialogue with them. And faith itself descends into the weakness and entanglements of specific, historic and contingent events in order to know them, of that particular and irreplaceable *certain day* when the Uncreated Word became flesh. Faith can achieve this, because at the same time it ascends into the absolute stability and simplicity, into the most concrete and existential individuality of the divine Self, and because it knows historical events not as a process of historical knowledge, but by means of the supra-historical, eternal, prime Truth in Person, "declaring" itself to us and enlightening human hearts. (*RT,* pp. 196–97)

2. But the mystery of our state is that our nature and our reason, as we see them in the real and concrete existence, cannot by themselves alone attain the fullness and the perfection of that of which they are capable. All the more, if they set out to usurp that which is beyond their reach, they will become for us a snare, an occasion of sin and of death. With regard to eternal life, and absolute wisdom, faith alone—and reason which heeds faith—truly knows the road. (*LT,* **p. 47**)

3. [The] simplicity of gaze and straightforwardness of reason are generally rare in minds loaded with human wisdom. But who could flatter himself that he has kept them intact—except by the effect of faith, which can maintain everything and cure everything—in a time in which philosophical intelligence, debased and degraded by the chafing of innumerable errors, slowly poisoned by attentive educators, made cowardly and pusillanimous by the incessant itching to be modern and to conform to the age, cannot take one step forward without asking itself in terror whether the external world really does exist, whether reality is knowable, whether the principle of causality is not a synthetic judgment *a priori*, and reason a mechanism with blind shackles (and then what is the good of philosophising? and have these propositions themselves any meaning?) and whether our ideas, our consciousness and the intellectual evidence are not the residue of biological or sociological accidents. (***BPT,*** **p. 180**)

4. A living Christianity is necessary to the world. Faith must be actual, practical, existential faith. To believe in God must mean to live in such a manner that life could not possibly be lived if God did not exist. For the practical believer, gospel justice, gospel attentiveness to everything human must inspire not only the deeds of the saints, but the structure and institutions of common life, and must penetrate to the depths of terrestrial existence. (***RR,*** **p. 100**)

5. Not only can we not of ourselves have access to supernatural reality, but it is also utterly improbable that erudite reason, the reason of philosophers and savants, should by its own resources avoid the absurd presupposition of the impossibility of a properly supernatural order of things. In other words, from the real we naturally conclude the possible, and we take advantage of this to deny the possibility of what we have not experienced. So long as faith does not bring us into contact with the reality of the supernatural world, as does the sense with the material world, our intellect continues stupidly to deny the very possibility of such a world. (***BPT,*** **p. 299**)

6. The superanalogy of faith is more humble than metaphysical analogy; it wears the livery of poverty. But we know from God that it attains divine secrets which metaphysics knows not. Once designated by revelation as likeness of what is hidden in God, the mind perceives that such things as paternity and filiation can be referred to the transcendental order; they have the value of analogy of proper proportionality. Thus the names of Father, Son and Holy Ghost are not metaphorical; they designate (yet without containing or circumscribing) what the divine persons are intrinsically and formally. The word redemption is no longer metaphorical. It expresses intrinsically and formally the work accomplished by the Son of God. Under its livery of poverty the superanalogy of faith conceals a supernatural vigor. By it we attain, in light of the deity itself, the Divine Essence as it is naturally participatible by no creature, and as no created perfection of itself can show it to our reason. (**DK, pp. 242–43; CW 7, pp. 257–58**)

7. There have always been Christians for whom to know that Christ redeemed the sins of the world is a piece of purely intellectual information of the same caliber as the information that the temperature this morning was 54 degrees Fahrenheit. For them, stating the fact is enough, just as the reading of the thermometer is enough. They have every intention of using the information to get to heaven; but they have never been face to face with the reality of the mystery of the Redemption, with the reality of the sufferings of the Savior. They have never experienced the shock of recognition of faith, the scales have not fallen from their eyes. What I mean is that the way the modern intelligence functions risks making this manner of living our faith appear normal whereas it tends indeed to empty faith of its content. (**RR, p. 208**)

8. The soul does not actually use the formulas of faith as formal means of knowing; it allows concepts to slumber, but it does not "abstract from faith." Faith, the *lumen fidei*, enters more than ever into play; thus perfected in its mode by the gift of wisdom, it is the proximate and proportionate means of contemplation. (**DK, p. 449; CW 7, pp. 473–74**)

9. Today the spirit of faith must climb back up the slopes of an intelligence no longer accustomed to the knowledge of being. And it is doubtless possible that a heroic faith is all the more pure and sublime, the more it dwells in an intelligence the general tenor of which is alien to it. Nevertheless, the fact is that faith itself, in order to find normal conditions for its exercise, needs to dwell in an intelligence which has itself regained its normal climate. An intellect patterned exclusively on the mental habits of technology and the natural sciences is not a normal climate for faith. Natural intelligence, the kind which is to be found in common sense, is spontaneously focused on being, as philosophy is in a systematic and premeditated way. Never have men had a greater need for the intellectual climate of philosophy, metaphysics and speculative theology; probably this is why they appear so fearful of them, and why such great care is taken not to frighten men with them. Yet they are the one and only way of restoring the intellect to its most natural and deep-rooted functioning, and thus to bring back the paths of intelligence into the main highway of faith itself. (*RR,* pp. 210–11)

10. Faith is an obscure communion with the infinitely luminous knowledge which the divine Abyss has of itself. Faith instructs us in the depths of God. Faith stands above any human system, no matter how valid; it is concerned with the revealed data, with that very glory which cannot be named by any human name, yet has desired to make itself known to us in words which all may understand. The transcendence of faith entails a strange paradox: Faith in its own domain—in the things which are *of faith*—unites minds absolutely and upon certainties absolutely essential to human life; it alone can create such a unity of minds. But faith only creates unity of minds at the top; it does not create unity of doctrine or of behavior in any of the categories of our activities which touch only human affairs, affairs which are not *of faith.*

All the Catholic intellectuals before whom I am speaking are united in the Faith and in the discipline of the Church; for all other things, whether it be philosophy, theology, aesthetics, art, literature, or politics (although there are certain positions which none of them would hold since they are incompatible with Faith), they can and doubtless do hold the most various positions. The unity of faith is too lofty to impose itself upon human affairs, unless they have a necessary connection with faith. Faith itself wants reason to be free in human affairs and it guarantees this freedom. And intelligence is willing to be held captive, but by God alone, the Subsistent Truth.

Faith creates unity among men, but this unity is in itself a divine, not a human unity, a unity as transcendental as faith. (*RR,* p. 211)

CHAPTER FOURTEEN

FREEDOM

1. Man's difficult condition comes from the fact that he is not only a creature of nature but also one of reason and freedom—elements which are weak in him and yet are his indestructible fortitude and tokens of his abiding dignity. No failures or stains can efface his original greatness. (***RR*, p. 201**)

2. Thomist philosophy establishes the freedom of man in the very terms of intellect and being. It shows us in human will a bottomless pit which subsisting Good, which God alone can fill; and in human freedom a participated similitude of divine freedom, thanks to which, without being able to *create* anything properly speaking (*ex nihilo*), we, however, as we please, cause that to be which was not and also form ourselves; thanks to which we are persons and, like gods, intervene in the order of the world by acts of endless scope; so much so that the mystery of our *acting* is as marvelous and as terrifying for whoever can be conscious of it, as the very mystery of our *being*.

Thomist philosophy further shows us that free will is a property deriving from our very nature as beings endowed with intelligence: so that those who deny our *specific difference* must also deny our freedom. So also that freedom is not the absurd power of choosing without motive or in spite of motive, but the power of choosing according to reason; in the words of

Saint Thomas . . . : *vis electiva mediorum servato ordine finis,* the power of choosing the means while the ordination to the end—to the ultimate end, in short—remains fixed. For every creature this signifies: the power of obeying the eternal Law without being necessitated to do so. From which it follows that we are at the lowest degree among free beings, because in our choice (even with regard to the natural order taken in itself), we can only too greatly deviate from our true ultimate goal. For the power of choosing evil, of preferring apparent good to real good, far from being an essential attribute of freedom as such, is only a sign of the imperfection of all created freedom, and especially of the weakness and infirmity of human freedom. (*BPT,* pp. 274–75)

3. Man is not born free save in the basic potencies of his being; he becomes free, by warring upon himself and thanks to many sorrows; by the struggle of the spirit and virtue; by exercising his freedom he wins his freedom. So that at long last a freedom better than he expected is *given* him. From the beginning to the end it is truth that liberates him. (*EM,* p. 168)

4. What is essential to freedom is the power to act or to not act, to produce or withhold one's action. (*BPT,* p. 275)

5. The notion of Freedom is Very much wider than the notion of Free Will. Free Will is indeed the source and spring of the world of Freedom: it is a datum of metaphysics; we inherit it with our rational nature, we do not have to achieve it: it appears within us as an *initial* form of Freedom. But this metaphysical root must grow and develop in the psychological and the moral order. We are called upon to become in action what we are already in the metaphysical order: a Person. It is our duty by our own effort to make ourselves *persons* having dominion over our own acts and being to ourselves a whole. (*FMW,* pp. 29–30; CW 11, p. 19)

6. It is man's privilege to determine his own ends. The natural desire for happiness is a kind of empty frame: filling this frame with a picture or a painting depends on my free choice. Animals do not determine their ends, which are determined by nature, and are particular ends; they do not have

the intelligible notion of the good. In the case of human beings—and this is what distinguishes them from animals—they must determine their own ends and what constitutes their happiness.

Thus morality is appendant to the ultimate end, because we must determine freely, by a moral act, which to tell the truth is the *first* moral act, what will constitute for us the supreme end of our life.

We cannot help desiring happiness. The desire for happiness is a desire of nature, not a moral desire; there is no free choice with respect to happiness in general. But we must freely choose or determine *what* constitutes our happiness. We are obliged by nature to be free; we cannot escape this choice of happiness. We meet this sphinx as soon as we leave childhood, and at all the crucial moments of our life. The first and paramount moral question is to choose, as the good for the love of which all our acts are implicitly or explicitly performed, the end which is the *true* end of human life. This is the primary use of our free will. (***BP,* p. 91**)

7. The free act, in which the intelligence and will involve and envelop each other vitally, is thus like an instantaneous flash in which the active and dominating indetermination of the will operates in regard to the judgment itself which determines it; the will can do nothing without an intellectual judgment; and it is will that makes itself determined by judgment and by this judgment rather than by another one.

Far from being a simple function of the intelligence, by which the latter realizes ideas which in virtue of their mere object appear best, the will is an original spiritual energy of infinite capacity which has control over the intelligence and its judgments in the order of practical choice and makes what it wants appear best to the subject *here and now.* What constitutes the real mystery of free will is that while essentially needing intellectual specification, the exercise of the will has primacy over the latter and holds it under its active and dominating indetermination because the will alone can give it existential efficacy. (***EM,* pp. 162–63**)

8. The human will, which is rooted in the intellect, and which is able to determine itself, or to master the very motive or judgment which determines it and is made efficacious by the will itself, is spiritual in its operation and nature. Every material agent is subject to the universal determinism. Free will is the privilege, the glorious and weighty privilege, of an agent endowed with immaterial power.

We are responsible for ourselves; we choose for ourselves and decide on our own ends and our own destinies. (**RR, pp. 58–59**)

9. For a Thomist ... [the] formula—man makes history and history makes man—would mean that history has a direction, determined with regard to certain fundamental characteristics by the immense dynamic mass of the past pushing it forward, but undetermined with regard to specific orientations and with regard to the spirit or the manner in which a change, necessary in other respects, will be carried into existence. Man is endowed with a freedom by means of which, as a person, he can, with more or less difficulty, but really, triumph over the necessity in his heart. Without, for all that, being able to bend history arbitrarily according to his desire or fancy, man can cause new currents to surge up in history, currents which will struggle and compound with pre-existent currents, forces and conditions so as to bring to final determination the specific orientation, which is not fixed in advance by evolution, of a given period of history. If, in fact, human freedom plays in the history of the world a part which seems all the greater as the level of activity considered is more spiritual, and all the smaller as the level of activity considered is more temporal, this is because man, collectively taken, lives little of the properly human life of reason and freedom. It is not surprising, in view of this fact, that he should be "in submission to the stars" in a very large measure. He can, nevertheless, escape from them, even in his collective temporal life. And if we consider things from a sufficiently long perspective of centuries, it seems that one of the deepest trends of human history is precisely to escape more and more from fate. But here again we meet with the law of the double and antagonistic motion of ascent and descent together. Thus, the development of our material techniques seems, on the one hand, to make historical fate weigh more heavily on man; and, on the other hand, this same development offers man unexpected means of freedom and emancipation. In the end, which of these two aspects will be predominant depends on the free will and the free choice of man. (**PH, pp. 27–28**)

10. The connatural aspirations [of personality] tend to a relative freedom compatible with conditions here below, and the burden of material nature inflicts upon them from the very beginning a serious defeat because no animal is born more naked and less free than man. The struggle to win freedom in the order of social life aims to make up for this defeat. (*EM,* **p. 166**)

11. The act of free will as such is not *of this world.* Even in the natural order it does not belong to the world of creation, to the world of that which has been made. That is why the Angels, although the knowledge of all that belongs to the world of creation is due to them, do not know the secrets of hearts. The free will transcends the world of creation. (*SA,* **p. 33**)

12. *There is no scenario prepared in advance,* in which created agents would play parts and act as performers. We must purge our thought of this spurious idea of a play written in advance, in a time anterior to time—a play in which time unfolds, and the characters of time read, the parts. (*GE,* **p. 79**)

13. The free act is not only the act of the person as such, it is moreover— and this is perhaps the same thing—the revelation of the person to itself. Even with a 'super-comprehension of the causes', however perfect it may be supposed, you cannot foresee this act. Even God cannot do so. To be precise, God does not *foresee* our free acts, He *sees* them, all the moments of time being present to His creative eternity. And in so far as our free acts are good, He works them with us and causes them, for He is the primary cause of being. We have the initiative and the free initiative of our good acts and of our good acts in their entirety, but this is a *secondary* initiative, and not the *primary* one; the latter belongs to God alone. Our good acts are thus wholly from God as primary cause, and wholly our own as due to a secondary free cause. And this is easy to comprehend, once we have understood that freedom consists in an active and dominating indetermination and the mastery of will over judgment. How could this mastery and this high activity exercise themselves in me without the activating influx of the first Cause within me? And how could this activating influx, descending from the Life in Pure Act, destroy or diminish in me this dominating activity, at the very instant when it activates and vivifies it? It is great folly to seek the freedom of our will—which is a supreme degree of activity—in I know not what *asides*, isolating us from Him, without whom we can do nothing but evil and nothingness. (***SP,*** **pp. 103–4**)

14. [God] did not invent moral evil and sin. It was not He who had the idea of all the defilements and abominations and contempts that are spat into His Face; the betrayals, lecheries, cruelties, cowardices, bestial wickednesses, refined perversions, depravities of mind which it is given to His creatures to contemplate. Those were born solely of nihilation by human liberty. They came forth from that abyss. God permits them as a creation of our power to make the thing which is nothing. (***EE,*** **p. 120**)

15. A murder planned by a brilliant mind and executed with exceptional physical skill is a good crime; it is not a good action. Good action, bad action—these notions relate to the use of freedom with regard to the proper fulfillment of the human being. (***BP,*** **p. 38**)

16. We must . . . have a holy dread of letting ourselves be misled by all those devilish words formed with the prefix *fore* which our human, too human, language naturally causes us to employ. Properly speaking, God does not *fore*-see the things of time, He *sees* them, and He sees in particular the free options and decisions of the created existent which, inasmuch as they are free, are unforeseeable in themselves. Because they are all indivisibly possessed and measured by His own eternal Instant, He sees them in the pure existential freshness of their emergence into being at this or that instant of time, in the humility of their own instant of coming forth.

All this means—and let us mark this well in our minds—that God has the entire course of time physically present to His eternal Instant, and that He has it before His eyes in its entirety when He establishes all things from all eternity. (***GE,*** **pp. 78–79**)

17. Let no one say that man alters the eternal plan! That would be an absurdity. Man does not alter it. He enters into its very composition and its eternal fixity by his power of saying, No! (***EE,*** **p. 118**)

18. Without fallible freedom there can be no created freedom; without created freedom there can be no love in mutual friendship between God and creature; without love in mutual friendship between God and creature, there can be no supernatural transformation of the creature into God, no entering of the creature into the joy of his Lord. Sin—evil—is the price of glory. (*PE*, p. 19)

19. [The moral order] concerns man as belonging not only to the universe of nature and of creation, but to another universe, founded on the universe of nature but superior to it, the universe of freedom. In this universe of freedom, each person is a whole with respect to the world and with respect to God, the transcendent Whole; and each person can have the authentic initiative (second after God in the case of good, first in the case of evil) for a flowering or withering of being.

It is within this universe of freedom that human actions are morally good or evil (in agreement or not in agreement with reason)—in this particular universe, in this particular order of freedom, whose rule is reason, and whose absolutely primary rule is divine wisdom. In such an order, man may transgress, or not transgress, the regulations of this wisdom; he can do or not do evil. (*BP*, pp. 73–74)

20. The pursuit of the highest contemplation and the pursuit of the highest freedom are two aspects of the same pursuit. In the order of spiritual life, man aspires to a perfect and absolute freedom, and therefore to a superhuman condition; sages of all times give evidence of this. The function of law is a function of protection and education of freedom, the function of a pedagogue. At the conclusion of this tutelage the perfect spiritual man is freed from every servitude, even, St. Paul says, from the servitude of the law, because he does spontaneously what is of the law and is simply one spirit and one love with the Creator. (*PP*, p. 336)

21. But why, in the doctrine of St. Thomas, did God permit the sin of Adam, if not for Christ, for the Incarnation and for redemptive grace? And then one could say that just as the sin of Adam was permitted for the sake of the redeeming Incarnation, so freedom that can err was created for the love of charity between God and creature. (*PE*, p. 14)

22. As to Freedom, he [the philosopher] reminds society that freedom is the very condition for the exercise of thought. This is a requirement of the common good itself of human society, which disintegrates as soon as fear, superseding inner conviction, imposes any kind of shibboleth upon human minds. The philosopher, even when he is wrong, at least freely criticizes many things his fellowmen are attracted to. Socrates bore witness to this function of criticism which is inherent in philosophy. Even though society showed its gratitude to him in quite a peculiar way, he remains the great example of the philosopher in society. It is not without reason that Napoleon loathed *idéologues,* and that dictators, as a rule, hate philosophers. (***UP*, p. 9**)

23. Nineteenth Century bourgeois democracy was *neutral* even with regard to freedom. Just as it had no real *common good,* it had no real *common thought*—no brains of its own, but a neutral, empty skull clad with mirrors: no wonder that before the second world war, in countries that fascist, racist, or communist propaganda was to disturb or to corrupt, it had become a society without any idea of itself and without faith in itself, without any *common faith* which could enable it to resist disintegration. (***MS*, p. 110**)

24. Education is education for freedom. And the world within which it has to fulfill its duties is sick with a frustrated longing for freedom and beauty, and has unlearned the primary conditions and requirements of freedom.

A striking sign of the practical materialism which threatens the roots of freedom today is our current notion of work as supreme end and of leisure as sheer relaxation. Work is good in itself; it is the normal condition of man. But work is not the end and perfection of human life. Work is essentially a means—toward an end which is the free activity, perfecting man in his innermost life, of communion with truth and beauty, and of the gift of oneself in love. Such free and immanent activity presupposes work, of course; it can inspire work and superabound in it. But of itself it is leisure activity, requiring that *free time* where man can be within himself and listen to God within himself. It has its peak in the grace-given contemplation and love of those heroes in spiritual life who are the saints. But it is available to all in its lower degrees, through the fruits of knowledge, art and poetry—of the humanities—that are conveyed in the common heritage of mankind, and through that other kind of fruit which is self-sacrifice in devotion to those one loves. (***EM*, p. 101**)

25. As long as our world makes work the end of human life, and consequently confuses genuine leisure and its free activities with animal relaxation, hypnotic pleasure or amusement which has no value except as it has fun instead of spiritual delectation, as long as it claims to cultivate the mind but simply ignores the soul, it will foster serfdom, not freedom, and thwart with its own general behavior the effort of education toward liberation of the mind and toward helping man to become man. (*EM,* **p. 102**)

26. When man seeking for his own inner universe takes the wrong road, he enters the internal world of the deaf unconscious, while believing he enters the internal world of the spirit, and he thus finds himself wandering in a false kind of self-interiority, where wildness and automatism mimic freedom. (*CI,* **p. 95**)

CHAPTER FIFTEEN

GOD

1. For love ... does not deal with possibles or pure essences, it deals with existents. We do not love possibles, we love that which exists or is destined to exist. And in the last analysis it is because God is the Act of Existing Itself, in His ocean of all perfection, that the love of that which is better than all goodness is that in which man attains the perfection of his being. That perfection does not consist in reunion with an essence by means of supreme accuracy in copying the ideal; it consists in loving, in going through all that is unpredictable, dangerous, dark, demanding, and insensate in love; it consists in the plentitude and refinement of dialogue and union of person with person to the point of transfiguration which, as St. John of the Cross says, make of man a god by participation, 'two natures in a single spirit and love' in a single spiritual super-existence of love. (*EE,* **pp. 49–50**)

2. Only in God, only in Pure Act, is intelligence, which is then subsisting Intelligence, able to realize fully the fundamental exigencies of its nature and give birth to *another itself* substantial and personal, to a Word which is really a Son. It is only in the Holy Trinity that we see two functions coincide which everywhere else are separate, the uttering of the word and the generation of the son, that we see intelligence issue in a subsisting term, into which passes substantially the integrity of its own nature. (*AS,* **pp. 87–88**)

3. All our values depend on the nature of our God.

Now God is Spirit. To progress—which means for any nature, to tend toward its Principle—is therefore to pass from the sensible to the rational and from the rational to the spiritual and from the less spiritual to the more spiritual; to civilize is to spiritualize.

Material progress may contribute, to the extent that it allows man leisure of soul. But if such progress is employed only to serve the will to power and to gratify a cupidity which opens *infinite* jaws—*concupiscentia est infinita*—it leads the world back to chaos at an accelerated speed; that is its way of tending toward the principle. (*AS,* p. 75)

4. Scholastic philosophy takes care not to confuse the mode by which *we know* an object with the mode in which the object known *is*, and it establishes that we can know in a composite way and by means of a certain multiplicity of concepts, a reality which is, in itself, simple. In this case our intellect, while it has a composite knowledge, does not tell us *that* the object known is itself composite; quite the contrary, it tells us that the object known is simple. Is there a more famous application of this doctrine than the complex procedure by which we raise ourselves to the knowledge of God, the supremely One? (*BPT,* p. 139)

5. In God alone are subject and object identified in an absolute way, even as existence and understanding are identified. He knows Himself exhaustively and all things in Himself, because His act of knowledge is His very infinite essence. (*DK,* p. 110; **CW 7,** p. 117)

6. The act of divine knowledge, you know, has and can have but one single *object* properly speaking, one single specifying object, namely, God Himself, the divine essence itself. And by such an object the divine knowledge is infinitely and eternally filled to overflowing.

Whence follows the great Thomist thesis that all the other things besides Himself that God knows, He knows them in His essence and His own uncreated intelligibility, the sole determining object of His knowledge. (*GE,* pp. 69–70)

7. To avoid pantheism, it is not enough to say that God is distinct from the world as the centre of spurting is distinct from the rockets which shoot out,

or as the fountain-head is distinct from the springs into which it divides, or as the sap is distinct from the tree, or as any created cause is distinct from its effect. The world is absolutely distinct from God *by essence*; there is nothing, absolutely nothing in common, except by analogy, between the being of God and the being of the world. (*BPT,* p. 199)

8. In order properly to understand the essential difference between God and the world, it is not enough to recognize a God distinct from the world as one man is distinct from another, or a mind from a body, or one thing here below from any other thing here below, no matter how different they may be. *No word of ours* is applicable to God in the same way that it is to the things of which we have experience. Between Him and creatures it is being itself in its depths and its totality, the metaphysical structure of being that differs; in Him an infinity of being infinitely different, infinitely separated from all that, outside Him, we call being, from all being which appears and can appear before our eyes and before our reason. That is why *what* God *is,* is known to us in reflections and in riddles, we do not know it in itself: *nos non scimus de Deo quid est.* In this being of the deity, essentially different from the entire being of the world, is hidden and rooted the universe of the supernatural order (supernatural *quoad substantiam*), which is the divine life itself participated in. Scarcely does that life come down into the world, when the scandal of the cross and the hatred of the world immediately *illustrate,* in a tangible way, the *real and essential distinction between God and the world . . .* [ellipsis in original] (*BPT,* p. 201)

9. The dependence of man in relation to material conditions which he must learn to control is of course admitted. But it is said there is no dependence that he needs to acknowledge to an order of things superior to his will or to a God who has created him. In our view it is absurd to admit dependence in one case and to deny it in the other. How could man be dependent on *things* of an inferior order if he were not in his essence a dependent being, and if there were not therefore something above him on which he must depend? (*FMW,* p. 91; CW 11, p. 49)

10. God does not create essences to which He can be imagined as giving a last rub of the sandpaper of subsistence before sending them forth into existence! God creates existent subjects or supposita which subsist in the individual nature that constitutes them and which receive from the creative influx their nature as well as their subsistence, their existence, and their activity. (*EE,* **pp. 65–66**)

11. Loving the divine Subject more than myself, it is for Him that I love myself, it is to do as He wishes that I wish above all else to accomplish my destiny; and because, unimportant as I am in the world, I am important to Him; not only I, but all the other subjectivities whose lovableness is revealed in Him and for Him and which are henceforth, together with me, a *we,* called to rejoice in His life. (*EE,* **p. 76**)

12. I am known to God. He knows all of me, me as subject. I am present to Him in my subjectivity itself; He has no need to objectise me in order to know me. Then, and in this unique instance, man is known not as object but as subject in all the depth and all the recesses of subjectivity. Only God knows me in this wise; to Him alone am I uncovered. I am not uncovered to myself. The more I know of my subjectivity, the more it remains obscure to me. If I were not known to God, no one would know me. No one would know me in my truth, in my own existence. No one would know me—*me*—as subject. (*EE,* **p. 77**)

13. Finally, what enables us to speak of God, to name Him, to know Him, is the fact that being and the notions connected with being, the one, that is to say being as undivided, the true, that is, being as facing intelligence, the good, that is, being as facing will, etc., are notions which overflow any genus or any category of things and which, consequently, imply in their essence no limitation. These notions, which for that reason are called transcendental, are found in all that is; as a result, they do not belong exclusively to any species of beings; they are ascribed to the one and the other *by analogy;* a man is good in his manner as a fruit is good in its manner or a word is good in its manner, and being must indeed be an essentially *analogous* notion, since things which differ really from one another, and since all of them nevertheless are, all of them truly and properly have being. Hence we can attribute to God, truly and properly, all the realities or perfections of the transcendental order, such as being or those defined in relation to being, even though we first got our idea of them from the consideration of creatures. (***BPT*, pp. 194–95**)

14. According to St. Thomas, as God alone knows the secrets of the Freedom he has created so He alone can act upon that Freedom. He alone can pierce into that world. And why? Because He is the cause of all the Being of all that is. Wherever there is being, He is there as First Cause; and when I exercise an act of freedom He alone is there, with me and in me, since, in brief, this act being free does not depend on any cause within the order of creation save only grace.

And God is cause in an analogical and eminent sense. He is not cause in the same sense as any of the causes of which I have experience. He rules and transcends both the order of Necessity and the order of Contingence. When therefore He acts in me who act, His action is to supply the basic freedom of my act. It is just so far as I am a free agent and have dominion over my act that His power penetrates my being, causing, in His quality as First Cause, in me who am a second and free cause, the very mode of my action and the perfection that is proper to it as a free act. (***FMW*, pp. 26–27; CW 11, p. 17**)

15. Metaphysics cannot attain the Divine Essence in itself; and yet, it truly knows God in the divided mirror of transcendental perfections analogically common to the uncreated and to the created. In this mirror it grasps in the imperfect mode proper to finite things, realities which, brought to their pure state and overflowing all our concepts, pre-exist in the incomprehensible simplicity of the infinite. (***DK*, p. 248; CW 7, pp. 264–65**)

16. It is thus that we know God by analogy, in a glass darkly. It is thus that Christian wisdom, going from one extreme to the other with strength and gentleness, shows us that God infinitely exceeds our knowledge by His essence and at the same time, that we can know Him inadequately, but with an absolute truth, by His creatures; know Him with more certitude than we know our brother, our friend, our own heart; as it shows us at the same time the ineffable transcendence of the divine nature and the sovereign immanence of divine operation; as it shows us both the very redoubtable holiness and the superabundant mercy of Him Who is.

But in any case it is ever the idea of being which is our light. By it, even though it also is infinitely overflowed by the divine reality, by the *deity*, which is super-being just as it is super-goodness and super-beauty— it is by the idea of being that we give God the name which suits Him *par excellence*, and that we see His absolute distinction from the world; by it, because of its analogous value, we can found our knowledge of God without giving either agnosticism or pantheism the slightest hold. (***BPT,*** **pp. 195–96**)

17. God is beautiful. He is the most beautiful of beings, because, as Denis the Aeropagite and Saint Thomas explain, His beauty is without alteration or vicissitude, without increase or diminution; and because it is not as the beauty of things, all of which have a particularized beauty, *particulatam pulchritudinem, sicut et particulatam naturam.* He is beautiful through Himself and in Himself, beautiful absolutely. (***AS,*** **pp. 30–31**)

18. If nothing else had been loved by God, nothing else would have existed. And this would involve no change in Him. And yet for the creature there is nothing more real than to be loved by God; it then partakes in some way of the love that God has for Himself. The love of each particular creature is in God something intrinsic and formal and supremely real since it is His immanent act of subsisting Love and of absolute Freedom in face of every possible being which constitutes this particular creature, this thing and not another, as the object of His love. (***FMW,*** **p. 12; CW 11, pp. 9–10**)

19. God knows and loves all existents. They do not impinge upon His knowledge and His love after the manner of specifying objects. In the act by which He knows Himself and loves His own goodness, God embraces all existents as *effects* flowing from the infinite gratuitousness in which that act superabounds. (***EE,*** **p. 106**)

20. Atheist communism is only bourgeois deism turned the other way round. (***FMW,*** **p. 100; CW 11, p. 54**)

21. Let us consider now the problem of atheism from the philosophical and doctrinal point of view. It is a problem of capital importance.

What is it that an authentically philosophical conception of the human will tells us? That atheism is *unlivable* in its metaphysical root, it its absolute radicalism—if, at least, one can reach this limit.

For the will goes by nature to the good as such, to pure goodness. From the moment it acts, it acts for a final end which can only be a good that fulfills it absolutely. Now, where is this good in reality, if not in the being which is by itself the infinite plenitude of Goodness? Such, briefly, is the teaching of an authentic philosophy of the will. Thus every will, even the most perverse, desires God without knowing it. Although a will can choose other final ends, opt for other loves, it is still and always God that it desires under aberrant forms and contrary to its own choice.

Atheism, *if it could be lived* down to the very roots of the will, would disorganize, would kill metaphysically the will. It is not by accident, it is by an effect strictly necessary, inscribed in the nature of things, that every absolute experience of atheism, if it is consciously and rigorously conducted, provokes in the end psychic dissolution. (***IH*, pp. 59–60; CW 11, pp. 189–90**)

22. There is an atheism which declares that God *does not exist* and which makes its god of an idol; and there is an atheism which declares indeed that God exists, but which *makes of God himself an idol*, because it denies by its acts, if not by its words, the nature and the attributes of God, and His glory; it invokes God, but as a protecting genius attached to the glory of a people or of a State *against* all others, or as a demon of the race. (***IH*, p. 281; CW 11, p. 330**)

23. Those who call themselves *intellectuals* ordinarily affect a fine disdain for what we call the proofs of the existence of God, first, because in most cases they are ignorant of them; next, because in reality these proofs are not made for those whom Pascal called the 'demi-habiles,' the half-clever ones. They are too *simple* for such people. (***BPT*, p. 180**)

24. To demonstrate the existence of God is neither to subject Him to our grasp, nor to define Him, nor to seize Him, nor to manipulate anything except ideas which are inadequate to such an object, nor to judge anything except our own proper and radical dependence. The procedure by which reason demonstrates that God exists, puts reason itself in an attitude of natural adoration and of intellectual admiration. (**DK, p. 225; CW 7, p. 239**)

25. The existence of God is not for mankind a truth evident in itself, that is to say it is not enough, as Descartes believed, to have the idea of God to know that God exists: the ontological argument proves, in fact, only one thing: that Being *a se* exists necessarily, *if it exists;* it does not prove *that it exists*. It is not with one single ambitious leap, with an idea of our minds as starting-point, that God wishes us to go to Him; it is by passing through His creatures and by making use of the things He has made. But so easy is that way, so natural and spontaneous that passage, that man cannot exert his reason without heaven and earth showing him his Creator, to the point that the knowledge of the existence of God is for him a *dowery from nature,* it happens in him without instruction, as the first fruit of the activity of his living intelligence; and if he really rejects so natural an instinctive certitude it is because in that case his will is deflected or because he has been blinded by his teachers. (*BPT,* p. 181)

26. God is not Cartesian, God is not an idealist. His knowledge of things does not stop at His essence. He knows their essences in His uncreated essence which is His sole specifying *object*. But at the same time—because, by means of the creative idea which causes things to be in their own existence, this sole object *quod,* the divine essence, performs also the function of an object *quo*—the 'science of vision' descends even to things themselves in their existential singularity. It attains them even in the most profound recesses of their being and of their contingent existence, it probes the loins and the heart, the 'science of vision' is *par excellence* a science of *presentness.* The divine knowledge thus attains fully, exhaustively, existentially, all that there is of being, of the positive, of good, of the ontologically good and of the morally good, in creatures, because it itself causes or makes all of this. In the uncreated eternal intelligibility as light and in the uncreated essence as sole specifying object, it grasps as secondary term the created existent in its concrete singularity itself and its created existence itself totally and perfectly penetrated. (*GE,* **pp. 70–71**)

27. It is thus that the 'science of vision,' which knows all that it knows in the uncreated essence and the uncreated light, descends even to the created existent taken in its created existentiality and its created activity themselves and as such, knows it according to the very existence which it has *extra Deum*: just as, to employ Saint Thomas' comparison, "through the *species* of the stone that the eye has within it, the eye knows the stone *secundum esse quod habet extra oculum,* according to the existence that it has outside the eye." This is how—to tell you as best I can what the weak means at my disposal permit me to stammer on such a question—God knows in its presentness the human clay which His hands shape, knows it even to the most hidden core of itself and of its contingent and free activity, right down to the last depths and to the slightest tremblings of its subjectivity. (***GE*, pp. 72–73**)

28. Finite and wretched in self, man cannot pass to a super-human condition save by adhesion of intellect and will to a superior being. God being the perfection of personal existence and man being also, though precariously, a person, the mystery of the achievement of freedom is contained in the relation of these two persons. (***FMW*, p. 36; CW 11, p. 22**)

29. God is an All-powerful Cause because He gives to all things their being and their very nature and acts in them, more intimate to them than they are to themselves, in the way that is proper to their essential being; thus assuring from within the free action of those creatures that are by nature free. (***FMW*, p. 93; CW 11, p. 50**)

CHAPTER SIXTEEN

HISTORY

1. Christianity has taught us that history has a direction, that it works in a determined direction. History is not an eternal return; it does not move in circles. Time is linear, not cyclical. This truth was a crucial acquisition for human thought. (*PH,* **p. 2**)

2. It would be fitting to explain oneself first of all here on the question of the possibility of a philosophy of history. In the hands of the pure philosopher—the philosopher who recognizes only the light of natural reason—the philosophy of history, in my opinion, is bound either to fail in its own expectations, or to risk mystification, for it inevitably requires prophetic data. And where would the pure philosopher find prophetic data?

To my mind this question is capable of a positive solution only if we admit the notion of a philosophy of man in which the philosopher illumines philosophy and the knowledge of the natural order with the light of a more elevated knowledge, a knowledge received from faith and theology. Then only, while of course retaining a conjectural character on many points, can a philosophy of history constitute itself as worthy of the name of philosophy or of wisdom. (*IH,* **pp. 241–42; CW 11, p. 304**)

3. The devil hangs like a vampire on the side of history. History moves forward nonetheless and moves forward with the vampire. It is only in the Church as Church that the devil has no place. He takes part in the onward march of the world and in a sense instigates it. His chief activity is to do in his particular way (which is not a good way) what good folk omit to do, because they are asleep. That which is done is done badly, but it is done.

The Prince of this world takes possession of the things of time as far as these things are not redeemed by the blood of Christ. But time belongs to God: it is He who first wills movement and change. There is a passage full of strange meaning in the Hymn of Habacuc, in the Vulgate. It is there said that the devil goes before the feet of God: *et egredietur diabolus ante pedes ejus*. He runs before Him: as a traitor he prepares His ways.

Truth to tell, history is bicephalous. The head of all the good folk leads his party to the place where God will be all in all; the head of all the wicked leads his party to the place where the creature will be all things to itself. When the members of these two parties who at every instant are intermingled shall have finally separated, history itself will be at an end. (***FMW*, pp. 85–86; CW 11, p. 46**)

4. To my mind, it is to betray both God and man not to understand that history is in movement toward the kingdom of God, and not to wish that this kingdom come about. But it is nonsense to think that it will come about *in* history, which is invincibly made up of good and evil. Prepared by the growth of history, and by the mixing and progressive exhaustion of the human being that are accomplished there, it will come *at the end of history*; I mean in the time of the resurrected into which history will open. (***IH*, p. 59; CW 11, p. 189**)

5. Those who make it their first principle to advance with history, or to make history advance and to march in step with it, thereby bind themselves to collaborate with all the agents of history; they find themselves in very mixed company.

We are not co-operators with history; we are co-operators with God.

No doubt, to absent oneself from history is to seek death. Spiritual activity, which is above time, does not vacate time, it holds it from on high.

Our duty is to act on history to the limit of our power: yes, but God being first served. And we must neither complain nor feel guilty if history often works against us: it will not vanquish our God, and escape His purposes, either of mercy or of justice. The chief thing, from the point of view of existence in history, is not to succeed; success never endures. Rather, it is *to have been there*, to have been *present*, and that is ineffaceable. (***PH*, p. 59**)

6. The world is the domain *at once* of man, of God, and of the devil. Thus appears the essential ambiguity of the world and of its history; it is a field common to the three. The world is a closed field which belongs to God by right of creation; to the devil by right of conquest, because of sin; to Christ by right of victory over the conqueror, because of the Passion. The task of the Christian in the world is to contend with the devil his domain, to wrest it from him; he must strive to this end, he will succeed in it only in part as long as time will endure. (***TP*, p. 35**)

7. I have spoken of what may be described as the vertical movement of the human person within society. The dynamic tension between the person and society provokes still a second sort of movement, the latter horizontal. I refer to a movement of progression of societies themselves evolving within time. This movement depends upon a great law, which might be called the double law of the degradation and revitalization of the energy of history, or of the mass of human activity upon which the movement of history depends. While the wear and tear of time and the passivity of matter naturally dissipate and degrade the things of this world and the energy of history, the creative forces which are characteristic of the spirit and of liberty and are also their witness and which normally find their point of application in the effort of the few—thereby destined to sacrifice—constantly revitalize the quality of this energy. Thus the life of human societies advances and progresses at the price of many losses. It advances and progresses thanks to that vitalization or super-elevation of the energy of history springing from the spirit and from liberty, and thanks to technical improvements which are often ahead of the spirit (whence catastrophe) but which by nature ask only to be the instruments of the spirit. (***RM*, pp. 29–30**)

8. There is nothing more striking than the astounding and ever-increasing acceleration of history set in motion by the spiritual revolution foretold by the recitation of the humble *Magnificat* of a tiny virgin of Israel. (***UA,* p. 200**)

9. The idea of necessary historic Progress is fundamentally as self-contradictory as the idea of a square circle. Historic Progress involves evolution in time, evolution in time involves matter: but matter involves a radical appetite for the new, an appetite not for the other as perfect, but for the other as other: hence the absence of necessary Progress or even of necessary tendency toward the more perfect. The myth of Progress is an excellent example of the pseudo-idea, the idea which is at once "clear" for the imagination, and fundamentally absurd in itself. (***TS,* p. 114**)

10. If in our day the Myth of Necessary Progress still seduces certain minds, one reason is that being heirs of an age hostile to all hierarchies and distinctions, we too often confuse different planes of the energies of man, bundling together in one single vague image the most diverse activities, and making a general law of what is true only in certain special cases. (***TS,* pp. 160–61**)

11. There is a law of history, which I have often invoked, that in the things of this world and of human nature, wounded as it is, there is simultaneously progress in the line of good and in the line of evil. We have to accept this, and we have to think too, given the fact that the goodness with which God and the angels watch over human beings is greater than the propensity of human beings to become corrupted, that progress in the line of good is, after everything has been taken into consideration, greater and more profound, despite appearances and despite our groans, than progress in the line of evil. Primitive peoples were happier than we. But who would want to return to their condition? We know better than they just what the human being is made of, and we are more truly human than they were. A sparrow is less to be pitied than a human being, but we are worth much more than sparrow, "*multis passerbius pluris estis vos.*" (***UA,* p. 458**)

12. Human history grows thus, for it is not here a process of repetition, but of expansion and progress: it grows as an expanding sphere, drawing near at one and the same time to its double consummation—in the absolute from below where man is god without God, and in the absolute from above where he is God in God. (***IH*, p. 290; *CW* 11, p. 336**)

13. Here appears a basic difference between the Christian philosophy of history and the Hegelian, Marxian or Comtian philosophies of history. Be they dialectical or positivist, these philosophies of pure immanentist or atheist evolution are inevitably bound to a patent self-contradiction. On the one hand, they insist that Becoming is the only reality, and the process of change continues without end; and, on the other hand, they offer themselves as the definitive and final revelation, at the end of time, of the meaning of all history. The Christian philosophy of history is not liable to such inconsistencies. The end is beyond time, and never therefore can the movement of history come to a definitive and final state, or a definitive and final self-revelation, within time. Never can a Christian philosopher of history install himself, as Hegel, Marx and Comte did, at the end of time. (***PH*, p. 162**)

14. Given the contingency of matter and the free will of men, there are, at each moment of history, always two possible different directions open regarding the future. (***RON*, p. 193**)

15. The Sovereign Law of the Incarnation continues its influence here. While detaching the things of God's Kingdom from historical formations tending to bring into subjection that life which is freedom itself, that law of the Incarnation remains the law of superabundance and fruitfulness—the gift of self proper to love. And, consequently, the forces of Christianity must be involved again and anew in the flesh of humanity, to give birth, in the order of earthly civilization, to formations which are new and more pure.

Because Christian liberty is a pledged liberty, one which bears and transports the heavy mountains of history; because, and this is the very mystery of the Christian life, to the extent that this liberty becomes involved most deeply in history and the world, to that extent does it remain free; and bears witness to the fact that it arises neither from history nor from the world, but from the Living God. (***SP*, p. 197**)

16. Man is naturally frightened by the irreversibility of his own duration and the very newness of unpredictable events. He refuses to face them.

Hence the negation of time by archaic civilizations. They defended themselves against the dire reality of history either by constructing mythical archetypes, or by assuming a periodic abolishment and regeneration of time, and a periodic recurrence of the same historical cycles. (***PH*, pp. 36–37**)

17. Acceptance of time and of history was a conquest of Christianity and modern times. But this very acceptance would be of a nature to drive man to despair if he could not decipher some trans-historical meaning in the awful advance of time into the night of the unknown, thronged with perpetually new perils. (***PH*, p. 37**)

18. The "fair play" of God is the first law of the philosophy of history. He plays a fair game with free agents. From the moment that He decided to create the world, He decided to let them have their way, even though they might undo His work, and say *no*, even though they might, either in the manner of angels or in the manner of man, raise, like gods from below, nothingness against His love. He enlists us along with Himself in this enterprise. Our collaboration is required for its progress. This is the unheard-of paradox of the first three petitions in the Lord's Prayer, that, as has been said, they are prayers we address to God for God, for His Name, for His Kingdom, for His Will, for His own victory over the evil that he permits, that He does not will. He is the sovereign master and governor of history (in which He nevertheless has partners—the created free agents). And He is the cause only of the good, not of the evil of history. He is pure of the impurities of history, innocent of its crimes. Absolutely innocent. (***MP*, p. 189**)

19. The idea of a Christian renovation of temporal existence forces us to abandon the anthropocentric humanistic age, and especially the "capitalistic" and "bourgeois" epoch, in order to bring ourselves into a new world. If this is so, such a renovation has internal dimensions of incomparably greater height and breadth and depth than any other revolution; it is linked to a vast historical process of *integration* and *reintegration*. (***IH*, p. 229; CW 11, pp. 295–96**)

20. History gives us valuable information about the material conditions in which a man's thought has developed, but it can never effect the synthesis of that thought. (***DK*, p. 311; CW 7, p. 330**)

21. We are immediately confronted with a preliminary objection: how can a philosophy of history be possible, since history is not a science? History deals only with the singular and the concrete, with the contingent, whereas science deals with the universal and the necessary. History cannot afford us any explanation by universal *raisons d'être*. No doubt there are no "raw" facts; an historical fact presupposes and involves as many critical and discriminating judgments, and analytical re-castings, as any other "fact" does; moreover, history does not look for an impossible "coincidence" with the past; it requires choice and sorting, it interprets the past and translates it into human language, it re-composes or re-constitutes sequences of events resulting from one another, and it cannot do so without the instrumentality of a great deal of abstraction. Yet history uses all this in order to link the singular with the singular; its *object* as such is individual or singular. The explanation given by an historian, as historian, is an explanation of the individual by the individual—by individual circumstances, motivations, or events. The historical elucidation, being individual, participates in the potential infinity of matter; it is never finished; it never has (insofar as it is elucidation) the certainty of science. It never provides us with a *raison d'être* drawn from what things *are* in their very essence (even if it be known only through signs, as in the sciences of phenomena).

What can we answer? I would answer that the fact that history is not a science does not make a philosophy of history impossible, because it is enough for philosophy itself to be "scientific" knowledge and a formal or systematized discipline of wisdom. And it is in no way necessary that the subject matter with which philosophy deals should be a subject matter previously known and worked out by some particular science. For instance, we have a philosophy of art, though art is not a science. The philosophy of art deals with the same subject matter as art, but it deals with it from the philosophical point of view and in a philosophical light. Therefore, we have a philosophy of art which is essentially distinct from art itself, and which provides us with philosophical knowledge about a matter which has not been previously scientifically elucidated. And I would make a similar observation if it were a question of the philosophy of nature. A philosophy of nature was possible before any developed scientific knowledge of nature, or when our scientific knowledge of nature was quite unsatisfactory. Thus it is that in the case of the philosophy of history we have a "scientific" object insofar as this object is the object of philosophy, but not insofar as the subject matter was previously scrutinized by some other scientific discipline.

I would say, therefore, that the philosophy of history has the same *subject matter* as history, which is not a science. And I might add, symmetrically, that the philosophy of nature has the same subject matter as physics and chemistry, which are sciences. But the philosophy of history has another *object* than history. It is concerned with an objective content—in Scholastic terms, a *formal object*—other than that of history and of the historical explanation; just as the philosophy of nature has a formal object other than that of physics and chemistry. In the case of the philosophy of nature, however, the formal object of physics and chemistry is scientific, and the formal object of the philosophy of nature is another intelligible and universal object, a more intelligible and a more universal object, in the sphere of the knowledge of nature. But in the case of the philosophy of history, the formal object of history is not scientific—it is not universal, not necessary, not raised to the level of abstract intelligibility. And the formal object of the philosophy of history is the only abstract and universal object, disclosing intelligible "quiddities" or *raisons d'être*, i.e., the only "scientific" (or rather wisdom-fitting) object, in the sphere of historical knowledge.

What philosophy needs as a basis, I may add, is the certitude of facts, the general facts from which it starts. Philosophy works on factual material which has been established with certainty. Now scientific facts are not the only well-ascertained facts. I remember Pierre Duhem, the celebrated physicist and historian of the sciences, insisting many years ago that the data of the senses or of common sense are in general more certain (they are less precise, and therefore they are not useful for science itself) than scientific facts. Therefore the data of the senses or of the common knowledge of man, when philosophically criticized, may serve as matter for the philosopher of nature. And similarly the data of history—I don't refer to the recitation of the details of singular events, which is but a presupposed background, but to certain significant general facts and factual relations—may serve as matter for the philosopher of history, because history is capable of factual certitude. (**PH, pp. 2–6**)

22. I would add, parenthetically, that in the field of history, and precisely because history is not a science, a particular knowledge through connaturality is required of the historian—he must have some congeniality with the matter he is studying. For instance, he cannot really know military history if he has no experience of military things. Abstract knowledge is not enough—he must have a real human experience of military things if he is to be able to interpret what happened in some particular case. (*PH,* pp. 14–15)

23. The philosophy of history is the final application of philosophical truths, not to the conduct of the individual man, but to the entire movement of humanity. And therefore it is *moral* philosophy. (*PH,* p. 17)

24. It was the misfortune of the philosophy of history to have been *advertised* in the modern world by philosophers who were either the greatest falsifier[s] in divinity, or utter atheists. Only a spurious philosophy of history could be elicited by them. (*PH,* p. 35)

25. Hard experience has taught us that the kingdom of God is not meant for earthly history, but at the same time we have become aware of this crucial truth that it must be enigmatically prepared in the midst of the pains of earthly history. (*CD,* pp. 43–44)

26. It is disorder dearly bought to despise the Eternal order and to look forward to a new order which shall arise out of the mere surge of Becoming and the mere movement of history, an order accomplished and precipitated by those who know the secrets of history, the Levites of the revolutionary process, the elect of the god of immanence in whom the *Weltgeist* becomes conscious of itself. But it is disorder equally serious to forget that the order of human affairs is made in the making of history and that if it is to be what it ought to be it must be continuously created by ceaseless effort of reason and of will, of imagination and of virtue, rescuing from the evil of the time and fashioning with the tools that are at hand things consonant with the temporal and the eternal good of human beings. From this point of view certain instances of obvious disorder, of overthrow and of destruction, may represent the elimination in the process of history of deeper and less obvious disorder—and the price that has to be paid for the misdeeds and omissions of those who forget that justice is, in the language of St. Catherine of Siena, the sentinel of states. (*FMW,* pp. 80–81; CW 11, p. 44)

CHAPTER SEVENTEEN

HUMANISM

1. Man, forgetting that in the order of being and of good it is God who has the first initiative and who vivifies our freedom, has sought to make his own proper movement as creature the absolutely first movement, to give to his freedom-of-creature the first initiative of his good. It was therefore necessary that his movement of ascent be henceforth separated from the movement of grace; this is why the age in question [modern history] has been an age of dualism, of dissociation, of splitting in two, an age of humanism separated from the Incarnation, in which the effort of progress was to take on an inevitable character and itself contribute to the destruction of the human.

In short, let us say that the radical vice of anthropocentric humanism has been its being anthropocentric, and not its being humanism. (***IH*, p. 27; CW 11, p. 169**)

2. We are thus lead to distinguish two kinds of humanism: a theocentric or truly Christian humanism; and an anthropocentric humanism, for which the spirit of Renaissance and that of the Reformation are primarily responsible, and of which we have just been speaking.

The first kind of humanism recognizes that God is the center of man; it implies the Christian conception of man, sinner and redeemed, and the Christian conception of grace and freedom. . . .

The second kind of humanism believes that man himself is the center of man, and therefore of all things. It implies a naturalistic conception of man and of freedom.

If this conception is false, one understands that anthropocentric humanism merits the name of inhuman humanism, and that its dialectic must be regarded as the *tragedy of humanism*. (**IH, pp. 27–28; CW 11, p. 169**)

3. Let us say simply that humanism tends essentially to render man more truly human and to manifest his original greatness by enabling him to partake of everything in nature and in history capable of enriching him. It requires both that man develop the latent tendencies he possesses, his creative powers and the life of reason, and that he work to transform into instruments of his liberty the forces of the physical universe. Obviously, we cannot delete from the humanistic tradition the wisdom of ancient Greece, which, in its own terms, sought to attain "that which is better than reason, being the principle itself of reason." From this, one should take warning never to define humanism in such a way as to exclude from it all that is ordained to the supra-human and as to forswear all considerations of transcendence. (*TC,* **pp. 3–4**)

4. As concerns civilization, the man of Christian humanism knows that political life aims at a common good which is superior to a mere collection of the individual's goods and yet must flow back upon human persons. He knows that the common work must tend above all toward the improvement of human life itself, enabling everyone to exist on earth as a free man and to enjoy the fruits of culture and the spirit. He knows that the authority of those who are in charge of the common good, and who are, in a community of free men, designated by the people, and accountable to the people, originates in the Author of Nature and is therefore binding in conscience, and is binding in conscience on condition that it be just. The man of Christian humanism cherishes freedom as something he must be worthy of; he realizes his essential equality with other men in terms of respect and fellowship, and sees in justice the force of preservation of the political community and the prerequisite which, "bringing unequals to equality," enables civic friendship to spring forth. He is aware both of the tremendous ordeal which the advent of machinism imposes on human history, and of the marvelous power of liberation it offers to man, if the brute instinct of domination does not avail itself of the techniques of machinism, and of science itself, in order to enslave mankind; and if reason and wisdom are strong enough to turn them to the service of truly human aims and apply to them the standards of human life. The man of Christian humanism does not look for a merely industrial civilization, but for a civilization integrally human (industrial as it may be as to its material conditions) and of evangelical inspiration. (**RR, p. 197**)

5. If our humanism has failed, it is perhaps because it was centered in man alone, and was utilitarian, not heroic; because it tried to relegate death and evil to oblivion, instead of facing them and overcoming them by an ascent of the soul into eternal life; because it trusted in techniques instead of in love, I mean in Gospel love. (**RR, p. 202**)

6. In the present civilization, everything is referred to a measure which is not human, but external to man: primarily to laws belonging to material production, to the technological domination of nature and to the utilization of all the forces of the world for the fecundity of money. In a truly humanist culture, it is to man and his measure that the things of the world would be referred. The vocation of man is great enough, his needs and desires are sufficiently capable of growth, that we may rest assured that such a measure would not imply a renunciation of greatness.

Greatness demands both abundance and poverty; nothing great is done without a certain abundance, nothing great without a certain poverty. Can a man understand life at all if he does not begin by understanding that always it is poverty which superabounds in greatness? It is the tragic law of man's sin, not of his nature, that makes the poverty of some create the abundance of others: poverty of want and slavery, abundance or covetousness and pride. This is the law of sin which we must not accept, but fight. What would be in conformity with nature, and what we should demand in the social order of new forms of civilization, is that the poverty of each—neither penury nor misery, but sufficiency and freedom, renunciation of the spirit of riches, the gaiety of the lilies of the field—is that a certain individual poverty create a common abundance, superabundance, riches, and glory for all. (**IH, p. 191; CW 11, pp. 272–73**)

CHAPTER EIGHTEEN

INTELLECT AND INTELLIGENCE

1. A thousand doctrines can aggravate the condition of the intelligence, only one can cure it. (*TA,* p. 101)

2. If a figure of speech be permitted here, let us say that the work of the intellect can be compared to an immaterial magic. From the flux of singular and contingent things, as given to the apprehension of the sense, a first glance of the intellect reveals the world of corporeal substances and their properties. A second glance reveals quite another universe, the ideal world of the extended number. A third glance discloses still another, wholly different, universe, the world of being as being and all the transcendental perfections common to spirits and bodies, wherein we can attain purely spiritual realities, and the very principle of all reality, as in a mirror. (*DK,* p. 37; CW 7, p. 40)

3. The intellect is, in fact, of itself an *intuitive* faculty. When, fecundated by the intelligible form received in it, it produces in itself a living likeness of the thing known, which identifies it with the thing, not in the way the thing itself exists naturally, but in the immaterial way in which it, the intellect,

exists, it *directly* perceives the intelligible object which it thus discovers in the real and which is but one with the real. (***BPT*, p. 150**)

4. It is because human ideas attain being, or what things *are* (even if they do so in the most indirect manner, and in the symbols of physico-mathematical science); it is because human thought is a vital energy of spiritual intuition grasping things in their intelligible consistency and universal values; it is because thinking begins, not with difficulties, but with *insights,* and ends in insights whose truth is established by rational demonstration or experimental verification, not by pragmatic sanction, that human thought is able to illumine experience and to dominate, control, and refashion the world. At the beginning of human action, insofar as it is human, there is truth, grasped or believed to be grasped, for the sake of truth. Without trust in truth, there is no human effectiveness.

Thus, for Thomist philosophy, knowledge is a value in itself and an end in itself; and truth consists in the conformity of the mind with reality—with what is or exists independently of the mind. The intellect tends to grasp and conquer being. Its aim and its joy are essentially disinterested. And "perfect" or "grown-up" knowledge ("science" in the broad Aristotelian sense) reaches certainties which are valid in their pure objectivity—whatever the bents and interests of the individual or collective man may be—and are unshakably established through the intuition of first principles and the logical necessity of the deductive or inductive process. Thus, that superior kind of knowledge which is wisdom, because it deals not only with mastering natural phenomena but with penetrating the primary and most universal *raisons d'être* and with enjoying, as a final fruition, the spiritual delight of truth and the sapidity of being, fulfills the supreme aspiration of the intellectual nature and its thirst for liberation. (***EM*, p. 47**)

5. True existentialism is the work of reason. The act by virtue of which I exist and things exist, transcends concepts and ideas; it is a mystery for the intellect. But the intellect lives on this mystery. It does so in its most natural activity, which is as ordinary, daily and vulgar as eating or drinking: for the act of existing is indeed the very object of every achieved act of the intellect, that is, of every judgment. It is perceived by that intellectual intuition, immersed in sense-experience, which is the common treasure (all the more precious as

it is natural and imbues the depths of our thought) of all our assertions, of all this mysterious activity by means of which we declare either *ita est* or *fiat!* in the face of the world or at the moment of making a decision. Now, when the intellect passes the threshold of philosophy, it does so by becoming aware of this intellectual intuition, freeing its genuine power, and making it the peculiar weapon of a knowledge whose subject-matter is Being itself. I do not here refer to Platonic essences. I refer to the act of existing insofar as it grounds and centers the intelligible structure of reality, as it expands into activity in every being, and as, in its supreme, uncreated plenitude, it activates and attracts to itself the entire dynamism of nature. (**RR, p. 87**)

6. Intelligence lives, because what is proper to life is immanent action, action which dwells in the subject acting; and there is no action more immanent than that of the intellect engendering in itself a living fruit which dwells in it to enrich and perfect it.

The intellect lives because the intellectual light, the light of the formative intellect, is a participated likeness of the living divine Light. The intellect lives because under the action of that intellectual light and of objective reality, it produces, as long as truth requires it, new concepts, in the measure and likeness of things, which well up from the depths of its activity and which contain inexhaustible riches; for it is true as Bergson has expressed it, perhaps exaggerating a little, that each of the great philosophers has spent his whole life in developing, in every possible direction, a single intuition, in reality the intuition in question has been an *intellectual* intuition, a living intellectual perception expressible in ideas or concepts. (**BPT, p. 158**)

7. The speculative intellect knows only for the sake of knowledge. It longs to see, and only to see. Truth, or the grasping of that which is, is its own goal, and its only life.

The practical intellect knows for the sake of action. From the very start its object is not Being to be grasped, but human activity to be guided and human tasks to be achieved. It is immersed in creativity. To mould intellectually that which will be brought into being, to judge about ends and means, and to direct or even command our powers of execution—they are its very life.

Such a distinction does not deal with accidental circumstances. It is an essential distinction. For the entire dynamism of the intellect and its typical approach to its object depend on this very object, and they are basically different when the object is merely knowledge and when the object is action. (*CI,* p. 46)

8. Let us first of all remember that the intelligence sees by and in the concepts which it, in a living way, produces from its own depths. Everything in the way of concepts and ideal constructions that the intelligence—ceaselessly leading its insatiable hunger for reality over the whole extent of exterior and interior experience, the whole extent of truths already acquired, perpetually on the *hunt for essences,* as Aristotle put it—causes to surge up in itself is only to serve that *sense of being* which is indeed the deepest thing in the intelligence, and to achieve an intuitive discernment which is the act itself of the intelligence. In those matchless moments of *intellectual discovery,* wherein we seize for the first time upon a pulsing, intelligible reality in the seemingly infinite abundance of its possibilities for expansion, and wherein we feel rising and confirming itself in our deepest beings that intellectual word which makes such reality manifest, we then know well what the intuitive power of the intelligence is, and that it is exerted by means of concepts. (*RT,* p. 59)

9. Indeed, the philosopher knows that the intellect is spiritual and hence must emanate from a spiritual soul. He knows that between the soul of a simple animal and the soul of man there is an *absolute,* abyssal difference because the senses, enclosed in materiality, perceive only the particular, whereas the intellect perceives the universal and reflects upon itself (and this implies immateriality in both cases) so that *in its exercise* the intellect certainly does develop, as we see in the child; but as a *power* it is given, with the intellective or spiritual soul, from the very first instant when that soul is infused into an organism sufficiently elevated for an ultimate disposition of the matter to call for it there. To think (as some scientists and even some philosophers seem to do, what a pity) that what current speech calls animal intelligence, which is an interior sense (called estimative by the philosopher), can succeed, advancing step by step, in finally becoming intellect, is just as absurd as to think that an architect will one day reach the moon by building higher and higher towers, or that by dint of perfecting its scent a well-trained hunting dog will succeed some day, when his master has become an art dealer, in distinguishing a Rouault from a Vermeer or an authentic Picasso from a fake one. (**UA, p. 120**)

10. What is at the bottom of the reproaches addressed by the new philosophy to abstract knowledge is impatience with the laws and limitations peculiar to our nature. This philosophy will not resign itself to perceiving the real only by a variety of manifold faculties, to the inability to drain reality to the dregs, to the absence of an experimental knowledge of the essence of things. In this ambition of making nature transcend itself, an ambition which is usually accompanied by an incomprehension of or refusal to accept the supernatural order, must be seen, transported here into an anti-intellectualist thesis, the proper sin of absolute intellectualism.

It is true that we have not by our intellect direct knowledge of the singular—but we have our senses for knowing the singular! And it is equally barbarous to wish to sacrifice the senses to the intellect, or the intellect to the senses, for these two orders of faculties are made to cooperate in the same perfection of human nature. As to perceiving by one and the same faculty the singular and the general alike, the abstract and the concrete, that is reserved for Angels, for pure Intelligences. (**BPT, p. 161**)

11. Today all intellectual objectivity seems to be concentrated in the realm of science where, moreover, an admirable co-operation of minds can be seen. But in the realm of philosophy contemporary thought is most often, and increasingly, subjective and introverted.

And yet we may observe that rarely has so much intellectual talent been spent, rarely have so many truths—not only so many errors, but also so many truths—been circulated. Truths are running rampant. We meet them in every corner of our daily newspapers and weekly magazines, and in the speeches of our politicians. People are even beginning to notice that the world is perishable, and that science without wisdom is of no use to men. But the ordinary intellect hardly profits from this swarm of truths; it takes them in one on top of the other, along with the mass of errors which are also running rampant—a blotter soaking up everything without discrimination.

This means that setting forth and elaborating philosophically even the best-established truths is to little purpose if intellects are not purified, but instead remain intoxicated by the poisons which afflict the world. How can clear vision be expected of ailing eyes? How can a debilitated organism be expected to sort out the queer mixture it receives as food, and to assimilate what is healthy and burn what is poisoned?

As to the work of Christian thought, it thus happens that to many contemporary minds the meat furnished by the philosophy in which that thought reaches its highest fulfillment and greatest vigor, I mean Thomistic philosophy, appears as too strong a food. One solution consists in diluting or more or less adulterating the food itself, and in discarding articulate knowledge and its too rigorous disciplines. An argument in favor of this solution is the pressing need we feel to go to our neighbor's help. But in reality, I am afraid, this solution would serve both to weaken and diminish the verities, and to prolong or aggravate the attack of pernicious anemia which the powers of the subject are now undergoing.

The true solution would require that one succeed in strengthening these powers from within, in restoring the taste for truth within the minds of men, and in purifying and refreshing the sight of their eyes. Finally, in order to achieve these ends—and this is the point I want to make—there is only one remedy: to re-awaken in the world a sense of, and esteem for, contemplation. The world is prey to a great thirst, an immense mystical yearning which does not even know itself and which, because it remains without objective, turns to despair or neurosis. (**RR, pp. 48–49**)

12. [In its] vital operation of knowing, our intelligence is *dependent* upon some object not itself. It is not a mere subjective game: on the contrary, it is an act of subjection and submission to the object known; for whereas the intelligence of *God* is both the cause and the measure of the truth of things, things are both the cause and the measure of the truth of *our* intelligence; and it is precisely in this act of subjection to the object that its liberty consists. It is made for *being*, it is in its totality reaching out towards the object, towards the other *as* other; it needs the dominating contact of the object, but only that it may be enriched by it—in a victorious action which springs from its own living spontaneity, from its *autonomy*. For, as it does itself immaterially become the object, it is truly from itself that the act of knowing emanates, which perfects it—though from itself thus become the *other*, fertilised by being, rightly subjected to the real. That is what Kant did not see and what St. Thomas saw very clearly. Kant had a profound feeling of

the spontaneity of the intellectual nature, but because he believed that the act of knowing consists in *creating* the other, not in *becoming* the other, he foolishly reversed the order of dependence between the object of knowledge and the human intellect and made the human intellect the measure and law of the object.

... Since the *immanent* activity of our intellect is essentially *dependent* upon the object, there is neither repose nor happiness for it save when it is totally conquered (that is, convinced) and mastered by the object, because then only is it truly free because following the nature of its own activity. (*TS*, pp. 9–10)

13. Through the intellect, whose being and operation are immaterial and which perceives the eternal truths, man emerges above matter and time— *intellectus supra tempus*—and already takes his place, as it were, in eternity. And while the beings below him have as their end nothing but particular goods, he has as his end the absolute good, and he loves it and is capable of attaining beatitude. (*BPT*, pp. 247–48)

14. Now observe that this intelligibility which accompanies being, is in pure act only in the Divine Being. Not only is it the prerogative of God to be intellection in pure act, an act of knowledge in pure act, it is also His prerogative, indeed it is the same thing, to be intelligibility in pure act. You will therefore see at once that any philosophy which claims that all things should be perfectly transparent to the intellect, contain nothing whatever that baffles comprehension, must not be in the slightest degree opaque, any such system of absolute intellectualism is inevitably pantheistic. For it ascribes to creatures this intelligibility in pure act. If things are not God they must comprise a certain measure of unintelligibility in as much as they originate from nothingness. If in truth intelligibility accompanies being, it is obvious that in so far as anything is affected with nonentity it must possess a root of unintelligibility. Its relative nonentity is also a relative unintelligibility. (*PM*, p. 102)

15. If the liberty of the intellect were simply a claim to have no end other than its own satisfaction, in total independence of the hard but salutary domination of the object—it might seem that the service of the common good would be equivalent to an abdication of its liberty and a renouncing of that which constitutes its happiness, in subordination to the interests of action. But if there is no true liberty for the intellect save in submission to the object, if there is no true leisure for it save in the activity of knowing the object, then it is obvious that it will best serve the common interests of men precisely in assuring its own leisure and its own liberty, precisely in working *disinterestedly*—which means not simply that it may take pleasure in its own operation, but that it may be subjected to that which *is*. For men are nourished by being; as their body lives by bread, their mind lives by being, by truth, by beauty; they have a measureless need of a constantly renewed inpouring of these transcendentals. By the mere fact of applying itself to being, the intellect works for the good both of the City and of the universe. (*TS*, pp. 10–11)

16. Realism is lived by the intellect before being recognized by it. (*DK*, p. 79; CW 7, p. 83)

17. Our teaching, on the contrary, is that the intellect's natural realism tends to things from the point of view of the essence, both to carry them into the mind by decanting their universal value (which for the human intellect occurs only through abstraction) and yet by attaining them indirectly in their singular conditions of existence by reference to the sensible. We are speaking here about requirements connatural to our intellect itself. If we try to enter more deeply into the knowledge of individuals as such, we do so in order to face up to another demand, and first of all because we love them: it is love, then, which, for its own ends, uses the intellect to penetrate to the heart of the being it loves. (*DK*, p. 455; CW 7, p. 479)

18. Let us not forget, however . . . that when the Angelic Doctor thus points out the inferiority of knowledge by abstraction and by discursive reasoning it is in order to show the imperfection of human intellect in comparison with pure intelligences—"the human intellect is at the lowest degree in the order of intellects, *infimus in ordine intellectuum,* and the farthest removed from the perfection of the sovereign Intellect" . . . not to credit us with some intellectual intuition other than the one proper to us, or to demand of some supra-intellectual intuition that it compensate, in the very order of philosophical cognition, for the infirmity of our concepts, or to deprive the latter of the intuitive light without which they would not be formed. For Saint Thomas, human intellect—which following its natural bent ascends to the great common verities—knows only by filling itself with immaterial words or concepts and its natural means of progress in knowledge is the rational movement which, continually taking in fresh supplies of experience, leads it from the intellection of principles to the intellection of conclusions. (***BPT,* p. 31**)

19. Whatever *we* picture to ourselves is in fact bathed in intelligence, and in intelligence which is free, which has the upper hand over imagination. Therefore we have great trouble in depicting to ourselves any state in which—in the case of primitive man—imagination had the upper hand over the intellect; or in which—in the case of the animal—there is knowledge, but merely sensitive knowledge: knowledge by way of the senses, which admittedly are capable, in superior vertebrates, of *resembling* intelligence to a great extent. It is really impossible for a man to imagine how a dog is "thinking." But nevertheless there is a dog-knowledge which exists as a matter of fact, and is the object of the psychology of animals. We experience a similar difficulty when it comes to the magical state proper to the mental activity of the primitive man, a state utterly different from our logical state, and in which the imagination was the queen of the human mind. We might call our present state a daylight or solar state because it is bound up with the luminous and regular life of the intellect. And the magical state might be called a nocturnal state, because it is bound up with the fluid and twilight life of the imagination. (***PH,* pp. 99–100**)

20. We believe that intelligence is in and by itself nobler than the will of man, for its activity is more immaterial and universal. But we believe also that, in regard to the things or the very objects on which this activity bears, it is better to will and love the good than simply to know it. Moreover it is through man's will, when it is good, not through his intelligence, be it ever so perfect, that man is made good and right. A similar intermingling of roles is to be found in education, taken in its broadest sense. The upbringing of the human being must lead both intelligence and will toward achievement, and the shaping of the will is throughout more important to man than the shaping of the intellect. Yet, whereas the educational system of schools and colleges succeeds as a rule in equipping man's intellect for knowledge, it seems to be missing its main achievement, the equipping of man's will. What an infelicity! (*EC,* **p. 22**)

21. One man takes the created intellect as its own last end; another essentially subordinates the intellect to practical action; both of them offend against the true nature of the intellect and twist the human being from its true line. We must firmly grasp that it is only by considering the object, only by restoring the objective value of our powers of knowing, that we can escape from both these vices: so that we shall at once prevent the intellectuals from using the intellect against the good of man, and maintain in its fullness Aristotle's great idea of the royal liberty of the intellect. (*TS,* **p. 13**)

22. The requests (and worries) of the intelligence—they are real enough. Even in the mass media we find a hint of them. We are, after all, animals endowed with reason: hence heirs to quite a few worries and illusions, and a good many demands as well, both exacting and inevitable. The renewals to which we are summoned by the great chime of the Council [the Second Vatican Council] depend above all on an inspiration and spiritual élan awakened in the heaven of the soul. But such an inspiration and such an élan necessarily entail and require a vast labor of reason, renewing its own perspectives and grasping more thoroughly the articulations of the real. Only then can they recast our ordinary regime of thought and behavior. For this, neither mystical experience, nor faith, however desirable the first, and necessary the other, can suffice; both demand to be accompanied by an indispensable renewal in the order of intelligence. And if we stop to consider the present condition of the intelligence, we will see (yes, we have been chained up longer and more tightly than we like to think) that what such a renewal requires is, first and foremost, a breaking of barriers and chains, a liberation: liberation of the intelligence itself, and liberation in hearts of a love which has been terribly repressed and which cries out from the depths of the abyss—the love of Truth. I say "in hearts" because it is a question of love, and I say "love"—love of that truth which is the life of the intellect—because it is desire or the will, whose primary act is loving, which puts into operation all our powers, and hence also our intellect. (*TP,* **pp. 84–85**)

23. In the absolute order of metaphysical dignity, there is not among human beings anything better than the Intellect; but Charity is better than the best of human things. Here below it is of greater value than the intellect: nothing else is. The true reign of the heart demands the union of the soul with what is better than reason—what Aristotle calls the *Principle* of reason; and it is, therefore, absolutely inseparable from the reign of truth. (**TS, p. 41**)

CHAPTER NINETEEN

KNOWING AND KNOWLEDGE

1. Not to know what one is doing—it is thus, especially when it is a matter of self-forgetfulness due to a superior motion, that one makes the most beautiful things and performs the most generous acts. But not to know what one is doing—it is thus also that one commits the greatest crimes (and has the best chance also of being pardoned for them). All in all, other things being equal, it is better, however dangerous it be, and to whatever sanctions one expose oneself, to *know what one is doing.* (*SO,* p. 58)

2. All facts are not of the same *rank.* They do not constitute an indistinct and disorderly agglomeration gathered together in the market of sensible experience, to which the diverse sciences have to come to look for the commodities they need. Facts themselves belong to various orders or hierarchies of knowledge; they are common-sense facts, scientific facts (facts of interest to the sciences of nature), mathematical facts (facts like existence—the ideal existence—of underived continuous functions), logical facts, philosophical facts. (*DK,* p. 52; CW 7, p. 56)

3. There is a philosophical criticism of facts just as there is a scientific criticism of facts. (This criticism of facts, observations and experiments, is, as you know, an integral part of scientific work.) And when a fact which is the result of absolutely general observation has been judged and criticized by philosophy, it can no longer be called a fact of common observation, for the light of philosophical judgment and criticism has intervened to make it a philosophical fact in the strict sense of the word. The fact that something exists, that a multiplicity of things exists, that knowledge and thought exist, that becoming exists, these are all philosophical facts. (*PN,* p. 143)

4. There are two different *esse*'s, two levels of existence, for things: the proper existence they possess in order to maintain themselves outside nothingness, and the existence that supervenes upon them in their apprehension by the soul in order that they may be known. In order that the bindweed and apple may enter the sense of sight, they leave at the door the proper matter in which they subsist; and they lay aside their individuality in order to be able to enter understanding and reasoning. In the inner world of our understanding there is a whole multitude of distinct views or distinct concepts for things that exist undivided in the world of nature, and they lead quite a different life in the latter world than they do in the former. In the world of nature the lion eats the antelope; in the world of understanding the lion receives the predicate carnivorous by means of the copula. And the possibility of error arises simply from the disparity in the way things exist in these two worlds. That indicates that thought is not referred to the thing as a material transfer that coincides with its model: there is a gulf between the conditions or mode of thought and the conditions or mode of the thing. (*DK,* p. 86; *CW* 7, p. 91)

5. The Angel, because of the plentitude of intellectual light within him, knows at once what there is to know, infallibly and with perfect simplicity. As for us, on the contrary, we are forced to compose our knowledge from bits and pieces, with long detours, and skirting error at every moment, without our knowledge ever being completed. Thus the Angel and man each have a way of knowing proportionate to their nature. (*BPT,* p. 154)

6. The most lowly human knowledge, the knowledge quite common and patrimonial implied in language and nominal definitions, grasps quiddities, but in the most imperfect and least quidditative fashion, like a needle in a bundle of straw. (***DK*, p. 209; CW 7, p. 222**)

7. The aptitude for acquiring knowledge of things is not enough; he [man] must be able to express his knowledge verbally. From this necessity arose the system of conventional signs, called *language,* by which men communicate their thought: a wonderful instrument fashioned of articulate sound passing through the air, imparting through the most pliant and subtle of materials our innermost and most spiritual selves. (***IL*, p. 45**)

8. From the speculative point of view, knowledge of the world of existence, taken precisely as concrete and existent, belongs to the realm of experience and history, of factual observation, of certitudes of perception and memory, as well as of conjecture and of well-founded opinion. In short, it belongs to the realm of the work of the intellect as immersed in the activity of the senses. From the practical point of view, it belongs to the realm of art, of prudence and of knowledge by connaturality.

Science, knowledge in the strict sense of the word, considers only the intelligible necessities immersed in the reality of this world of existence. Each of our typical knowledges considers in it one, and only one, universe of intelligible necessities, while if there is a supreme knowledge, a knowledge-in-chief, a knowledge of first principles, it will consider all these different universes together, not in such a way as to replace the particular knowledge that concerns itself with each of them, but in order to know that knowledge itself, to defend and justify its principles, and thus to establish unity. What are, then, at least in their most general types, these diverse universes of intelligibility which our intellect brings into focus when it works while, disengaged from the activity of the senses? . . . The Aristotelian tradition recognizes three principal universes, which correspond to what Thomists call the three degrees or orders of abstraction. They are: the universe of the principles and laws of sensible and mobile nature, or the world of *Physica*; the universe of quantity as such, or the world of *Mathematica*; the universe of being and of the intelligible objects which of themselves do not require matter as a condition of their real existence, or the world of *Metaphysica*. (***DK*, pp. 136–37; CW 7, pp. 145–46**)

9. It is impossible to over-emphasise the importance of the problem of universals. It is for want of attention to it that so many philosophers and scientists of modern times cling to the naïve belief that science must be a copy of pure and simple, a tracing of the individual reality; serve up the stock arguments of ignorance against abstraction, the essential pre-condition of all human knowledge; and when treating of the principles of the sciences, especially of mathematics, spin elaborate theories, devoid of solid foundation, whose sole result is to render knowledge totally impossible. (*IP,* p. 121)

10. Knowledge itself can only be affirmed to be this or that if it is taken to be something distinct from the act by which it is thought. (***DK,* p. 86; CW 7, p. 91**)

11. There is a gulf between the conditions or mode of thought and the conditions or mode of the thing. (***DK,* p. 86; CW 7, p. 91**)

12. First principles are seen intellectually. Quite otherwise than by empirical observation. I do not see a subject-thing in which a predicate-thing would be contained as in a box. I see that the intelligible constitution of one of these objects of thought cannot subsist if the other is not posited as implying it or as implied by it. This is not a simple observation as of a fact known by the senses; it is the intellection of a necessity. Besides, first principles impose themselves absolutely, in virtue of the notion of being itself. Their authority is so independent and so rooted in the pure intelligible, they are so far from being the result of a simple inductive generalization, or of apriori forms destined to subsume the sensible, that sensible appearances are in some way disconcerted by them and lend themselves only with ill grace to illustrate the fashion in which they rule things. I affirm the principle of identity and I look at my face in a mirror; already it has aged; it is no longer the same. (*DK,* p. 215; *CW* 7, p. 229)

13. No leisure time will be enough for man to experience the joys of knowledge, of art and poetry, of devotion to great human causes, of communicating with others in the dreams and anxieties of the mind, of silently conversing with himself and silently conversing with God. (*RON,* pp. 157–58)

14. Generally speaking, as the "practical man" is the dupe *par excellence* of all the utopias, so the man who calls himself a "realist" with a certain tone of assurance and of gloomy satisfaction calls himself this because reality is usually in the right as against him. Only believing in force, but also only believing in what can be seen immediately, he puts his trust in any grandeur, provided that it has underneath it neither foundations nor roots. Many who believe themselves "realists" are in fact, empiricists and nominalists who think by dialectical commonplaces. (***IH*, p. 225; CW 11, p. 293**)

CHAPTER TWENTY

MAN

1. Man has more grandeur than the Milky Way; but how easy evil is for him, how inevitable (if one considers the species collectively) it is, in a being in which sense and instinct, and the animal unconscious, ask only to elude or to twist the judgment of the mind. As for suffering, it is already a frightful thing to see an animal suffer, but the suffering of beasts is of small account in comparison with the suffering that pierces a flesh united to spirit, or spirit itself. (*MP*, p. 453)

2. In answer to our question, then, "What is man?" we may give the Greek, Jewish, and Christian idea of man: man as an animal endowed with reason, whose supreme dignity is in the intellect; and man as a free individual in personal relation with God, whose supreme righteousness consists in voluntarily obeying the law of God; and man as a sinful and wounded creature called to divine life and to the freedom of grace, whose supreme perfection consists in love. (*EC,* **p.** 7)

3. Nothing is more necessary to man than to *discern*, and nothing does he find more difficult. Ordinarily we work with intellectual instruments that we have not taken the trouble to sharpen, we use steam-hammers to crush

a fly, and telegraph posts to mount a butterfly; and we bring the paws of bears to the task of following out and drawing apart the threads of a spider's web. (***TS*, pp. 173–74**)

4. Thomist philosophy lays stress on the basic psychosomatic unity of the human being (one single substance composed of matter and a spiritual "form" or entelechy), thus affording us a philosophical key for a sound interpretation of great modern discoveries in neurology and psychiatry. Also, it lays stress on the notion of human personality. Man is a person, who holds himself in hand by his intelligence and his will. He does not exist merely as a physical being. There is in him a richer and nobler existence: he has spiritual superexistence, through knowledge and love. He is thus, in some way, a whole, and not merely a part; he is a universe unto himself, a microcosm in which the great universe can be encompassed through knowledge. Through love he can give himself freely to beings who are to him, as it were, other selves; and for this relationship no equivalent can be found in the physical world. (***EM*, p. 52**)

5. Every man is a man in his very essence, but no man is man in essence, that is, exhausts in himself all the riches of the various perfections of which human-kind is capable. In this sense all the diversity of perfections and virtues distributed through the generations of men in space and time is but a varied participation in the common and inexhaustible potentialities of man. (***RT*, p. 20**)

6. But man does not know himself through his own essence. His substance is hidden from him, he perceives himself only as refracted by the world of his acts which itself refracts the world of things; if he does not fill himself with the universe he remains empty to himself. (***AP*, p. 89**)

7. It is a paradox of human nature that for all its weakness and wretchedness it responds more readily to a call to superhuman than to ordinary human effort. For the sake of some "mystical" cause of absolute value that is yet incarnate in contingent reality and experience the mass of men will suffer much evil and endure it with love. The history of social democracy in our time makes it plain to demonstration that without an ardent love of such a kind achievement is impossible. (*FMW,* p. 182; *CW* 11, pp. 94–95)

8. Understand that between men who belong to a same intellectual family there can be serious disagreements on particular points, without for all that the unity of their fundamental views and of their common universe of thought being broken. These particular disagreements are even a good sign—they show that their common effort aims only at truth, and consequently shuns all conformism and lives by freedom. (*GE,* p. 20)

9. How should we all be called upon thus to love one another in God if we were not all equal in our condition and specific dignity as rational creatures? (*RT,* p. 19)

10. Racism, on its irrational and biological basis, sets itself against Christianity by rejecting all universalism, and by breaking even the natural unity of the human family, so as to impose the hegemony of a so-called higher racial essence. (*SP,* p. 16)

11. Racism is existentially related to [a] demonic pseudo-theism, since, in its reaction against individualism and in its thirst for communion, it seeks that communion in human animality, which, once separated from the spirit, is no longer anything but a biological inferno. In the metaphysics of the social concrete, the god of the community of blood cannot but be the demon of the blood. Racist neo-paganism is thus inferior to the paganism of classical antiquity, which at least had the piety of the eternal Laws and of supreme divinity. It revives only the basest features of paganism. (*TC,* p. 21)

12. It is sometimes said . . . that racism is neo-paganism: this is an insult to the pagans, who never lapsed into such brutish materialism. The cult of so-called predestined animal blood (in reality the vehicle of original sin and all those divisions among men of which this sin is the principle), is the cult most fundamentally opposed to the Christian cult of the redeeming and vivifying blood of the Word Incarnate, by means of which all who do not reject divine grace are brought into the supernatural unity of the "race" of God and the Sons of God.

From a social and cultural point of view, racism degrades and humiliates to an unimaginable degree reason, thought, science and art, which are thenceforth subordinated to flesh and blood and divested of their natural "catholicity." It brings to men, among all the modes of barbarism which threaten them to-day, a barbarism in itself the most inhuman and the most desperate of all. For . . . it rivets them to biological categories and fatalities from which no exercise of their free will will enable them to escape. (**AN,** pp. 14–15)

13. It would be a great mistake to look upon racism as an irrationalist doctrine: racism is not a doctrine of irrationalism, it is the very surging up of irrationalism as an elemental force getting rid of all doctrine, truth and rational structure. Communistic atheism is utterly dogmatic; it is an error asserting itself as truth. Racist pseudo-theism or paratheism causes any dogma or intellectual conviction to dissolve and rot. It hates and disrupts any idea and sense of truth. Thus its mad religiosity is linked with utter nihilism. (**TC,** pp. 23–24)

14. The spirit of racism is attached to the hate of the God of Calvary and of the God of Sinai. (**TC, p. 43**)

15. Not only are laws of racial or religious discrimination fundamentally unjust; they also are for the state an avowal of impotence and political immaturity. Just laws, equal for all, should suffice to check evil, whencesoever it may arise, and to promote good, whencesoever it may come. (**RT,** pp. 191–92)

16. The third "moment" [in the dialectic of modern culture] consists in a progressive retirement of man before the forces of matter. In order to rule over nature as a demiurge man is in fact obliged more and more to subordinate his intelligence and his life to necessities not human but technical and to forces of the material order that he sets in motion and that invade our human life. God dies: Man now materialist thinks he can only be man or superman if God is not God. (**FMW, p. 95; CW 11, p. 51**)

17. *A resurrection of metaphysics and a new expansion of charity:* before all else this is the prerequisite for the return to human unity, to that unity which was perfect only in the Garden of Eden and in the heart of Christ in Gethsemane, but the longing for which will never cease to haunt us. (***TA,* p. 62**)

18. It is the privilege of the human intelligence to understand other languages than the one it itself uses. It is none the less true that if, instead of being men, we were patterns of Pure Ideas, our nature would be to devour each other in order to absorb into our own world of thought whatever other such worlds might hold of truth. (***UP,* p. 34**)

19. Thus it is, by that *admirable connection of things,* that according to Saint Thomas's expression, the human soul is a "sort of horizon, and as it were the confines of the corporeal and the incorporeal world." Thus it is that in man the virtues and activities of bodies and of spirits combine and rejoin, and that, assembling in himself, so to speak, the material universe of which he is the summit, and reflecting in his soul the eternal light, man is by nature designated to offer freely to God, in the name of all beings, sacrifice and thanksgiving. (***BPT,* p. 248**)

20. It is written that God made garments of skin for Adam and Eve in their exile. In like manner, through His prophets, then His incarnate Son and His Church, He has made for us garments woven of words and notions to clothe the nakedness of our mind till the day it sees Him. (***DK,* p. 243; CW 7, p. 258**)

21. Man's labour in its first and humblest stage is a co-operation with God the Creator, and Christianity's rehabilitation of labour in the moral order is bound up with revelation, in the dogmatic order, of creation *ex nihilo.* (***SP,* p. 139**)

22. Supported by revealed dogma, the Christian idea of man and of the human person has not been shaken by Darwinism. But the rationalist idea of the human person has received a mortal blow. (***IH,* p. 29; CW 11, p. 170**)

23. Man is both *homo faber* and *homo sapiens,* and he is *homo faber* before being in truth and actually *homo sapiens* and in order to become the latter. (***SP,* p. 139**)

24. Man is not born free, except in the basic potencies of his being: he becomes free, by warring upon himself and enduring many hardships. Through the work of the spirit and virtue, by exercising his freedom he wins his freedom, so that, at long last, a freedom better than he expected is *given* him. From the beginning to the end, it is truth which liberates him. (*PP,* **p. 18**)

25. I should like to put it in this way: there are two ways of looking at man's mastery of himself. Man can become master of his nature by imposing the law of reason—of reason aided by grace—on the universe of his own inner energies. That work, which in itself is a construction in love, requires that our branches be pruned to bear fruit: a process called *mortification.* Such a morality is an ascetic morality.

What rationalism claims to impose upon us today is an entirely different morality, anti-ascetic, exclusively technological. An appropriate technique should permit us to rationalize human life, *i.e.,* to satisfy our desires with the least possible inconvenience, without any interior reform of ourselves. What such a morality subjects to reason are material forces and agents exterior to man, instruments of human life; it is not man, nor human life as such. It does not free man, it weakens him, it disarms him, it renders him a slave to all the atoms of the universe, and especially to his own misery and egoism. What remains of man? A consumer crowned by science. This is the final gift, the twentieth century gift of the Cartesian reform.

Technique is good—mechanics is good. I disapprove of the spirit of archaism which would suppress the machine and technique. But if mechanics and technique are not mastered, subjected by force to the good of man, that is to say entirely and rigorously subordinated to religious ethics and made instruments of an ascetic morality, humanity is literally lost. (*DD,* pp. 182–83)

26. St. Thomas says clearly that a donkey does not have a natural desire to become a lion, because this would involve a desire to destroy what it is, that is to say, a donkey. But intelligence, love, personality, are not destroyed in passing from an inferior to a superior degree of being. Far from being destroyed, these transcendental perfections are then more than ever themselves. That is why there exists in us, as reasonable animals, a natural desire, which is not exactly of ourselves but of a transcendental element within us, to pass beyond the human condition: which does not take place, of course, without some accidents, and which too often makes us want to be unreasonable animals. But precisely because these desires to pass beyond the human state are not desires of our own specific nature, but are only the product of a transcendental element in us, they remain inefficacious and conditional. We have no right to have them granted; if they are granted to some extent it is only through grace. These aspirations tend to the super-human; they torment us without satisfying us. We cannot rightfully claim their fulfilment, because they are not specific (connatural) aspirations of human nature, but only metaphysical (transnatural) aspiration of a transcendental element within us. Truly speaking, it is only in God himself, in the uncreated Being, that these aspirations find their fulfilment. (*SP,* **p. 106**)

27. How then shall we characterize the cultural significance of Cartesian dualism? . . . Let us say that this dualism carries along with it both an anthropocentric angelism and materialism of civilization. On the balance-sheet must be written: division of man, rupture of the human life. They began by putting the human self above everything else, an angelic self—nay, a divine self. It is so perfectly one that no plurality of powers or of faculties is to be distinguished in it! Its substance is the very act of thinking.

This Cartesian man, naturally good in so far as he is reason, will later become the man of Rousseau, naturally good in so far as he is sentiment and instinct, and whom social life and reflection corrupt. He has no further need to perfect himself, to build himself up by his virtues, he has only to blossom forth, to display himself by virtue of sincerity. It is as though one were to tell a fertilized egg to be sincere and not to have the hypocrisy to construct its form by its own efforts, through a host of morphogenetic choices and differentiations which cruelly limit its availability.

Reflection has progressed prodigiously. Never has man more carefully scrutinized his innermost recesses. Never has he experienced so heart-rending a nostalgia for freedom. Yet how is he truly to know freedom? His personality escapes him, he is a prey to that duality. (***DD*, pp. 183–84**)

28. Now it happens that being made to act, we do not merely act, we claim to know in a disinterested fashion. A strange ambition, which probably comes from the fact that, having succeeded too well in our effort to impose

our contingency on matter, we have at our disposal unforeseen leisure, a sum of available energy which we use then in reflection; a deceptive ambition, though not altogether illusory, which gives us nobility but which makes of us, as it were, strangers wretchedly alone in a world where everything is made for brute force and for action. (***BPT*, p. 69**)

29. There are two things in which our nature has not the strength to believe: death, which we see, and perfect happiness, which we do not see. (***MP*, p. 76**)

30. Human duration knows two states which differ by nature: the state of peace and the state of war. The first proceeds as if salvation were assured, requires of each one that he contribute for his part to maintain, to continue salvation, already acquired (for example, in society, practice of métiers; in religion, practice of "religious duties," going to Mass), tend to an organization, a regular functioning, a harmony, in which immediate salvation is no more than a condition of that which flowers above it. On the contrary, the state of war proceeds as if salvation were absolutely jeopardized, always in question, and requires of each one that he abandon everything in order to find salvation. (***NB*, p. 23**)

31. As regards man himself, modern man (I mean that man who seemed himself to be modern, and who starts now entering into the past) modern man knew truths—without *the* Truth; he was capable of the relative and changing truths of science, incapable and afraid of any supra-temporal truth reached by Reason's metaphysical effort or of the divine Truth given by the Word of God. Modern man claimed human rights and dignity—without God, for his ideology grounded human rights and human dignity on a godlike, infinite autonomy of human will, which any rule or measurement received from Another would offend and destroy. Modern man trusted in peace and fraternity—without Christ, for he did not need a Redeemer, he was to save himself by himself alone, and his love for mankind did not need to be founded in divine charity. Modern man constantly progressed toward good and toward the possession of the earth—without having to face evil on earth, for he did not believe in the existence of evil; evil was only an imperfected stage in evolution, which a further stage was naturally and necessarily to transcend. Modern man enjoyed human life and worshipped human life as having an infinite value—without possessing a soul or knowing the gift of oneself, for the soul was an unscientific concept, inherited from the dreams of primitive men. And if a man does not give his soul to the one he loves, what can he give? He can give money, not himself.

As concerns civilization, modern man had in the bourgeois state a social and political life, a life in common without common good or common work, for the aim of common life consisted only of preserving everyone's freedom to enjoy private ownership, acquire wealth, and seek his own pleasure. Modern man believed in liberty—without the mastery of self or moral responsibility, for free will was incompatible with scientific determinism; and he believed in equality—without justice, for justice too was a metaphysical idea that lost any rational foundation and lacked any criterion in our modern biological and sociological outlook. Modern man placed his hope in machinism, in technique, and in mechanical or industrial civilization—without wisdom to dominate them and put them at the service of human good and freedom; for he expected freedom from the development of external techniques themselves, not from any ascetic effort toward the internal possession of self. And how can one who does not possess the standards of human life, which are metaphysical, apply them to our use of the machine? The law of the machine, which is the law of matter, will apply itself to him, and enslave him. (*RR*, pp. 186–87)

32. The answers which philosophers have given to the problem of human nature correspond strictly with the position they adopt towards the problem of abstraction. (*IP*, p. 131)

33. I am taking it for granted that you admit that there is a human nature, and that this human nature is the same in all men. I am taking it for granted that you also admit that man is a being gifted with intelligence, and who, as such, acts with an understanding of what he is doing, and therefore with a power to determine for himself the ends which he pursues. (*RM*, p. 60)

CHAPTER TWENTY-ONE

MARX AND MARXISM

1. The pursuit of the kingdom of God in history, the redemptive mission of the proletariat, the universalism of the revolutionary gospel, the nostalgia for communion (not the "communion of the saints" but communion in social life and in the work of history), the march toward the transformation or transfiguration of man finally achieving his true name, not to speak of the kind of political simulacrum of the Church offered to us by the Party and the conscience of the Party—all these features derive from ideas of Christian origin, distorted and recast. (***MP*, p. 241**)

2. We witness another spectacle, a spectacle quite the contrary of a continuation, aggravation and exasperation of anthropocentric humanism in the direction which it followed from its origin, in the direction of rationalistic hopes, now constituted no longer solely as philosophical religion, but as a lived religion. This other development arises from taking all the consequences of the principle that *man alone, and through himself alone, works out his salvation.*

   The purest case of this tendency is that of Marxism. No matter how strong some of the pessimistic aspects of Marxism may be, it remains attached to this postulate. Marx turned over Hegelianism; he remained rationalistic nevertheless, so much so that for him the movement proper to matter is a *dialectical* movement. In Marxist materialism, it is not irrational instinct or biological mysticism, but reason which decapitates reason. (*SP,* pp. 5–6)

3. In spite of the belligerent pessimism imprinted on it by Marxism, communism has as metaphysical root an absolute optimistic philosophy of man, that great optimistic mysticism which began with rationalism and was continued by the Encyclopedists, then by Jean-Jacques Rousseau, then by utopian socialism, on the one hand, and Hegelian philosophy, on the other. Practically, it denies that man is a creature of God, because it is unwilling to recognize in man that which comes from nothingness. Because of this optimistic basis, it does not profess to be totalitarian; the totalitarian principle is immanent in it as a vice and fatality, which is not avowed. (*SP,* pp. 9–10)

4. What distinguishes Marxism is not simply that it teaches that economics is preponderant—other schools have committed and are now committing this same error—but that it makes all the forms of life, with all their values and all their efficacy, dependent on—they are not denied, but subordinated to—this human material absolute in dialectic movement. To use Aristotle's language again, let us say that material causality thus becomes purely and simply the primary causality. (*IH,* p. 50; CW 11, p. 184)

5. Marx is fundamentally preoccupied with man and with the human: one might say that the things of the person—of the human person who is individual, who insofar even as individual constitutes a universe—escape his view. Hence the congenital infirmity of his humanism. Hence his strangely monist and immanentist conception of work itself as a kind of common and absolute substance in which the essence of man actualizes itself, and which has reference of itself neither to specifying objects or goods, nor to the creative activity of the person as such with its own rightful exigencies. (*IH,* **p. 186; CW 11, p. 269**)

6. The obligation to be in connivance with history is just as strong, as total, as fundamental for Marx as for Hegel. It is difficult for the observer who is determined to maintain the freedom of the critical mind not to conclude from this that in the last analysis Marx is vanquished by the false God of

Hegel, of whom it must be asked that his will be done on earth not *as* it is done *in heaven* but *as* the *earth* exhibits it, and asked while bowing the knee to history. (*MP,* p. 233)

7. The Marxist philosophy of history is but Hegel's very philosophy of history which has grown atheistic (instead of pantheistic and anthropo-theistic) and which makes history advance toward the divinization of man thanks to the dialectical movement of matter. (*PH,* p. 24)

8. Marxism is a humanism—an atheistic humanism in which the anthropocentric humanism of the rationalist centuries reaches its full realization.

But this humanism is a humanism of the generic-human-being, a humanism of human nature expanded and consummated in human society—it knows nothing of the human person as such. Because it does not want to recognize anything which carries with it a reflection of the divine transcendence, it is purely and simply ignorant of what distinctively constitutes the person (the fact of being a whole, a universe in itself). While it sees correctly that man is only man in society, it does not understand that in the last analysis this is only in order to transcend society (the society of creatures). In short, it conceives of the individual only as a *social being*; the individual is in no sense a whole and in no way emerges above the social whole. The social whole is not composed of wholes. Not only is the individual a part of society, but he has no reality and no true human dignity except insofar as he is a part of society. All of this is pure Hegel, wrenched out of the Hegelian metaphysical perspective. (*MP,* pp. 238–39)

9. Marx's humanism is pre-eminently a humanism of that *Manichaean* type.... It asks that we thrust into darkness, to the extent to which it has been religious, a whole part of the human heritage.

On the contrary, Christian humanism, integral humanism, is capable of assuming all, because it knows that God has no opposite and that everything is irresistibly carried along by the movement of the divine government. It does not reject into darkness all that which, in the human heritage, relates to heresies and to schisms, to the aberrations of the heart and of reason; *oportet haereses esse.* It knows that the historical forces invaded by error have served God despite themselves, and that despite themselves there has passed through them all along modern history, at the same time as the surge of the energies of illusion, the surge of Christian energies in temporal existence. (*IH,* **pp. 91–92; CW 11, p. 210**)

10. Marx ... expected from the communist Jerusalem, where deified man reveals himself to himself, such a fulness of humanity that the senses and work will have come to belong to sorts of glorified bodies in a materialist eschatology, exulting at one and the same time in self-communion, and in the autonomy and the pure selflessness of their finally reconquered, or rather self-created generic essence. (*MP,* **p. 253**)

CHAPTER TWENTY-TWO

METAPHYSICS AND METAPHYSICIANS

1. Metaphysics, the supreme human science, possesses a characteristic in common with the Gospels. What is most precious and most Divine is hidden under what seems most commonplace. So is it with the Catholic religion in general. There is nothing esoteric about it. It conceals the most precious mysteries under the simplest teaching which it proclaims from the housetops. This, in due proportion, is also true of metaphysics. For the little word "is," the commonest of all words, used every moment everywhere, offers us though concealed and well concealed, the mystery of being as such. It is from the most ordinary object of common knowledge that the metaphysician educes it, draws it out of its ironical commonplace to look it full in the face. There is, however, a difficulty in this connexion of which we should be warned, namely that in an old civilisation it is not easy to recover the perceptions prior to language. The triteness of language blunts the mind's power to perceive its significance. With good reason then do we seek to recover a fresher and purer perception, liberated from the routine and mechanism of words. This, in my opinion, is one of the motives of certain contemporary essays in metaphysics. Their authors are seeking this fresh and pure intuition, they are seeking it in defiance of language, therefore as far as possible from *being,* precisely because there is no *word* commoner or in more current use.

It must, however, be sought where it is hidden, and that is precisely in the most ordinary being, expressed by the most commonplace and the tritest of all words. (***PM*, p. 89**)

2. Metaphysics, like any science of the real, is nothing if it is not based upon observation and experience. (***BPT*, p. 206**)

3. There is a sort of grace in the natural order presiding over the birth of a metaphysician just as there is over the birth of a poet. The latter thrusts his heart into things like a dart or rocket and, by divination, sees, within the very sensible itself and inseparable from it, the flash of a spiritual light in which a glimpse of God is revealed to him. The former turns away from the sensible, and through knowledge sees within the intelligible, detached from perishable things, this very spiritual light itself, captured in some conception. The metaphysician breathes an atmosphere of abstraction which is death for the artist. Imagination, the discontinuous, the unverifiable, in which the metaphysician perishes, is life itself to the artist. While both absorb rays that come down from creative Night, the artist finds nourishment in a bound intelligibility which is as multiform as God's reflections upon earth, the metaphysician finds it in a naked intelligibility that is as determined as the proper being of things. They are playing seesaw, each in turn rising up to the sky. Spectators make fun of their game; they sit upon solid ground. (***DK*, p. 2; CW 7, p. 2**)

4. Metaphysics demands a certain purification of the intellect; it also takes for granted a certain purification of the will and assumes that one has the courage to cling to things that have no use, to *useless* Truth.

However, nothing is more necessary to man than this uselessness. What we need is not truths that serve us but a truth we may serve. For that truth is the food of the spirit. And, by the better part of ourselves, we are spirit. Useless metaphysics puts order—not any sort of police order, but the order that has sprung from eternity—in the speculative and practical intellect. It gives back to man his balance and his motion, which, as is well known, means to gravitate, head first, to the midst of the stars, while he hangs from the earth by his two legs. Throughout the whole extent of being, metaphysics reveals to him authentic values and their hierarchy. It provides a center for his ethics. It binds together in justice the whole universe of his knowledge by guaranteeing the natural limits, harmony and subordination of the different sciences. And that is more important to the human being than the most luxuriant proliferation of the mathematics of phenomena. Indeed, what does it profit to gain the whole world and lose the integrity of reason? Besides, we are so weak that the limpid peace dispensed by a healthy metaphysics may quite well be less favorable to experimental discovery than the musings or the eagerness of a mind buried deep in the sensible. The sciences of nature may very well enjoy fishing in troubled waters; but perhaps, too, we have a right to deem ourselves amply surfeited by the benefits of that dissipation.

Metaphysics sets us down in the midst of the eternal and the absolute; it causes us to pass from the show of things to the knowledge of reason (in itself stronger and more certain than mathematical certitudes, even though less adapted to our grasp), to the knowledge of the invisible world of divine perfections spelled out from their created reflections.

Metaphysics is not a means; it is an end, a fruit, a good at once self-justifying and delightful, a knowledge for the free man, the finest and naturally most regal knowledge, the door to the leisure of the great speculative activity in which intellect alone can breathe, set, as it is, on the very peak of causes. (***DK*, pp. 4–5; CW 7, pp. 4–5**)

5. He who has not meditated on the angels will never be a perfect metaphysician. (***DK*, p. 221; CW 7, p. 235**)

6. The theologian considers personality in the world of the deity, the metaphysician in the world of being insofar as it is being, the psychologist in the world of inner phenomena, the moralist in the world of action. Most often these considerations remain disjointed, which engenders in the mind a species of pluralism of the worst kind.

It then happens, when levels are muddled by chance, that the *person* of the metaphysician finds himself astray in the dictionary of the psychologist. The latter, satisfying himself and with reason that the metaphysical person is neither this phenomena nor that one, takes it for an "illusion of common-sense." One barleycorn would be more to his liking. (*AP,* pp. 51–52)

7. True, timeless metaphysics no longer suits the modern intellect. More exactly, the latter no longer squares with the former. Three centuries of empirio-mathematicism have so warped the intellect that it is no longer interested in anything but the invention of apparatus to capture phenomena—conceptual nets that give the mind a certain practical dominion over nature, coupled with a deceptive understanding of it; deceptive, indeed, because its thought is resolved, not in being, but in the sensible itself. By advancing in this fashion, not by linking new truths to already acquired truths, but by substituting new apparatus for outmoded apparatus; by handling things without understanding them; by gaining ground against the real bit by bit, patiently, through victories that are always piecemeal and provisory—by acquiring a secret taste for the matter with which it conspires—thus has the modern intellect developed within this lower order of scientific demiurgy a kind of manifold and marvelously specialized touch as well as wonderful instincts for the chase. But, at the same time, it has wretchedly weakened and disarmed itself in the face of the proper objects of the intellect, which it has abjectly surrendered. It has become quite incapable of appreciating the world of rational evidence except as a system of well-oiled gears. Henceforth, it has to take its stand either against all metaphysics (old-fashioned positivism) or in favor of a pseudo-metaphysics (new-styled positivism). (*DK,* p. 3; CW 7, pp. 2–3)

8. Metaphysics is of no use in furthering output of experimental science. Discoveries and inventions in the land of phenomena? It can boast of none; its heuristic value, as they say, is absolutely nil in that area. From this point of view, there is nothing to be expected of it. There is no tilling of the soil in heaven. (*DK,* pp. 3–4; CW 7, pp. 3–4)

9. Nothing is more valuable in metaphysics than the notion of immanent activity, the mark of mind. But it is in a very different meaning that the word *immanence* is understood in current speech and that the sages of anthropocentric humanism have affirmed the principle of immanence. This principle signifies for them that all things are contained in the heart of man and in his history.... The dependence of man in relation to material conditions which he must learn to control is of course admitted. But it is said there is no dependence that he needs to acknowledge to an order of things superior to his will or to a God who has created him. In our view it is absurd to admit dependence in one case and to deny it in the other. How could man be dependent on *things* of an inferior order if he were not in his essence a dependent being, and if there were not therefore something above him on which he must depend? (*FMW*, p. 91; CW 11, p. 49)

10. The gods envy us metaphysical wisdom (the doctrinal inheritance which alone allows us to attain that wisdom without too grievously mingling error with it, is itself constantly misunderstood); man never holds it except on a precarious claim. And how could it be otherwise? What more beautiful paradox than a science of things divine achieved by human means, an enjoyment of liberty, proper to spirits, gained by a nature which is "a slave in so many ways"? Metaphysical wisdom is at the purest degree of abstraction because it is farthest removed from the senses; it opens out onto the immaterial, onto a world of realities which exist or can exist separately from matter. But our means of making the ascent must also mark our limits. By a kind of natural necessity, abstraction, the lot of all human science, brings with it, along with a multiplicity of partial and complementary insights, the rigid law of logical movement, the slow elaboration of concepts, the complexity and vast mechanism, weightier than air, of the winged apparatus of discourse. Metaphysics would like to contemplate in the purest way, to reach beyond reasoning and to enter the realm of pure intellection; it aspires to the unity of simple vision. It comes close to it, as to an asymptote. It does not reach it. (*DK*, p. 5; CW 7, p. 5)

11. Metaphysical wisdom is in its essence a purely natural wisdom. It is in terms of natural and rational evidences that this wisdom is entirely developed. And though, from the point of view of exercise, one should, as Plato said, philosophize with all one's soul, from the point of view of specification, it is the intellect alone which is here engaged. Metaphysical wisdom is illumined by the intelligibility of being disengaged and in a pure state (I mean without intrinsic reference to any construction of the imagination or to any experience of sense), at the highest degree of abstractive intuition.

Its formal object is *being* according to its proper mystery—*being as being,* as Aristotle said.

If positivism, old and new, and kantism do not understand that metaphysics is authentically a science, a knowledge of achieved and completed type, it means that they do no[t] understand that the intellect *sees.* For them, sense alone is intuitive, the intellect having only a function of connexion and of unification. Let them be silent! for we cannot say 'I,' we cannot utter a noun of the language, without testifying that there are objects in things, that is, centres of visibility, which our senses do not reach but which our intellect does. Of course, there is no *angelistic,* intellectual intuition, in the sense of Plato and Descartes—I mean an intuition which does not need the mediation of the senses; of course there is nothing in the intellect which does not originally derive from sensible experience. But it is precisely the activity of the intellect which disengages from this experience and brings to the fire of immaterial visibility in act, the objects which sense cannot decipher in things, and which the intellect sees. This is the mystery of abstractive intuition. And in these objects which it sees, the intellect knows, without seeing them directly, the transcendent objects which do not exist in the world of sensible experience. This is the mystery of analogical intellection. The problem of metaphysics reduces itself finally to the problem of abstractive intuition and to the question whether, at the summit of abstraction, being itself, in so far as it is being—permeating the world of sensible experience, but yet exceeding this world on all sides—is or is not the object of such an intuition. It is this intuition which makes the metaphysician. Everybody does not have it. And if we ask why positivism, old and new, and kantism ignore this intuition, we shall be bound finally to admit that it is because there are philosophers who see, and philosophers who do not see. (***SP*, pp. 39–40**)

12. Metaphysics . . . would not find itself faced with any major difficulty if the created existent always exercised its liberty in the line of good. But we know well enough that this is not the case. (***EE*, p. 88**)

13. Remember, too, that metaphysics is supremely difficult, by reason of its object which, being purely immaterial, is, to our reason, "as light to the eye of an owl." It follows that it must be the part of a very small number, and that there are moments when the deposit of wisdom could be transmitted only by the very slenderest spiritual thread. It follows also that philosophy is something other than the immense mass of the notions of philosophers, and that if all mathematicians co-operate in the growth of mathematics, and all scientists in the growth of science, all philosophers do not co-operate— at any rate directly—in the growth of philosophy. When they go wrong on principles, the direct effect of their work is towards the deterioration of philosophy; and thus, while the law of progress dominates the eternal metaphysics of the human intellect, the law of pure change, of alteration and corruption, the tyranny of the other as such, the appetite for change proper to matter, constantly intervenes to frustrate philosophical effort outside the spiritual organism of philosophy scientifically formed. (*TS,* **p. 160**)

14. Printing has freed the plastic arts from the pedagogical function that was incumbent upon them in the days of the cathedrals. Sciences of phenomena have freed metaphysics from the trouble of explaining things of sensible nature, and from so many illusions which had followed upon it for Greek optimism. We must congratulate ourselves on this purification of metaphysics. It is less pleasant to state, however, that in the practical order, the government of earthly things, to the extent that it demands a heavier material work of intellect, is more and more separated from the life it leads beyond time. The earth is no longer in need of a moving angel; man pushes it by the strength of his arm. Spirit ascends to heaven.

Yet, man is flesh and spirit, not held together by a thread, but substantially united. The fact that human affairs cease to be cut to the measure of man (since some of those affairs take their rhythm from the energies of matter, while others look for their standards to the exigencies of a disincarnate spirituality) constitutes for man a frightful metaphysical disjunction. It is quite believable that the shape of this world will pass away on the day that this tension becomes so great that our heart will break. (***DK,*** **p. 15; CW 7, p. 16**)

15. Language is inevitably loaded with intelligence and with ontology. (***SP,*** **p. 25**)

16. Like mathematics, metaphysics emerges above time. It causes a universe of intelligibility other than that of the experimental sciences (and of the Philosophy of Nature) to stand out in things and thereby grasps a world of eternal truths, valid not for a particular moment of contingent realization, but for all possible existence. Unlike the Philosophy of Nature, it has no need to find its terminus in the verifications of the sense in order to establish these truths which are superior to time. But, unlike mathematics, it always looks, in establishing these truths, to subjects which exist or can exist. In short, it does not abstract from the order to existence. The mathematical praeter-real does not imply matter in its notion or definition, but, enclosed in a genus, it can (when it can exist) exist only in matter. The metaphysical trans-sensible, since it is transcendental and polyvalent (analogous), is not only free from matter in its notion and definition but can also exist without it. That is why the order to existence is embowelled in the objects of metaphysics. To admit beings of reason as object would be unworthy of the science of being as being. If moreover . . . metaphysics descends to the actual existence of things in time, and rises to the actual existence of things outside time, it is not only because actual existence is the sign par excellence of the intrinsic possibility of existence, but also and especially because existence itself is . . . the seal of all perfection, and cannot remain outside the field of the highest knowledge of being. (**DK, p. 218; CW 7, pp. 231–32**)

17. Metaphysics uses the concept of existence in order to know a reality which is not an essence, but is the very act of exisiting. (**EE, p. 34**)

18. The object of metaphysics is not in the least the world of the universal known in the most general and therefore least determined fashion. In other words, it is not the generic classes of the things of nature. It is an entirely other world, the world of the superuniversal, the world of transcendental objects which, disengaged as such, do not demand, as genera do, to be completed by progressive differentiations coming as from outside, but offer a field of intelligibility which has in itself its own ultimate determinations. And those objects can be realized outside the mind in individual subjects which do not fall under the senses and so are outside the whole order of the genera and differentiations of the world of experience. That is why metaphysics is a perfect knowledge, a true science. (**DK, p. 217; CW 7, p. 231**)

19. St. Thomas goes so far as to say that the things pertaining to moral science are known especially through experience. It is nonetheless true that metaphysics supplies the first foundation. (**FMW, p. 19; CW 11, p. 13**)

CHAPTER TWENTY-THREE

MORAL PHILOSOPHY

1. The art of morality is not the art of living morally *with a view to* attaining happiness; it is the art of *being happy* because one lives morally. (*MP,* p. 14)

2. Moral philosophy proposes to regulate action *from afar*, and therefore, to act *from afar* upon the will through knowledge itself. It is in view of this end that it organizes its materials into a practical context and discovers the ontological articulations which are concerned with action by adapting to its practical end a conceptual equipment, to wit, those modes of defining and judging which are typically speculative. Unlike prudence, which consists formally in *directing* and not in *knowing*, the truth of judgments in moral philosophy consists formally in knowing, I mean *knowing* as the foundation of *directing.* (***DK*, p. 456; CW 7, p. 481**)

3. And now, as a corollary to my reflections on the progress of moral conscience, I would emphasize that moral philosophy presupposes moral experience, the historical experience of mankind. Moral philosophy, as indeed all philosophical knowledge, comes about through concepts and judgments. It supposes a developed rational knowledge. It entails a scientific justification of moral values by a demonstrative determination of what is consonant with reason, and of the proper ends of the human essence and of human society. But it is a kind of after-knowledge. The moral philosopher submits to critical examination, elucidates, sorts out, justifies, re-interprets, formulates in a more systematic or more pungent manner the natural morality of mankind, I mean the moral standards and regulations which are spontaneously known to human reason in such or such an age of culture. As a result, it is rather infrequent that a moral philosopher is in advance with respect to his time.

In other words, moral philosophy is a reflective knowledge, and in this we have a token of its difference from metaphysical knowledge. Metaphysics is not a reflective knowledge—it is not a reflection on common sense. It states its own truths, and nobody can judge a metaphysician, except in the name of a higher wisdom. But any kind of virtuous man, even one completely ignorant in philosophy, can judge a moral philosopher, if the moral philosopher teaches something wrong. I see in this a sign that moral philosophy is a reflective knowledge. And therefore, while it can happen, of course, that a moral philosopher may have broader horizons than the common people of his time, and may see things that they do not see, nevertheless, in general, the work of theoretical reflection cannot replace in moral matters the slow advances of consciousness, conscience, and experience in mankind. And this means not only an advance in rational knowledge, but primarily an advance in our lived awareness of our basic inclinations—an advance which may be conditioned by social changes. Thus for many centuries moral philosophers and common consciousness stressed the obligations of man prescribed by natural law. But there are also rights of man, which were, of course, implicitly recognized, especially by Christian thinkers. (***PH,* pp. 109–10**)

4. There is good reason to distinguish between a *philosophical* knowledge of moral values and a *natural, pre-philosophical* knowledge of these values. This distinction must be made because moral philosophy presupposes moral experience. There is a moral knowledge, of the average man and of common experience, which precedes philosophical knowledge. People didn't wait for philosophy before acquiring a morality.

If it is a question of the *philosophical* knowledge of moral values, it occurs, like all philosophical knowledge, by means of concepts and judgments.

It supposes a highly developed rational knowledge, and involves a scientific justification of values by a clearly demonstrable determination of what is consonant with reason and with the ends peculiar to the human essence and to human society. We are in the presence of the explaining, justifying, demonstrating function of truth, which belongs to moral philosophy. Moral philosophy is a reflective knowledge, no doubt not in the same sense as logic, but after all a knowledge of the second look. (*BP,* pp. 51–52)

5. The notion of right and the notion of moral obligation are correlative. They are both founded on the freedom proper to spiritual agents. If man is morally bound to the things which are necessary to the fulfillment of his destiny, obviously, then, he has the right to fulfill his destiny; and if he has the right to fulfill his destiny he has the right to the things necessary for this purpose. The notion of right is even more profound than that of moral obligation, for God has sovereign right over creatures and He has no moral obligation toward them (although He owes it to Himself to give them that which is required by their nature). (*RM,* p. 65)

6. Moralists are unhappy people. When they insist on the immutability of moral principles, they are reproached for imposing unlivable requirements on us. When they explain the way in which those immutable principles are to be put into force, taking into account the diversity of concrete situations, they are reproached for making morality relative. In both cases, however, they are only upholding the claims of reason to direct life.

The worst temptation for mankind, in the epochs of dark night and universal perturbation, is to give up Moral Reason. Reason must never abdicate. The task of ethics is humble but it also magnanimous in carrying the mutable application of immutable moral principles even in the midst of the agonies of an unhappy world, as far as there is in it a gleam of humanity. (*MS,* pp. 74–75)

7. Moral obligation is resolved in the ontological. It is not the pure and a priori "you should" of Kantian ethics, the empty form of duty imposing itself by itself and without reason, like a commandment which has descended from the Sinai of pure practical reason upon the empirical and phenomenal self. That was an illusory magnification of moral obligation, transforming the fear of the Lord into terms of pure philosophy.

Nor is moral obligation a result of external constraint exercised by society and social taboos, which supposedly penetrates the individual psyche and creates hereditary conditioned reflexes, hereditary habits and mental pressures. A mere psychological transference of social fear is not an explanation of moral obligation, but simply its destruction.

Moral obligation essentially relates to the structure of human nature and to the practical function of reason, to the fact that human beings are endowed with reason and that reason has the idea of good and evil and commands us to do what is good and to avoid what is evil, that is to act in conformity with reason itself. (***BP*, pp. 178–79**)

8. But in many cases, which, in truth, form the stuff of our moral life, man finds himself confronted by a diversity of conflicting duties and multiple rules which crisscross in a complex of circumstance where the problem 'What ought I really do?' is posed. This is the time when he must have recourse to the *regulae arbitrariae* of prudence; to those rules which not only take account of all the objective peculiarities of given conditions, but which become decisive only by reason of the subject's deepest attractions (which, by supposition, are duly oriented) and the inclinations of his virtues. (***EE*, p. 53**)

9. The most prudent decision can sometimes appear irrational and inexplicable—its reasons being hidden in the substance of the subject. And when we subsequently recall the decision, being removed from the actual (though not conceptually perceptible) glow in which it was bathed, we may doubt retrospectively of its prudence and even of its freedom. (***EE*, p. 54**)

10. In actual fact, the principles of morality are neither theorems nor idols, but the supreme rules of a concrete activity which aims at a work to be done in such-and-such circumstances, with the help of more proximate rules and with the help, finally, of the rules *never traced in advance* of the virtue of prudence, which apply the ethical precepts to particular cases in the climate of a concretely upright will. They do not seek to devour human life, but to build it up. (***IH*, p. 218; CW 11, p. 289**)

11. There is a mistake to be avoided on the intellectualism of St. Thomas. He proclaims unceasingly the superiority of the intellect over the will, considered according to the absolute hierarchy of the faculties: and he maintains the pure sovereignty of the intellect in the order of speculative knowledge. But, on the other hand, he maintains, that it is by the will that man is good or bad, using the words "good" and "bad" absolutely and without qualification: he makes judgment depend, in the order of practical and prudential activity, on the appetitive faculties—the faculties, that is, of the will—and upon their rectification: and above all, he most definitely affirms the pre-eminence, considered according to the conditions of this world, of love in human life. He teaches that in heaven, thanks to the light of glory, which will render it capable of direct knowledge of God, the intellect will enjoy its primacy: for it is by the intellect that we shall hold our beatitude, possessing God by the vision of His essence; but equally clearly he teaches that here below, while it is better to know inferior things than to love them, and although man never loves save what he knows in some manner, yet it is better to love God than to know Him: because love draws us to the thing that we love as it is in itself, according to *its* mode of existing, whereas knowledge renders the thing that we know present in us according to the mode and the capacity of our mind. (*TS,* **pp. 37–38**)

12. The basic systematic notions of moral good, value, end, norm, are like the intellectual fibers of the structure of moral thought. It is important to recognize the fact that the examination and the justification of these notions belongs to metaphysics, even though the notions themselves are not metaphysical, but essentially moral notions. They are *philosophical* moral notions, whose final elucidation depends on metaphysics; their meaning will inevitably escape us if we refuse to make our intellect work at the level of philosophical visualization and remain fixed at the level of empirical knowledge, that is to say, of sensory knowledge. We run into this difficulty all the time because the contemporary cast of mind, accustomed to empirical knowledge and dazzled by it, risks taking it for knowledge pure and simple. So a special effort must be made to pass from one level of knowledge to another and to understand that the notions we are speaking of can only have meaning if we think of them not from the perspective of the sciences of phenomena and the experience of the senses, but of philosophical intellection. (*BP,* **p. 27**)

13. The same moral case never appears twice in the world. To speak absolutely strictly, precedent does not exist. Each time, I find myself in a situation requiring me to do a new thing, to bring into existence an act that is unique in the world, an act which must be in conformity with the moral law in a manner and under conditions belonging strictly to me alone and which have never arisen before. Useless to thumb through the dictionary of cases of conscience! Moral treatises will of course tell me the universal rule or rules I am bound to apply; they will not tell me how I, the unique I, am to apply them in the unique context in which I am involved. No knowledge of moral essences, however perfect, meticulous, or detailed it may be and however particularised those essences may be (though they will always remain general); no casuistry, no chain of pure deduction, no science, can exempt me from my judgment of conscience, and, if I have some virtue, from the exercise of the virtue of prudence, in which exercise it is the rectitude of my willing that has to effect the accuracy of my vision. In the practical syllogism, the major, which enunciates the universal rule, speaks only to the intellect; but the minor and the conclusion are on a different plane; they are put forward by the whole subject, whose intellect is swept along towards the existential ends by which (in virtue of his very liberty) his appetitive powers are in fact subjugated. (*EE*, pp. 51–52)

14. Practical philosophy does not suffice to regulate action. It knows in a theoretical, speculative, explanatory way things which need not only to be explained but also to be done. It gathers into a scientific system all the knowledge necessary to regulate action from afar, that is, all the rules for action which the intellect can discern by adapting to practical use an equipment and a mode of discerning the true which is typically speculative. The most expert and competent philosopher in ethical matters can be disconcerted by the smallest act to be done, and he can himself lead an immoral life. (*DK*, p. 313; CW 7, p. 332)

15. Right practical knowledge, as the immediate regulator of action, is the virtue of prudence. It judges and commands what is to be done here and now. As we know, this virtue is both intellectual and moral; it is connected with the moral virtues and necessarily presupposes the rectitude of the will. In this field the intellect does not work alone, but depends upon the will and its dispositions. It is in relation to the direction of the *agere* and to the rectitude of the will that its judgment is true or false. (***DK*, p. 314; CW 7, p. 333**)

16. For by necessity of nature man cannot exercise his freedom, man cannot act except in the desire for happiness. But what man's happiness is, what human happiness consists of, that is not inscribed in the necessary functioning of his nature, this is above this necessary functioning. Because man is a free agent. Thus he has to decide for himself what kind of supreme good his happiness consists of in actual fact, he must choose his own happiness or supreme good, and the fate of his moral life depends on the fact of his choice being made or not according to the truth of the matter. (***RA*, p. 30**)

17. The office of the moral law is that of a pedagogue, to protect and to educate us in the use of freedom. At the end of this period of instruction we are enfranchised from every servitude, even from the servitude of law, since Love has made us one in spirit with the Wisdom that is the source of Law. The perfect soul serves neither law nor fear. (***FMW*, p. 39; CW 11, p. 23**)

18. Moral life is possible for the human being only if the value of his acts is an ethical absolute which stands forth like a rock from the river of facts, events, phenomena, time and history. And because every knowledge whose object is something absolute and superior to time stands forth above time and, so far as it is true, is immutably true, this ethical absolute must be the object of immutable truths bearing on the value of our acts, unless the moral life of the human being is no more than a mirage or a mystification. That is why every moral theory, whether it be relativist or materialist, which makes fun of the "eternal truths" (the expression is not appropriate, let us rather say supra-temporal truths), betrays the moral life it undertakes to explain. That man makes progress only with the greatest difficulty in the knowledge of these truths which are immutable by nature, that he can occasionally more or less lose consciousness of them, that at the various moments of evolution what he knows of them may be mixed with all kinds of elements which depend on infinitely variable social conditions and historical situations, that is quite another story. But it is a sign of childishness to think that a truth ceases to be true because the myopic see it badly or the blind do not see it at all. (***MP*, p. 288**)

19. It is the very transcendence of God which makes it impossible that the love for God upon which all right moral life depends should emanate from the intellectual creature (even in the natural order) by virtue solely of his creation, or of the dynamism of his nature at its first instant. (***SA*, p. 34**)

20. For Greek philosophy, duty was only what was fitting, the *officium*. In our civilization, the sacred sense of duty developed as linked to religion, to the Decalogue. Thus we see that morality, in the existential conditions of humanity, is actually strengthened, either by social constraint which hardens it, or by religious faith in the transcendent God, which purifies it. (***BP*, p. 171**)

21. Christian morality is a morality of beatitude, but first and foremost it is a morality of the divine Good supremely loved. (***MP*, p. 79**)

22. If men often use morality badly, it is also that they neglect to take into consideration another moral truth, which is a primary one: morality demands that we apply its rules to our own conduct, it does not demand that we avenge them on the person of another when that other has been unfaithful to them: that is the business of the eternal Judge, and, in a very imperfect measure, of human judges and human educators: it is not the business of each one of us in relation to each other.

Man, thou art not thy brother's judge; thou art a sinner as he is, and he is thy brother: there, in a general way, be it a question of private ethics or of political ethics, is the fundamental datum of our behavior toward others. *Omnes quidem peccaverunt, et egent gloria Dei.* We must judge the moral value of the acts committed by another; but not the soul of another. We must not be silent, we must denounce vigorously the injustice: but we are not charged with dispensing the divine retributions. Christ, who hated sin, was the friend of sinners. When another has become guilty of some fault, we may have to change our conduct with regard to him, because we no longer have confidence in him, because he puts in jeopardy certain goods over which we have to watch. But *unless we have, by some title or other, a jurisdiction over him*, we are not required to exhibit in our behavior toward him our reprobation of his fault. As though one were to render oneself an accomplice of the fault that a man has committed, not to treat this man as guilty and not to manifest thus by a social sign the purity of our conscience! This naïve form of Pharisaism belongs to the "closed morality" of the social group; so much the more developed as the society in question is the more primitive, it justifies itself morally only by reflex considerations of social pedagogy, and in relation to a certain good, itself vital, which is the formation of common opinion. But it in no way constitutes an absolute and unconditional exigency of morality—the Gospel has instructed us on this once and for all: "Let him that is without sin cast the first stone." (*IH,* pp. 222–23; CW 11, p. 292)

23. Love of God and fraternal love are one indivisible charity. And it is on this charity that Christianity makes the whole moral life of the human being depend. The whole law is contained in the precept to love God with our whole soul, and in the precept to love all men as our brothers, and these two form one single precept. (*MP,* p. 83)

24. A trifle then, a certain act of giving, of giving away, of forgiving, made almost without thinking, a little water offered to a poor man, a little suffering accepted through pity, a refusal to demand one's due, the simple fact of being present at the material or moral distress of another, or of listening to his despair, a word said for justice or for truth, any task whatever undertaken and pursued through fidelity to some singular call and with a little fraternal love; or else, on the contrary, an exceptionally great act, the long acceptance of a suffering which revolts nature, or of an intolerable burden carried in order to relieve the needs of an ungrateful person, a sacrifice in which the soul truly immolates what it most treasures; there is no common measure for the different kinds of "bewilderment" in question. It is sufficient that there passes into them the force of a love which has no bounds and which is like the breath of Uncreated Love; a human life has borne fruit. (*MP,* p. 447)

25. The fact is, I believe, that in the background of all our moral difficulties there is a fundamental problem which is ineluctably posed for each of us, and which in practice is never fully resolved, except in those who have entered into the ways of perfection: the problem of the relation of man to the human condition, or of his attitude in the face of the human condition.

This condition is that of a spirit united in substance with flesh and engaged in the universe of matter. It is an unhappy condition. In itself it is such a miserable condition that man has always dreamed of a golden age when he was more or less freed of it, and so miserable that on the plane of revelation, the Christian religion teaches that mankind was created, with the grace of Adam, in a superior condition in which it was free of sin, of pain, of servitude and of death, and from which it fell through its own fault. The Judeo-Christian tradition also teaches that after the end of history and in a new world the human condition will be supernaturally transfigured. Those who believe neither in the state of innocence nor in original sin put the golden age at the end of history, not at the beginning, and fancy that man will attain it in the last stage of his terrestrial adventure, through his own liberating effort, thanks to science and to radical social transformations; others, who want no part of consoling illusions, try to escape the spectacle of this planet by surrendering to some powerful passion which distracts them day after day from themselves and from the world, or by the ardor of a despairing pity which in a way appeases their hearts while it corrodes them little by little.

Indeed, the tragic perplexity in which we are placed consists in the fact that we can neither refuse the human condition nor accept it purely and simply.... As to refusing the human condition, it is clear that it is a question there only of a moral disposition. Such a refusal belongs to the world of dream; but man nourishes himself on dreams, and a dream which has its roots in the depths of the individual psychology of the subject can determine his fundamental attitude in life. (*MP,* **pp. 452–53**)

26. Natural law is an unwritten law. Man's knowledge of it has increased little by little as man's moral conscience has developed. The latter was at first in a twilight state. Anthropologists have taught us within what structures of tribal life and in the midst of what half-awakened magic it was primitively formed. This proves merely that the knowledge men have had of the unwritten law has passed through more diverse forms and stages than certain philosophers or theologians have believed. The knowledge which our own moral conscience has of this law is doubtless still imperfect, and very likely it will continue to develop and to become more refined as long as humanity exists. Only when the Gospel has penetrated to the very depth of human substance will natural law appear in its flower and its perfection. (***MS,* p. 90**)

27. Man's right to existence, to personal freedom, and to the pursuit of the perfection of moral life, belongs, strictly speaking, to natural law. (***MS*, p. 100**)

28. The final objective of law is to make men morally good. Civil law would adapt itself, with a view to the maximum good of which the multitude is capable, to various ways of life sanctioned by various moral creeds, but it should resist changes which were requested through sheer relaxation of morality and decaying mores. And it should always maintain a general orientation toward virtuous life, and make the common behavior *tend*, at each level, to the full accomplishment of moral law. (***MS*, p. 171**)

29. The person as intellectual *maker* is the ground of the right of property; the person as moral agent is held to the "common use" of the things he has appropriated. (***FMW*, p. 197; CW 11, p. 103**)

30. The common good is not only a system of advantages and utilities but also a rectitude of life, an end, good in itself or, as the Ancients expressed it, a *bonum honestum*. . . . Only on condition that it is according to justice and moral goodness is the common good what it is, namely, the good of a people and a city, rather than a mob of gangsters and murderers. (***PG*, p. 53**)

CHAPTER TWENTY-FOUR

MYSTERY AND MYSTICISM

1. We must believe the mystics about God, as we do the physicists about matter; both are competent, they both know whereof they speak. (*BPT*, p. 328)

2. It is clear that mystical experience and infused contemplation are, indeed, seen to be the normal, rightful end of the life of grace. They could even be said to be the summit towards which all human life tends: for, in this fallen and redeemed world wherein grace presses in on every side, human life tends towards the Christian life since every man belongs by right to Christ, the head of the human race; and Christian life itself... tends to the mystical life. (*DK*, p. 259; CW 7, p. 275)

3. Mystical wisdom judges the things of God through an affective experience which touches the very thing that lies hidden in faith. To the very extent that divine reality is hidden to us—being absolutely transcendent as regards every created idea—this secret wisdom experiences it: You are truly a hidden God, a savior God: and the more hidden, the more you are a savior and giver of life; the soul cherishes these dark shadows of faith because it knows they are fruitful. It knows, it feels that in them alone can it intimately taste and judge them by experience, the depths of its God. (*DK,* p. 262; CW 7, p. 279)

4. It is a scandal to the intellect, a profound offence against the sense of order, to see psychologists and sociologists—or even philosophers and metaphysicians—lay hands on mystical experience in order to judge its nature by their own light, that is to say, to systematically misunderstand it. The philosopher needs to be initiated into one or the other of the lower sciences, to mathematics, for example, when he wants to deal with certain questions. He ought, in the same way, to borrow light from a higher science when he seeks to deal, even for his own philosophical ends, with an object that essentially surpasses philosophy. (**DK, p. 288; CW 7, p. 306**)

5. If anti-mystical tendencies were completely systematized, they would turn Christianity into a mere moral system, while it is, first of all, a theological communion. (**SP, p. 147**)

6. And so, it is with the senses that in every animal immateriality has its very first beginning. But in all of them it stops there, except in that animal endowed with reason, in whom this immateriality which begins with the senses is destined in our case to come to full bloom in the higher faculties because our soul is spirit. Sensation is an *immutatio spiritualis*. We must not let all the evil that the majority of moralists tell us about the senses and sensuality lead us to forget the great dignity of these senses in us.

It seems to me that in reflecting on this we notice that many things are changing. Ascetical and mystical writers do well to put us on guard against the senses and their pleasures, which are not "*delectationes propter se quaerendae*," pleasures to be sought for themselves. But would they not do well also to teach us first of all to understand and respect this spirituality in the rough which begins with the senses? To respect the senses is not a bad way to learn that it is stupid to abuse them. (**UA, p. 409**)

7. It remains nevertheless true, provided that one understands correctly that which one says, that on Good Friday, *a divine Person died* (a human death), the Word Incarnate died, died of love and voluntarily. It is a very shocking expression, but if one refuses shocking expressions, one renounces glimpsing however little the mystery of the Cross. *Unus de Trinitate mortuus est*, one of the members of the Trinity has died, it is the formula which the

Second Council of Constantinople has employed. Here is the scandal of the Cross. (**GJ, pp. 139–40**)

8. The more theology knows God from a distance the more it wants to know Him through experience. The more mystical wisdom knows God by way of experience, the more it aspires to the vision of Him. And each time the higher disciplines gives to the soul that which it has been encouraged by the lower discipline to desire. (**SW, p. 25**)

9. Natural spirituality has techniques which are well determined and are, moreover, good and useful. This apparatus of techniques strikes everybody who begins to study comparative Mysticism. Now, the most obvious difference between the Christian and the other mystics is the freedom of the former from any techniques, recipes or formulas. It is, essentially, not esoteric or *reserved to specialists*. (**SP, p. 149**)

CHAPTER TWENTY-FIVE

NATURAL LAW AND HUMAN RIGHTS

1. Nature has its own reality, its own dignity, its own finalities; yet it is not an absolute; distinct from grace, it is neither separate nor independent from grace; grace is added to it not like a cap stuck on top of some professor's head, but like a divine graft which at once makes man participate in a supernatural life and exalts his natural life itself within the very order of this natural life. (*RT,* p. 182)

2. The Gospel has proclaimed the equal dignity of all men; but as concerns the affairs of the Master of the vineyard with men, which are, I repeat, affairs of the heart, the Gospel is far from being egalitarian. (***GE,* p. 105**)

3. Far from being dispensed from the obligations that every man has in the social and political order, the Christian knows that in addition he must as Christian bring the witness of the spirit into even the world of violence and contradiction. The Christian philosopher knows that he must elaborate, under the sky of the supreme principles of which the Church holds the de-

posit, a social and political philosophy that faces the risks and perils on the earth of human and profane history, or that is realistic enough to gain a hold upon the living historical work occurring under our eyes and yet at the same time free enough to affirm the political primacy, which the present world never ceases to deride, of the dignity of the human person, of the common good of the assembled multitude, and of moral and spiritual values.

He knows that he must keep an attitude open to the future and an attention alert not to mistake the slightest movements which a little hope appears that the dove of the spirit of God lurking in the depth of those waters now darker than ever; an attention at the same time alert to maintain in the midst of the vicissitudes of becoming those truths which do not change. It would certainly be easier to make a good[1] university career teaching the great principles, even false ones, with contentment and security. (*LI*, p. 123)

4. The Thomist idea of man coincides with the Greek, Jewish, and Christian idea: man as an animal endowed with reason, whose supreme dignity is in the intellect; and man as a free individual in personal relation with God, whose supreme righteousness consists in voluntarily obeying the law of God; and man as a sinful and wounded creature called to divine life and to the freedom of grace, whose supreme perfection consists in love. (*EM*, pp. 51–52)

5. Man evolves in history. Yet his nature as such, his place and value in the cosmos, his dignity, his rights and aspirations as a person, and his destiny do not change. Consequently, the secondary aims of education have to be adjusted to changing conditions in successive historical periods; but as concerns the primary aim, as well as the intrinsic domination it exercises on the secondary aims, it is sheer illusion to speak of a ceaseless reconstruction of the aims of education. (*EM*, p. 52)

6. We are no longer held to the multitude of ceremonial precepts nor to the juridical rules of the Mosaic Law; we are held to other ceremonial precepts less onerous and less numerous. And while we are ever held to the moral

---

1. Correction of translation "mood university career." Original: "une belle carrière universitaire."

precepts of the Law, we are held thereto as to the requirements of the very life and freedom which are within us, not as to requirements which (as long as only the Law, and not Christ's grace, is relied upon) do us violence and exceed our capacity. Thus the New Law is less burdensome than the Old Law, though it prescribes a more difficult purity and holiness. If the New Law requires many less things beyond the prescriptions of the natural law, and many less ceremonial observances than the Old Law, in return it requires that which is the most difficult of all: purity in the hidden movements and internal acts of the soul. (And it demands that we nurture the *spirit* of the counsels of the Gospel.) But love makes light the yoke of this higher perfection.

Thus it must be said that we are no longer "under the Law," which is to say that we are quit of the regimen of the Law. We are quit of that condition of humanity wherein the government of its actions had, as its basic rule, no longer the natural light and the internal promptings of conscience, as in the days of the Patriarchs, and not as yet the promulgation of the Gospel, as after Christ's coming, but the promulgation of the written law transmitted by Moses. We have passed under the regimen of the New Law, which is a law of freedom. (**PH, p. 84**)

7. The image of man involved in integral humanism is that of a being made of matter and of spirit, whose body may have emerged from the historical evolution of animal forms, but whose immortal soul directly proceeds from divine creation. He is made for truth, capable of knowing God as the Cause of Being, by his reason, and of knowing Him in His intimate life, by the gift of faith. Man's dignity is that of an image of God, his rights derive as well as his duties from natural law, whose requirements express in the creature the eternal plan of creative Wisdom. Wounded by sin and death from the first sin of his race, whose burden weighs upon all of us, he is caused by Christ to become of the race and lineage of God, living by divine life, and called upon to enter by suffering and love into Christ's very work of redemption. Called upon by his nature, on the other hand, to unfold historically his internal potentialities by achieving little by little reason's domination over his own animality and the material universe, his progress on earth is not automatic or merely natural, but accomplished in step with freedom and together with the inner help of God, and constantly thwarted by the power of evil, which is the power of created spirits to inject nothingness into being,

and which unceasingly tends to degrade human history, while unceasingly and with greater force the creative energies of reason and love revitalize and raise up this same history. (***RR*, pp. 195–96**)

8. But since man is endowed with intelligence and determines his own ends, it is up to him to put himself in tune with the ends necessarily demanded by his nature. This means that there is, by very virtue of human nature, *an order or a disposition which human reason can discover and according to which the human will must act in order to attune itself to the necessary ends of the human being. The unwritten law, or natural law, is nothing more than that.* (***RM*, p. 61**)

9. Natural law is not a written law. Men know it with greater or less difficulty, and in different degrees, running the risk of error here as elsewhere. The only practical knowledge all men have naturally and infallibly in common is that we must do good and avoid evil. This is the preamble and the principle of natural law; it is not the law itself. Natural law is the ensemble of things to do and not to do which follow therefrom in *necessary* fashion, and *from the simple fact that man is man*, nothing else being taken into account. (***RM*, 62–63**)

10. Natural Law—strictly speaking, Natural Law for man—is moral law, because man obeys or disobeys it freely. We might compare natural law in general with an algebraic equation according to which a curve develops in space. But with man the curve must conform freely to the equation. (***CR*, p. 214**)

11. The aim of society is its own *common good*, the good of the social body. But if we fail to grasp the fact that this good of the social body is a common good of *human persons*, as the social body itself is a whole made up of human persons, this formula would lead in its turn to other errors, of a collectivist type—or to a type of state despotism. The common good of society is neither a mere collection of private goods, nor the good proper to a whole, which (as in the case of the species with regard to its individual members, or the hive with regard to the bees) draws the parts to itself alone, and sacrifices these parts to itself. It is the good human life of the multitude, of a multitude of persons, the good life of totalities at once carnal and spiritual, and principally spiritual, although they more often happen to live by the flesh than by the spirit. The common good of society is their communion in the good life; it is therefore common *to the whole and to the parts,* to the parts, which are in themselves wholes, since the very notion of *person* means totality; it is common to the whole and to the parts, over which it flows back and which must all benefit from it. Under pain of being itself denatured, it implies and demands the recognition of the fundamental rights of the person (and the rights of the family, in which persons are enmeshed in a more primitive way of communal living than in political society). It involves, as its *chief* value, the highest possible attainment (that is, the highest compatible with the good of the whole) of persons to their lives as persons, and to their freedom of expansion or autonomy—and to the gifts of goodness which in their turn flow from it. (***RM*, pp. 8–9**)

12. Every human person has the right to make its own decisions with regard to its personal destiny, whether it be a question of choosing one's work, of marrying the man or woman of one's choice or of pursuing a religious vocation. In the case of extreme peril and for the safety of the community, the State can forcibly requisition the services of each of us and demand that each risk his life in a just war; it can also deprive criminals of certain of their rights (or rather sanction the fact that they themselves forfeited them); for example, men judged unworthy of exercising parental authority. But the State becomes iniquitous and tyrannical if it claims to base the functioning of civil life on forced labor, or if it tries to violate the rights of the family in order to become master of men's souls. (***RM*, p. 78**)

13. In the first place, both economic life and political life depend on *nature* and *reason,* I mean *nature* as dominated by material forces and laws and by deterministic evolution, even when the human mind interferes in the process with its technical discoveries—and on *reason* as concerned with the ends of human existence and the realm of freedom and morality, and as freely establishing, in consonance with Natural Law, an order of human relations. In the second place, it is nature and matter that have the upper hand in the economic process; and it is reason and freedom that have the upper hand in the political, the genuinely political process. (***MS*, p. 190**)

CHAPTER TWENTY-SIX

THE PERSON

1. Essentially, then, the human person is a member, a member of Adam or a member of Christ. The grace which makes him a member of Christ cuts him off from the body of Adam, to which he only remains attached through concupiscence, but without the human person acting henceforth in the virtue (or rather the failing) of original sin and Adam's weakness.

Each of us carries Adam's weakness within himself, but in the case of a righteous man it is a wound inflicted by another, whereas in the case of the sinner it is a weakness born of his own substance and origin, a weakness of the body of which he is a part, a wound upon which he feeds and lives. (***RR*, p. 74**)

2. The subject, or suppositum, or person has an essence, an essential structure. It is a substance equipped with properties and which is acted upon and acts by the instrumentality of its potencies. The person is a substance whose substantial form is a spiritual soul; a substance which lives a life that is not merely biological and instinctive, but is also a life of intellect and will. It is a very simple-minded error to believe that subjectivity possesses no intelligible structure, on the ground that it is an inexhaustible depth; and to conceive of it as without any nature whatsoever for the purpose of making of it an absurd abyss of pure and formless liberty.

These observations allow us to understand why many contemporary philosophers, while they talk of nothing but person and subjectivity, nevertheless radically misunderstand those words. They remain light-heartedly ignorant of the metaphysical problem of . . . *subsistence*. . . . They do not see that personality, metaphysically considered, being the subsistence of the spiritual soul communicated to the human composite, and enabling the latter to possess its existence, to perfect itself and to give itself freely, bears witness in us to the generosity or expansivity of being which, in an incarnate spirit, proceeds from the spirit and which constitutes, in the secret springs of our ontological structure, a source of dynamic unity and unification from within.

Because analysis wearies them, they are ignorant of what the proper life of the intelligence consists in, and in what the proper life of the will consists. They do not see that, because his *spirit* makes man cross the threshold of independence properly so-called, and of self-inwardness, the subjectivity of the person demands as its most intimate privilege communications proper to love and intelligence. They do not see that, even before the exercise of free choice, and in order to make free choice possible, the most deeply rooted need of the person is to communicate with *the other* by the union of the intelligence, and with *others* by the affective union. Their subjectivity is not a *self*, because it is wholly phenomenal. (***EE*, pp. 81–82**)

3. The notion of person is an *analogous* notion which is realized in different degrees and on essentially different planes of ontological being. The human being is a person, that is to say a universe or whole of a spiritual nature, endowed with freedom of choice and intended to enjoy freedom of autonomy. He is no more a *pure person* than he is *pure intellect*. On the contrary, just as he is at the lowest level of intellectual beings, so is he also at the lowest level of personality. To forget this would be to confuse the personality of man with the personality of Angels or again of the Divine Persons in Whom alone (because the Divine Person is subsistent Being and subsistent Freedom of Autonomy) is realized in purest form—in Pure Act—the perfection denoted by the word Personality, which is, as St. Thomas says, the highest perfection that exists in the whole realm of Nature. (***FMW*, p. 47; CW 11, pp. 27–28**)

4. Only the person is free; only the person possesses, in the full sense of these words, inwardness and subjectivity—because it contains itself and moves about within itself. The person, St. Thomas says, is that which is noblest and highest in all nature. (***EE,* p. 68**)

5. But the intuition of subjectivity is an existential intuition which surrenders no essence to us. We know *that which* we are by our phenomena, our operations, our flow of consciousness. The more we grow accustomed to the inner life, the better we decipher the astonishing and fluid multiplicity which is thus delivered to us; the more, also, we feel that it leaves us ignorant of the essence of our self. Subjectivity *as subjectivity* is inconceptualisable; is an unknowable abyss. It is unknowable by the mode of notion, concept, or representation, or by any mode of any science whatsoever—introspection, psychology, or philosophy. How could it be otherwise, seeing that every reality known through a concept, a notion, or a representation is known as object and not as a subject? Subjectivity as such escapes by definition from that which we know about ourselves by means of notions. (***EE,* pp. 69–70**)

6. At the very beginning and above all, subjectivity is known or rather felt in virtue of a formless and diffuse knowledge which, in relation to reflective consciousness, we may call unconscious or pre-conscious knowledge. (***EE,* p. 70**)

7. Subjectivity is not known, it is felt as a propitious and enveloping night. (***EE,* p. 70**)

8. To know that I am known as subject in all the dimensions of my being is not only to know that my truth is known, and that in this knowledge justice is done me; it is also to know that I am *understood*. Even though God condemn me, I know that He understands me. The idea that we are known to Him who scrutinises the loins and the heart dissolves us at first in fear and trembling because of the evil that is within us. But on deeper reflection, how can we keep from thinking that God Who knows us and knows all those poor beings who jostle us and whom we know as objects, whose wretchedness we mostly perceive—how can we keep from thinking that God Who knows all these in their subjectivity, in the nakedness of their wounds and their secret evil, must know also the secret beauty of that nature which He has bestowed upon then, the slightest sparks of good and liberty they give

forth, all the travail and the impulses of good-will that they drag from the womb to the grave, the recesses of goodness of which they themselves have no notion? The exhaustive knowledge possessed by God is a loving knowledge. To know that we are known to God is not merely to experience justice, it is also to experience mercy. (*EE*, pp. 78–79)

9. Subjectivity marks the frontier which separates the world of philosophy from the world of religion. This is what Kierkegaard felt so deeply in his polemic against Hegel. Philosophy runs against an insurmountable barrier in attempting to deal with subjectivity, because while philosophy of course knows subjects, it knows them only as objects. Philosophy is registered whole and entire in the relation of intelligence to object; whereas religion enters into the relation of subject to subject. For this reason, every philosophical religion, or every philosophy which, like Hegel's, claims to assume and integrate religion into itself, is in the last analysis a mystification. (*EE*, p. 72)

10. It is something to know that God is a transcendent and sovereign Self; but it is something else again to enter oneself and with all one's baggage—one's own existence and flesh and blood—into the vital relationship in which created subjectivity is brought face to face with this transcendent subjectivity and, trembling and loving, looks to it for salvation. This is the business of religion. (*EE*, p. 73)

11. Being the only subject which is a subject for me in the midst of a world of subjects which my senses and my intelligence can know only as objects, I am at the centre of the world.... With regard to my subjectivity in act, I *am* the centre of the world ('the most important person in the world'). My destiny is the most important of all destinies. Worthless as I know myself to be, I am more interesting than all the saints. There is me, and there are all the others. Whatever happens to the others is a mere incident in the picture; but what happens to me, what I myself have to do, is of absolute importance. (*EE*, pp. 74–75)

12. The person is a whole, but it is not a closed whole, it is an *open* whole. It is not a little god without doors or windows, like Leibnitz's monad, or an idol which sees not, hears not, speaks not. It tends by its very nature to social life and to communion.

    This is true not only because of the needs and the indigence of human nature, by reason of which each one of us has need of others for his material, intellectual and moral life, but also because of the radical generosity inscribed within the very being of the person, because of that openness to the communications of intelligence and love which is the nature of the spirit, and which demands an entrance into relationship with other persons. To state it rigorously, the person cannot be alone. It wants to tell what it knows, and it wants to tell what it is—to whom, if not to other people? (**RM, pp. 5–6**)

13. Now the Christian knows that there is a supernatural order, and that the ultimate end—the absolute ultimate end—of the human person is God causing His own personal life and eternal bliss to be participated in by man. The direct ordination of the human person to God transcends every created common good—both the common good of the political society and the intrinsic common good of the universe. Here is the rock of the dignity of the human person as well as of the unshakeable requirements of the Christian message. Thus the indirect subordination of the body politic,—not as a mere means, but as an end worthy in itself yet of lesser dignity—to the supra-temporal values to which human life is appendent, refers first and foremost, as matter of fact, to the supernatural end to which the human person is directly ordained. To sum up all this in one single expression, let us say that the law we are faced with here is the *primacy of the spiritual.* (**MS, pp. 149–50**)

14. The human person is ordained directly to God as to its absolute ultimate end. Its direct ordination to God transcends every created common good—both the common good of the political society and the intrinsic common good of the universe. Here is the fundamental truth governing the entire discussion—the truth in which nothing less than the very message of Christian wisdom in its triumph over Hellenic thought and every other pagan wisdom, henceforth toppled from their dominion, is involved. (**PG, p. 15**)

15. Society cannot exist without the personal gift and the perpetual surplus which derive from persons, without the wellsprings of generosity hidden in the very depths of the life and liberty of persons, and which love causes to flow forth. (*RM,* p. 36)

16. Materialistic conceptions of the world and life, philosophies which do not recognize the spiritual and eternal element in man cannot escape error in their efforts to construct a truly human society because they cannot satisfy the requirements of the person, and, by that very fact, they cannot grasp the nature of society. Whoever recognizes this spiritual and eternal element in man, recognizes also the aspiration, immanent in the person, to transcend, by reason of that which is most sublime in it, the life and conditions of temporal societies. Thus temporal society can be erected in accordance with the proper laws of its own nature. Its genuine character as a society of persons is understood. The natural tendency of the person to society, and the relation by which it morally and legally belongs to the society of which it is a part are also understood. (***PG,*** **pp. 100–101**)

17. Immortality is not a more or less precarious, successful or unsuccessful survival in other men, or in the ideal waves of the universe. Immortality is a nature-given, inalienable property of the human soul as a spiritual substance. (***RR,*** **p. 64**)

18. As to the human person, he is but a person in embryo. He is, as with all created persons, not only subject to realities other than himself as to the specifying objects of his knowledge and of his will, but he is also subjected to laws he has not made, as measures regulating his actions. And this is the first defeat, inflicted upon the aspirations of the person as such, a defeat far deeper in men than in angels.

Moreover, the human person is involved in all the miseries and fatalities of material nature—the servitudes and the needs of the body, heredity, ignorance, selfishness, and the savagery of instincts. This is the second defeat, inflicted upon the person as such, and this defeat originates not in the transcendence of God, but in the burden of nature. The human person! This unfortunate being, threatened by the entire universe, which seems ready to crush him, pretends to be a whole, to be a person! He is, indeed, a whole and a person! He is a person in the metaphysical root of personality. But for subjects both spiritual and bodily, which participate in the same specific nature, which are opaque to themselves, and whose normal state is movement, this metaphysical root, hidden in the depths of being, manifests itself only through a progressive conquest of itself by itself, accomplished in time. Man must win his personality, as well as his freedom, and he pays dearly for it, and runs many risks. He is a person in the order of doing only if his rational energies, and virtues, and love, give such a face to the torrential multiplicity which inhabits him, and freely imprint on him the seal of his radical, ontological unity. In this sense, the one knows real personality and real liberty, while the other does not. (*SP,* p. 107)

19. Man and angel are both *persons,* and in that light not parts but real *wholes;* for the person signifies in itself, wholeness. Neither man nor even the angel are persons in the perfect and absolute state, but they are in a real sense persons—however wretchedly that condition of person is realised in man. (*PE,* p. 11)

20. Dependent though he may be upon the slightest accidents of matter, the human person exists by virtue of the existence of his soul, which dominates time and death. It is the spirit which is the root of personality.

The notion of personality thus involves that of wholeness and independence. To say that a man is a person is to say that in the depth of his being he is more a whole than a part and more independent than servile. It is this mystery of our nature which religious thought designates when it says that the person is the image of God. A person possesses absolute dignity because he is in direct relationship with the realm of being, truth, goodness, and beauty, and with God, and it is only with these that he can arrive at his complete fulfillment. His spiritual fatherland consists of the entire order of things which have absolute value, and which reflect, in some manner, a divine Absolute superior to the world and which have a power of attraction toward this Absolute. (*EC,* pp. 8–9)

21. The conviction each of us has, rightly or wrongly, regarding the limitations, deficiencies, errors of others does not prevent friendship between minds. In such a fraternal dialogue, there must be a kind of forgiveness and remission, not with regard to ideas—ideas deserve no forgiveness if they are false—but with regard to the condition of him who travels the road at our side. Every believer knows very well that all men will be judged—both himself and all others. But neither he nor another is God, able to pass judgment. What each one is before God, neither the one nor the other knows. Here the "judge not" of the Gospels applies with its full force. We can render judgment concerning ideas, truths, or errors; good or bad actions; character, temperament, and what appears to us of man's interior disposition. But we are utterly forbidden to judge the innermost heart, that inaccessible center where the person day after day weaves his own fate and ties the bonds binding him to God. When it comes to that, there is only one thing to do, and that is to trust in God. And that is precisely what love for our neighbour prompts us to do. (*UP,* pp. 35–36)

22. When we say that a man is a person, we do not mean merely that he is an individual, in the sense that an atom, a blade of grass, a fly, or an elephant is an individual. Man is an individual who holds himself in hand by intelligence and will. He does not exist only in a physical manner. He has spiritual super-existence through knowledge and love; he is, in a way, a universe in himself, a microcosm, in which the great universe in its entirety can be encompassed through knowledge; and through love he can give himself completely to beings who are to him, as it were, other selves, a relation for which no equivalent can be found in the physical world. The human person possesses these characteristics because in the last analysis man, this flesh and these perishable bones which are animated and activated by a divine fire, exists "from the womb to the grave" by virtue of the very existence of his soul, which dominates time and death. Spirit is the root of personality. The notion of personality thus involves that of totality and independence; no matter how poor and crushed he may be, a person, as such, is a whole and subsists in an independent manner. To say that man is a person is to say that in the depths of his being he is more a whole than a part and more independent than servile. It is to say that he is a minute fragment of matter that is at the same time a universe, a beggar who communicates with absolute being, mortal flesh whose value is eternal, a bit of straw into which heaven enters. It is this metaphysical mystery that religious thought points to when it says that the person is the image of God. The value of the person, his dignity and his rights belong to the order of things naturally sacred which bear the imprint of the Father of being, and which have in Him the end of their movement. (*PP,* p. 14)

CHAPTER TWENTY-SEVEN

THE PERSON AND THE INDIVIDUAL

1. Let us first speak briefly of individuality. Suffice it to recall that, according to St. Thomas Aquinas, the *individuality* of inanimate and animate things is rooted in *matter,* so far as matter has uniquely distinct determinations with respect to location in space. The word matter designates here, not a concept used in physics, but in philosophy: that of the *materia prima,* pure potentiality, able neither to *be* nor to *be thought* by itself, and from which all corporeal beings are made. Prime matter or 'matter absolute' is a kind of nonbeing, a simple power of receptivity and of substantial mutability, an avidity for being. And, in every being made of matter, this avidity bears the imprint of a metaphysical energy—'form' or 'soul'—which constitutes with matter a substantial unity, and which determines the latter to be that which it is, and which, by the simple fact that it is ordained to inform matter, is particularized to such and such a being, sharing with other beings, equally immersed in space, the same specific nature.

According to this doctrine, the human soul constitutes, with the matter which it informs, a unique substance, both spiritual and fleshly. It is not as Descartes believed: the soul is not *one thing*—thought—existing as a complete being; and the body *another thing*—extension—existing in its own way as a complete being. But soul and matter are two substantial co-principles of one and the same being, of a single and unique reality whose name is man. It is because each soul is made to animate a particular body (which derives its matter from the germinative cells from which it springs with all their load of heredity); it is because each soul has a substantial relation, or rather *is* a substantial relation with a particular body; it is for these reasons that it has in its very substance individual characteristics which differentiate it from every other human soul. For man, as for all other corporeal beings—as for the atom, the molecule, the plant, the animal—individuality has its primary ontological root in matter. Such is the doctrine of St. Thomas concerning individuality.

I said that matter is an avidity for being, without determination, an avidity which receives its determination from form. One might say that in each of us, *individuality,* being in one that which excludes from one all that other men are, is the narrowness in being, and the 'grasping for oneself,' which, in a body animated by a spirit, derives from matter.

Man, in so far as he is a material individuality, has but a precarious unity, which wishes only to slip back into multiplicity; for matter as such tends to decompose itself. In so far as we are individuals, each of us is a fragment of a species, a part of this universe, a single dot in the immense network of forces and influences, cosmic, ethnic, historic, whose laws we obey. We are subject to the determination of the physical world. But each man is also a person and, in so far as he is a person, he is not subject to the stars and atoms; for he subsists entirely with the very subsistence of his spiritual soul, and the latter is in him a principle of creative unity, of independence and of freedom. (*SP,* pp. 48–50)

2. Such are, if I have succeeded in describing them correctly, the two metaphysical aspects of the human being: individuality and personality, each with their own ontological physiognomy. Let us note, that we do not represent two separate things. There is not in me one reality called my individuality and another called my personality. It is the same entire being which, in one sense, is an individual and, in another sense, a person. I am wholly an individual, by reason of what I receive from matter, and I am wholly a person, by reason of what I receive from spirit: just as a painting is in its en-

tirety a physico-chemical complex, by reason of the colouring materials out of which it is made, and a work of beauty, by reason of the painter's art.

Let us note, moreover, that material individuality is not something bad in itself. No, it is something good, since it is the very condition of our existence. But it is precisely in relation to personality that individuality is good; what is bad, is to let this aspect of our being predominate in our actions. No doubt, each of my acts is an act of myself-the-individual, and an act of myself-the-person. But even as it is free and engages my whole self, each of my acts is drawn *either* into the movement which tends to the supreme centre toward which personality strives, *or* into the movement which tends towards dispersion, to which, if left to itself, material individuality is bound to fall back.

Now it is important to observe that man must complete, through his own will, what is sketched in his nature. According to a commonplace expression, which is a very profound one, man must become what he is. In the moral order, he must win, by himself, his freedom and his personality. In other words, his action can follow either the slope of personality or the slope of individuality. If the development of the human being follows the direction of *material individuality,* he will be carried in the direction of the 'hateful ego', whose law is to *snatch,* to absorb for oneself. In this case, personality as such will tend to adulterate, to dissolve. If, on the contrary, the development follows the direction of *spiritual personality,* then it will be in the direction of the generous self of saints and heroes that man will be carried. Man will really be a person, in so far as the life of spirit and freedom will dominate in him that of passion and of the senses. (**SP, pp. 52–53**)

3. But why is it that a person, as person, seeks to live in society? It does so, first, because of its very perfections, as person, and its inner urge to the communications of knowledge and love which require relationships with other persons. In its radical generosity, the human person tends to overflow into social communications in response to the law of superabundance inscribed in the depths of being, life, intelligence and love. It does so secondly because of its needs or deficiencies, which derive from its material individuality. In this respect, unless it is integrated in a body of social communications, it cannot attain the fullness of its life and accomplishment. Society appears, therefore, to provide the human person with just those conditions of existence and development which it needs. It is not by itself alone that it reaches its plenitude but by receiving essential goods from society.

Here the question is not only of his material needs, of bread, clothes and shelter, for which man requires the help of his fellowmen, but also, and above all, of the help which he ought to be given to do the work of reason and virtue, which responds to the specific feature of his being. To reach a certain degree of elevation in knowledge as well as a certain degree of perfection in moral life, man needs an education and the help of other men. In this sense, Aristotle's statement that man is by nature a political animal holds with great exactitude: man is a political animal because he is a rational animal, because reason requires development through character training, education and the cooperation of other men, and because society is thus indispensable to the accomplishment of human dignity. (*PG,* pp. 47–49)

4. It is the human *person* who enters into society; as an individual, it enters society as a part whose proper good is inferior to the good of the whole (of the whole constituted of persons). But the good of the whole is what it is, and so superior to the private good, only if it benefits the individual persons, is redistributed to them and respects their dignity.

On the other hand, because it is ordained to the absolute and is summoned to a destiny beyond time, or, in other words, because of the highest requirements of personality as such, the human person, as a spiritual totality referred to the transcendent whole, *surpasses* and is superior to all temporal societies. From this point of view, or if you will, in respect to things *which are not Caesar's* both society itself and its common good are indirectly subordinated to the perfect accomplishment of the person and its supra-temporal aspirations as to an end of another order—an end which transcends them. A single human soul is worth more than the whole universe of material goods. There is nothing higher than the immortal soul, save God. With respect to the eternal destiny of the soul, society exists for each person and is subordinated to it. (*PG,* pp. 60–61)

5. A person as such is a whole, open and generous. Indeed if human society were a society of *pure persons,* the good of society and the good of each person would be one and the same. Yet man is very far from being a pure person; the human person is a poor, material individual, an animal born more poverty-stricken than all other animals. Even though the person, as such, is an independent whole, and that which is noblest in all nature, the human person is at the lowest level of personality, stripped and succorless; a person destitute and full of needs. Because of these deep lacks and in accordance with all the complements of being which spring from society and without which the person would remain, as it were, in a state of latent life, it happens that when a person enters into the society of his fellows, he becomes a *part* of a whole larger and better than its parts—a whole which transcends the person in so far as the latter is a part of that whole—and whose common good is other than the good of each one and other than the sum of the good of all. Nonetheless, it is by very reason of *personality* as such, and of the perfections which it carries with it, as an independent and open whole, that the human person seeks to enter into society. (**RM, pp. 11–12**)

6. It is thus in the nature of things that man sacrifices his temporal goods, and if necessary his life itself, for the sake of the community, and that social life imposes upon the life of the person, taken as part of the whole, many a constraint and many a sacrifice. But even as these sacrifices and constraints are demanded and accepted by justice and by friendship, even so they raise the spiritual level of the person. When man gives his life for the community's sake, he accomplishes, through an act of such great virtue, the moral perfection by which the person asserts his supreme independence as regards the world. By losing himself temporally for the city's sake, the person sacrifices himself in the truest and most complete fashion, and yet does not lose the stakes; the city serves him even then, for the soul of man is not mortal, and there is an eternal life.

In brief, while the person as such is a *totality*, the individual as such is a *part*; while the person, as person or as totality, demands that the common good of temporal society should flow back to him, and while through his ordination to the transcendent whole, he even surpasses the temporal society, the same person, as an individual or as part, is inferior to the social whole, and must serve the common cause as a member of the whole. (*SP,* **pp. 58–59**)

7. As individuals, we are subject to the stars. As persons, we rule them. (*TR*, **p. 21**)

CHAPTER TWENTY-EIGHT

PERSONALITY

1. In each of us there dwells a mystery, and that mystery is the human personality. We know that an essential characteristic of any civilization worthy of the name is respect and feeling for the dignity of the human person. We know that in defense of the rights of the human person, just as in defense of liberty, we must be ready to give our lives. What worth deserving of such sacrifice is then contained in man's personality? What precisely do we mean when we speak of the human person?

Whenever we say that a man is a person, we mean that he is more than a mere parcel of matter, more than an individual element in nature, such as is an atom, a blade of grass, a fly or an elephant. Where is the liberty, where is the dignity, where are the rights of an individual piece of matter? There would be no sense in a fly or an elephant giving its life for the liberty, dignity, or rights of the fly or the elephant. Man is an animal and an individual, but unlike other animals or individuals. Man is an individual who holds himself in hand by his intelligence and his will. He exists not merely physically; there is in him a richer and nobler existence; he has spiritual superexistence through knowledge and through love. He is thus in some fashion a whole, not merely a part; he is a universe unto himself, a microcosm in which the whole great universe can be encompassed through knowledge; and through love he can give himself freely to beings who are, as it were, other selves to him. For this relationship no equivalent is to be found in the physical world. All this means, in philosophical terms, that in the flesh and bones of man there lives a soul which is a spirit and which has a greater value than the whole physical universe. However dependent it may be on the slightest accidents of matter, the human person exists by virtue of the existence of its soul, which dominates time and death. It is the spirit which is the root of personality. (*RM,* **pp. 2–3**)

2. Now *personality* is an even deeper mystery [than *individuality*], whose profound significance it is still more difficult to discover. In order to embark upon the philosophical discovery of personality, the best way is to consider the relation between personality and love. . . .

What I love is the deepest reality, the most substantial, hidden, *existing* reality in the beloved—a metaphysical centre, deeper than all qualities and essences which I can discover and enumerate in the beloved. That is why such enumerations pour endlessly from the lover's mouth.

Love aims at this centre, without separating it from the qualities—in fact, merging into one with them. This centre is in some way inexhaustibly a source of existence, of goodness and of action, capable of giving and of *giving itself*—and capable of receiving not only this or that gift from another, but another self as gift and giver.

Thus, through considering the very law of love, we are introduced to the metaphysical problem of the person. Love does not aim at qualities, or at natures, or at essences, but at persons. . . .

In order to be able to *give oneself,* one must first exist, and not only as the sound which passes in the air, or this idea which crosses my mind, but as a thing which subsists and which by itself exercises existence. And one must not only exist as other things, one must exist in an eminent way, by possessing oneself by holding oneself in hand and by disposing of oneself; that is, one must exist through a spiritual existence, capable of enveloping itself by intelligence and freedom, and of *super-existing* in knowledge and free love. That is why the Western metaphysical tradition defines the person by independence: the person is a reality, which, subsisting spiritually, constitutes a universe by itself and an independent whole (relatively independent), in the great whole of the universe and facing the transcendent Whole, which is

God. And that is why this philosophical tradition sees in God the sovereign personality, since God's existence consists itself in a pure and absolute super-existence of intellection and love. The notion of personality does not refer to matter, as does the notion of individuality applied to corporeal things. It refers to the highest and deepest dimensions of being; personality is rooted in the spirit, in so far as the latter stands by itself in existence and super-abounds in it. Metaphysically considered, personality, being in one's substance a signature or a seal enabling one freely to perfect and freely to give this substance, evidences in each of us that expansiveness of being which, in a corporeal-spiritual being, is linked to the spirit, and which constitutes, in the secret depths of our ontological structure, a source of dynamic unity and of inner unification. (*SP*, pp. 50–51)

3. The notion of personality thus involves that of totality and independence; no matter how poor and crushed a person may be, as such he is a whole, and as a person, subsists in an independent manner. To say that a man is a person is to say that in the depth of his being he is more a whole than a part and more independent than servile. It is to this mystery of our nature that religious thought points when it says that the human person is the image of God. The worth of the person, his liberty, his rights, arise from the order of naturally sacred things, which bear upon them the imprint of the Father of Being, and which have in Him the goal of their movement. A person possesses absolute dignity because he is in direct relationship with the absolute, in which alone he can find his complete fulfillment. His spiritual fatherland consists of the entire order of things which have absolute value, and which reflect, in some way, an Absolute superior to the world and which draw our life towards this Absolute. (***RM*, pp. 3–4**)

4. The personality of the wise is still very precarious and mingled! How much poor plaster there is on the stoic's austere mask. The privileges of personality—the pure life of intelligence and liberty, the pure agility of the spirit, which is self-sufficient for action as for being—and so deeply buried in our case in the matter of our fleshly individuality that we can only free them by being ready to fall to earth and die there in order to bear divine fruit; and we shall only know our true face if we receive the white stone on which God has written our new name. Truly perfect personality is only found in saints. (*TR*, **p. 25**)

5. What is modern individualism? A misunderstanding, a blunder; the exaltation of individuality camouflaged as personality, and the corresponding degradation of true personality. (*TR,* **p. 21**)

6. Personality, which it is metaphysically impossible to lose, suffers many a defeat in the psychological and moral spheres. It risks contamination from the miseries of material individuality, from its pettiness, its vanities, its bad habits, its narrowness, its hereditary predispositions, from its natural regime of rivalry and opposition. For the same being who is a person, and subsists through the subsistence of his soul, is also an individual in a species, and dust in the wind. (*SP,* **p. 108**)

7. It is in man because he is animal and also spirit that the characteristic law of individuation enters most deeply into composition with that of personality and tends to thwart it. For the metaphysical root of personality is the subsistence of Spirit and, in all corporal beings, the root of individuality lies in matter. This is the reason why *personality* in the case of man is precarious and always in peril and must be achieved by a kind of progress. (*FMW,* **pp. 47–48; CW 11, p. 28**)

8. Any man who, in a primary act of freedom deep enough to engage his whole personality, chooses to do the good for the sake of the good, chooses God, knowingly or unknowingly, as his supreme good; he loves God more than himself, even if he has no conceptual knowledge of God. (*RA,* **p. 31**)

9. History is an unimaginable drama of the confrontation of free personalities, of the eternal divine personality and our own personality. And how real is the being and existence of these created personalities! If we wish to get beyond the nightmare of a banal 'indefinite pronoun' existence, of 'one' instead of 'I'—by which all our imaginations are oppressed in modern conditions; if we want to awake to the consciousness of ourselves and *our* own existence, we may indeed read Heidegger, but we would surely do better to read the Bible. The behaviour of the patriarchs, of Moses, David, Job and Ezekiel before God will teach us what *personal existence*, as distinguished from 'anonymous' existence, is; the existence of an *Ego*. They have no shame in existing and in existing in their own name precisely because they are in the all-powerful hand of Him who made them. Everything in Holy Scripture is dialogue: it is always a question of 'Thou' and 'I.' (***SW*, p. 16**)

10. Insofar as man participates in the metaphysical privileges of spirit and personality, he has aspirations which transcend human nature and its possibilities, and which consequently may be called trans-natural aspirations: the longing for a state in which he would know things completely and without error, in which he would enjoy perfect communion with spirits, in which he would be free without being able to fail or to sin, in which he would inhabit a realm of unfading justice, in which he would have the intuitive knowledge of the First Cause of being.

Such a longing cannot be fulfilled by nature. It can be fulfilled by grace. The immortal soul is involved and engaged in the great drama of the Redemption. If, at the moment of its separation from the body, at the moment when its choice is immutably fixed forever, the immortal soul prefers its own will and self-love to the will and gift of God, if it prefers misery with pride to the blessing of grace, then it is granted what it has wished for. It has it, and it will never cease wanting and preferring it, for a free choice made in the condition of a *pure* spirit is an eternal choice. If the soul opens itself to the will and gift of God, Whom it loves more than its own existence, then it is granted what it has loved, it enters forever into the joy of the uncreated Being, it sees God face to face and knows Him as it is known by Him, intuitively. (***RR*, pp. 63–64**)

11. A person is a center of liberty; a person confronts things, the universe, God; talks with another person, communicates with him by understanding and affection. The notion of personality, however complex it may be, belongs primarily to the ontological order. It is a metaphysical and substantial perfection which unfolds in the operative order in psychological and moral values.

The first metaphysical root of personality is what is called subsistence. Subsistence presupposes a (substantial) nature that is individual or singular (i.e., having the ultimate of actuation and determination in the very line of nature or essence). What it properly signifies, insofar as it gives the final completion to the order of created things, is that this nature, from the fact that it is endowed with subsistence, cannot communicate with any other substantial nature in the very act of existing, it is, so to speak, absolutely enclosed in itself with regard to existence. My person exists before acting; and it possesses its existence, as it possesses its nature, in a way absolutely proper to it and incommunicable. Not only is its nature singular, it owns so completely the existence which actuates it that it desires to keep it to itself alone; it can share this existence with no other. (***DK*, p. 231; CW 7, pp. 245–46**)

12. Subsistence is for the nature an ontological seal, as it were, of its unity. When this nature is complete (a separated soul is not a person) and above all when it is capable of possessing itself, of taking itself in hand by the intellect and the will, in short, when it belongs to the spiritual order, then the subsistence of such a nature is called personality.

Such, in the terminology of the Schoolmen, is the metaphysical notion of personality. This is the notion we all use . . . when we say that every man has a personality, is a person, endowed with free will. But for subjects that are corporeal as well as spiritual and who share the same specific nature so that the personality of each supposes its individuation by matter, and who are obscure to themselves, and for whom change is the proper condition, this metaphysical root, hidden in the depth of being, is only manifested by a progressive conquest of the self by the self accomplished in time. Man must win his personality as he wins his liberty; he pays dearly for it. He is a person in the order of acting, he is *causa sui* only if rational energies and virtues, and love—and the Spirit of God—gather his soul into their hands—*anima mea in manibus meis semper*—and into the hands of God, and give a face to the turbulent multiplicity that dwells within him, freely seal it with the seal of his radical ontological unity. In this sense, one knows true personality and true liberty; another knows them not. Personality, while metaphysically inalienable, suffers many a check in the psychological and moral register. There it runs the risk of contamination by the miseries of material individuality, by its meannesses, its vanities, its bad habits, its narrownesses, its hereditary predispositions, by its natural regime of rivalry and opposition. For that same man who is a person, and subsists in his entirety with the subsistence of his soul, is also an individual in a species and dust before the wind. (***DK*, p. 232; CW 7, pp. 246–47**)

13. The paradox of consciousness and personality is that each of us is situated precisely *at the centre* of this world. Each is at the centre of infinity. And this privileged subject, the thinking self, is to itself not object but subject; in the midst of all the subjects which it knows only as objects, it alone is subject as subject. We are thus confronted by subjectivity as subjectivity. (***EE*, p. 68**)

14. In struggling with Things and Nature, Greek art is always turned toward them. Man, privileged as his figure may be, remains an object in Nature and a thing in the cosmos, subordinate to the perfection and divinity of the universality of Things. A certain individualism starts to assert itself, it is true, but only as to the artist's individual talent or mastery, not as to his individual self-interiority. The Greek artist had less self-forgetfulness, perhaps than the Chinese, but only in so far as he was concerned with his own excellence in the face of beholders or competitors, rather than with his own inwardness in the face of Things. The inner mystery of personality was not yet revealed to man. (***CI*, p. 21**)

CHAPTER TWENTY-NINE

PHILOSOPHERS

1. All great philosophers have recognized the existence of and necessity for an intuition from which their wisdom is suspended. It is on the nature of this intuition that they are divided: as much, to tell the truth, as on the nature of the human being, which Aristotle alone was able to contemplate with quiet glance as an animal endowed with reason. The genuine and nourishing intuition of human knowledge and of philosophy is not an intellectual angelistic intuition reserved for the wise like the Platonist intuition of separate Ideas or Spinoza's knowledge of the third genus; nor an intellectual angelistic intuition accessible to all, like the Cartesian intuition of thought and of clear ideas; nor a supra-individual intellectual intuition like the Hegelian communion of the universal spirit with itself; nor a supra-intellectual intuition continuing the intellect and transcending all sense experience like the ecstasy of Plotinus; nor a "supra-intellectual" intuition running counter to intellect and plunging into sense experience, like the folding back by which, in Schopenhauer, the will becomes conscious of itself; or like the Bergsonian intuition of duration. It is a *human intellectual intuition,* the intellection of being which, suprasensible in itself, is directly grasped in the sensible in which it is immanent, and pursued into the pure spiritual analogically attained—an intellection at first rudimentary, and naturally progressive, like everything

human, and due to the essentially human process (too human, like everything human) of the abstraction of intelligibles. (*BPT,* pp. 30–31)

2. But Aristotle must be studied, not only in his attitude to Plato, but absolutely in his attitude to *that which is.* For Plato did no more than furnish him with the occasion to wrestle with the problem of being. Aristotle won the match, leaving us his great concepts of *potentiality* and *act, matter* and *form,* the *categories,* the *transcendentals,* the *causes,* as weapons wherewith to wage the same intellectual contest, and teaching us, as a true master of wisdom, to rise above the study of visible and perishable things to contemplation of the living, imperishable reality which knows no change. (*IP,* p. 65)

3. What shall be said of philosophers who wish to reach truth by despising intellect, and find something better than the light which enlightens every man coming into this world? It is not the overwhelming power of glory, it is the fascination of change without substance which will end the adventure. (*BPT,* p. 281)

4. Truly, philosophers play a strange game. They know very well that one thing alone counts, and that all their medley of subtle discussions relates to one single question: why are we born on this earth? And they also know that they will never be able to answer it. Nevertheless they continue sedately to amuse themselves. Do they not see that people come to them from all points of the compass, not with a desire to partake of their subtlety but because they hope to receive from them one word of life? If they have such words why do they not cry them from the housetops, asking their disciples to give, if necessary, their very blood for them? If they have no such words why do they allow people to believe they will receive from them something which they cannot give? For mercy's sake, if ever God has spoken, if in some place in the world, were it on the gibbet of one crucified, He has sealed His truth, tell us; that is what you must teach. Or are you indeed masters in Israël only to be ignorant of these things? The moment it is a question of divine things and our salvation, the question to be answered first is the one which comes before everything else: is there a Revelation?

Thus it is that reason leads the philosopher to a living person greater than himself, Whose name is ineffable. And certainly, once having reached this point he will be able to learn enough to renew his science from top to bottom. But will the philosopher follow reason to the very end? (***BPT,* p. 298**)

5. And why should a philosopher not have many more fears than anyone else? Does he not know the sad story of the many ways in which simple and sane common sense can be impaired by ideological cultivation? Is he ever sure that the long habit of a certain system as well as the inevitable friction due to many different kinds of errors has not caused a distortion or attenuation of the natural vigour of his reason? (***BPT,* p. 297**)

6. Not only can we not of ourselves have access to supernatural reality, but it is also utterly improbable that erudite reason, the reason of philosophers and savants, should by its own resources avoid the absurd presupposition of the impossibility of a properly supernatural order of things. In other words, from the real we naturally conclude the possible, and we take advantage of this to deny the possibility of what we have not experienced. So long as faith does not bring us into contact with the reality of the supernatural world, as does the sense with the material world, our intellect continues stupidly to deny the very possibility of such a world. (***BPT,* p. 299**)

7. The philosopher is led to broach questions (most often thankless) of a practical kind by the sense of his responsibility toward souls, a sense which wins him no man's gratitude and of which even he realizes the absurdity—for what indeed is this pretended responsibility, seeing that no one listens? In the long run his talk is for the angels. (***FMW,* p. 188; CW 11, p. 98**)

8. Before sewing one must cut. A philosopher who is in search of the nature of things is obliged to begin with sharp distinctions. These distinctions may seem brutal. They simply deal with certain essences taken in themselves: and how could we bring out otherwise the intelligibility of things from the confused flux of existence? To isolate an essence does not imply any disregard for the complexity and continuity of the real. It is indispensable in order to analyze this complexity and continuity in a correct manner—and finally to become aware of their very richness and meaning. (***CI,* p. 44**)

9. The philosopher in remaining philosopher is of little use to men. But to remain philosopher and act as philosopher, one must maintain everywhere

the liberty of philosophy and in particular to affirm ceaselessly the independence of the philosopher from whatever political parties there are. I belong to neither the left nor the right.

The independence of the philosopher—that is required by the very nature of a knowledge that is of itself a wisdom, and even when it is applied in the strictest way to the contingent still dominates it. The independence of the philosopher stands witness to the liberty of the intellect in the face of the passing instant. (*LI*, p. 122)

10. The slope of modem intelligence is slanted against us. Well, slopes are made to be climbed. The intellect has not changed its nature; it has acquired habits. Habits can be corrected. Second nature? But the first nature is always there; and the syllogism will last as long as man does. It is less bothersome for the philosopher to be out of intellectual step with his time than it is for the artist. Besides, things happen quite differently in the one case than in the other. The artist pours out his creative spirit into a work; the philosopher measures his knowing-spirit by the real. It is by leaning for support, at first, on the intellect of his age, by concentrating all its languors and fires in a single focal point, and then driving it to the limit, that the artist has the opportunity to refashion the whole mass. But the concern of the philosopher is, above all, to seize upon the object, to cling to it desperately, with such tenacity that a break-through is finally effected in the mass which confronts him, achieving a regrouping of forces and a new course of action. (*DK*, p. 3; CW 7, p. 3)

11. The Greek thinkers had set out with high hopes of knowing everything, and climbing the sky of wisdom in a single step. As a result of this immoderate ambition, and because they lacked discipline and restraint in handling ideas, their concepts were embroiled in a confused strife, an interminable battle of opposing probabilities. The immediate and obvious result of these attempts at philosophising seemed the bankruptcy of speculative thought. It is not, therefore, surprising that this period of elaboration produced a crisis in the history of thought, at which an intellectual disease imperilled the very existence of philosophic speculation. This intellectual disease was sophistry, that is to say, the corruption of philosophy. (*IP*, p. 47)

12. Philosophers imbued with Cartesian principles call every authentic realism a "naive realism." And although it is pointed out to them that when such a designation is applied to Aristotelian-Thomistic realism it is itself childish, they will not be undeceived because, as far as they are concerned, naiveté is to start with an act of knowledge about things rather than with an act of knowledge about knowledge. Good! The mind does, indeed, have to choose its path right from the start; an original decision is demanded of it, and it is a decision that will dictate its entire fate. But the first act of reflection shows that the person who has made his choice in keeping with nature, and without challenging the first light shed upon his heart (I mean the first objective evidence), has chosen wisely. And it indicates that the person who has made his choice against nature in demanding a second light before following the first one, has chosen absurdly: for he would fain start with what comes second.

One cannot think about a "thought thing" until after one has thought about a "thinkable thing"—a thing "good for existing," i.e., at least, a possible real. The first thing thought about is being independent of the mind. The *cogitatum* of the first *cogito* is not *cogitatum,* but *ens.* We do not eat what has been eaten; we eat bread. To separate object from thing, the objective *logos* from metalogical being, is to violate the nature of intellect, to flee from the first evidence of direct intuition, and at the same time, to mutilate reflexive intuition (the very reflexive intuition on which we would make everything depend) in the very first of its immediate data. Idealism sets an original sin against the light at the beginning of the whole philosophical edifice. (***DK,* pp. 107–8; CW 7, pp. 114–15**)

13. As his contemporary Heraclitus was the slave of *change,* Parmenides was the slave of *being.* He had eyes for one thing alone: what is is, and cannot not be; being is, non-being is not. Parmenides was thus the first philosopher who abstracted and formulated the principle of *identity* or non-contradiction, the first principle of all thought. (***IP,* p. 45**)

14. Anguish is no more than one form of the spiritual experience of the philosopher. In proportion as he goes forward, the philosopher moves through other states: he knows the intellectual joy (into which nothing human penetrates) of decisive intuitions and illuminating certainties—a sort of intoxication with the object which is almost cruel—and sometimes the freezing exaltation of the glance that denudes and destroys; and sometimes the revulsion of handling those animal skeletons and bones of the dead of which Goethe speaks; and sometimes the ardour which wounds him on every side for the infinite search which men carry on and for all captive truths; sometimes the pity for error with its ambiguities; and sometimes the great solitude or distress of the spirit; and sometimes the sweetness of going forward in the maternal night. What I should like to stress is that the spiritual experience of the philosopher is the nourishing soil of philosophy; that without it there is no philosophy; and that, even so, spiritual experience does not, or must not, enter into the intelligible texture of philosophy. The pulp of the fruit must consist of nothing but the truth. (*EE,* pp. 146–47)

15. The philosopher in society witnesses to the supreme dignity of thought; he points to what is eternal in man, and stimulates our thirst for pure knowledge and disinterested knowledge, for knowledge of those fundamentals—about the nature of things and the nature of the mind, and man himself, and God—which are superior to, and independent of, anything we can make or produce or create—and to which all our practice is appendent, because we think before acting and nothing can limit the range of thought: our practical decisions depend on the stand we take, on the ultimate questions that human thought is able to ask. That is why philosophical systems, which are directed toward no practical use and application, have ... such an impact on human history. (*UP,* p. 7)

16. Needless to say, a philosopher may set aside his philosophical pursuits and become a man of politics. But what of a philosopher who remains simply a philosopher, and acts only as a philosopher?

On the one hand we may suppose, without fear of being wrong, that he lacks the experience, the information, and the competence which are proper to a man of action: it would be a misfortune for him to undertake to legislate in social and political matters in the name of pure logic, as Plato did.

But, on the other hand, the philosopher cannot—especially in our time—shut himself up in an ivory tower; he cannot help being concerned about human affairs, in the name of philosophy itself and by reason of the very values which philosophy has to defend and maintain. He has to *bear witness* to these values, every time they are attacked, as in the time of Hitler when insane racist theories worked to provoke the mass murder of Jews, or as today before the threat of enslavement by communist despotism. The philosopher must bear witness by expressing his thoughts and telling the truth as he sees it. This may have repercussions in the domain of politics; it is not, in itself, a political action—it is simply applied philosophy.

It is true that the line of demarcation is difficult to draw. This means that no one, not even philosophers, can avoid taking risks, when justice or love are at stake, and when one is face to face with the strict command of the Gospel: *haec oportuit facere, et illa non omittere,* "these ought ye to have done, and not to leave the other undone." (***UP**,* pp. 14–15)

17. Here we touch upon one of the primary roots of Kant's system: namely his theory of judgment and of the concept, an arbitrary presupposition resulting from a reaction against sensualistic nominalism, which reaction was itself incapable of rising above nominalism, and consequently able only to aggravate the error. If Kant had discerned the true nature of judgment he would have understood that in an existential judgment of experience, the mind, compelled by sensory intuition, declares to be identical in reality two notions, two concepts each of which has its own intelligible content; and that the intelligible content of the predicate "existing" being an essentially analogous object of thought, the mind is justified in applying this predicate, purified of all empirical significance, to purely intelligible subjects which experience, in the light of the first intellectual principles, requires as being its *raison d'être.* (***DD**,* p. 141)

18. It is quite true that economic conditions, like all conditions generally of the material order, are of basic importance in the destiny of spiritual activities among men, that they have a constant tendency to enfeoff them, and that in the history of culture they make one body with them. From this point of view, the cynicism of Marx, like that of Freud, has brought many truths to light. But it is nonsense to take material conditioning, no matter how real it may be, as the prime determining reason—were it only as regards its historical existence—of a spiritual activity, and as that which above everything else discloses its significance for human life. (***IH**,* p. 49; ***CW** 11,* pp. 183–84)

CHAPTER THIRTY

PHILOSOPHY

1. Thus philosophy, alone among the branches of human knowledge, has for its object everything which is. But in everything which is it investigates only the first causes. The other sciences, on the contrary, have for their object some particular province of being, of which they investigate only the secondary causes or proximate principles. That is to say, of all branches of human knowledge philosophy is the most sublime.

It follows further that philosophy is in strictest truth *wisdom*, for it is the province of wisdom to study the highest causes: *sapientis est altissimas causas considerare*. It thus grasps the entire universe in a small number of principles and enriches the intellect without burdening it. (***IP*, pp. 79–80**)

2. Philosophy, therefore, and particularly the first philosophy or metaphysics, because it is wisdom and the supreme science, judges, governs, and defends the other sciences. But the ruler is certainly not dependent upon those whom he governs. We therefore conclude that philosophy is independent of the inferior sciences, or at any rate depends on them only in the sense that a superior, when he is not strong enough to be self-sufficient, depends on the servants or instruments which he employs. It was for this reason that Aristotle regarded philosophy as the science pre-eminently *free*. (***IP*, p. 88**)

3. The trouble is that one can no more philosophize with non-philosophical instruments than paint with a flute or a piano. (*UP*, p. 54)

4. Philosophy, taken in itself, is above utility. And for this very reason philosophy is of the utmost necessity for men. It reminds them of the supreme utility of those things which do not deal with means, but with ends. For men do not live only by bread, vitamins, and technological discoveries. They live by values and realities which are above time, and are worth being known for their own sake; they feed on that invisible food which sustains the life of the spirit, and which makes them aware, not of such or such means at the service of their life, but of their very reasons for living—and suffering, and hoping. (*UP*, pp. 6–7)

5. We succeed in gaining an intimate knowledge of the real in philosophy, wherein we study things not from the particular point of view of their specific diversity, but from the universal point of view of transcendental being soaked into them. (*DK*, p. 31; **CW 7, p. 34**)

6. Modern philosophies grow out of what has gone before, but rather by way of contradiction: the scholastics by way of agreement and further development. The result is that philosophy in our day is like a series of episodes simply stuck end to end, not like a tree where each is organically related to each and all to the roots. But given all that, I grant you that even those who hold it to be the primary duty of every thinker worth his salt to give men a *new* conception of the universe, cannot, in fact, advance a step or set forth their discoveries without making use of the results of those who have gone before them; so true is it that the labour of the mind, by its very nature, demands a collaboration running through the years. (*TS*, pp. 5–6)

7. It is non-sense to think of making the bearing or posture of Jacob in the night of his combat with the angel the attitude of metaphysics, with its special way of coming to grips with the law of things. It is non-sense to think of making the bearing or posture of Minerva in her search for causes the attitude of faith, with its special manner of tackling the dialogue with the God of faith. We do not philosophise in the posture of dramatic singularity; we do not save our souls in the posture of theoretical universality and detachment from self for the purpose of knowing. (*EE*, p. 125)

8. Insuperable disagreements which divide philosophers . . . do indeed exist. But in one sense there is more continuity and stability in philosophy than in science. For a new scientific theory completely changes the very manner in which the former ones posed the question, whereas philosophical problems remain always the same, in one form or another. Nay more, basic philosophical ideas, once they have been discovered, become permanent acquisitions in the philosophical heritage. They are used in various, even opposite ways: they are still there. (*UP,* **p. 6**)

9. Whoever insists on being "modern," and believes that the era of freedom began with Descartes, the development of philosophy in the last three centuries ends in a truly tragic alternative. While metaphysics, obstinately intent on deducing evidence, vainly seeks its equilibrium, passes from system to system and finally proclaims its total helplessness, positive science alone—and by that we mean the physico-mathematical knowledge of matter—imposing itself upon the world by the extraordinary abundance of its actual results and by its utilitarian applications, appears to be possessed of the rules of truth. The only philosophy which seems to rest on tested principles is the philosophy which that physico-mathematical knowledge has in tow, and which is a mere automatic generalization of it. Moreover, this mechanistic philosophy lays open claim to sovereignty, declares itself ready to explain everything by certain infinitesimal beginnings taken from matter or from sense experience, and treats with the conqueror's scorn the timorous little vestiges of spiritualism which some distinguished minds try to set up against it, begging the favor of a few conclusions, after having capitulated on all the principles. That, then, is the last word of intelligence! If one aspires to the absolute and refuses to be satisfied with half-measures, there remains only the choice between two doctrines: either radical mechanism, the abandoning of all that makes thought worthy of being thought; or radical skepticism, which is intellectual despair and the abandoning of thought. (*BPT,* **pp. 65–66**)

10. It would be imprudent to judge philosophy by philosophers, art by artists, the ideal by idealists, order by officials, and piety by the pious! (*TS,* **p. 182**)

11. Are materialist mechanicism and agnostic relativism, which claim to annex the positive sciences, the last word of philosophy? And is it not possible to discover, equi-distant from materialism and rhetorical or *a priori* spiritualism, a philosophy which attains the absolute, the absolute truth, and which thus restores the great spiritualist theses, without however contradicting in any way the acquisitions of science, and keeping constant contact with experience?—These questions may seem elementary. But precisely because they are elementary, they are fundamental. And we are bound to confess that the philosophy issuing from Descartes and Kant is not capable of solving them satisfactorily. (***BPT*, p. 121**)

12. Existential existentialism was thus like a man struggling in the coils of a gigantic reptile. By an astounding mistake, and as the effect of an inevitable illusion, this protest of a faith, caught in a Babylonian captivity, came forth into the world dressed in the livery of Babylon. It was a religious protest *in the guise of a philosophy*—a philosophy directed against the professionals of philosophy; and this was, of course, most comforting. But also (and here an entire tragedy was involved), it was a philosophy *against philosophy*. (***EE*, p. 126**)

13. The philosophy that is not ancient is very soon old. If a philosophy belongs to the present moment *by its substance and its principles,* surely you must see that its very newness (not being a newness of growth or of achievement, but only a matter of being newly born in time), is a sign that it is inferior to the intellect in that it is subject to the law of matter: for time is a measure of matter's changing. It is true, of course, that philosophy is a human thing: it is in time by the subject wherein it resides—in the philosopher, that is. It must, then, be of the present moment *by its application to the real and by the use made of it.* If it is not ... it will have no hold upon men. (***TS*, p. 58**)

14. It is no great accomplishment for a philosophy to be dramatic, it need only give way to its human penchants. But there are two ways for a philosophy not to be so: either not to appreciate the drama of human life, or to be too keenly aware of it. (***CP*, p. 48**)

15. There is no worse philosophy than a philosophy that despises nature. A knowledge that despises what is, is itself nothing; a cherry between the teeth holds within it more mystery than the whole of idealist metaphysics. A philosophical distortion of the maxims of the saints cut off from love, in which alone these maxims have their meaning, would lead one to think that creatures are nothing so that one might love nothing, and to humiliate them before God in order to give oneself the right not to render them their due. (*DK,* pp. 335–36; CW 7, pp. 356–57)

16. We must detest Manichean idealism which, in condemning the humility of our nature, at the same time destroys any sublimity in it. It is one and the same activity in us, essentially immanent and virtually productive, that engenders concept and perceives what is, that perceives in conceiving and conceives in perceiving. It conceives in order to perceive; it abstracts, it enunciates, it reasons in order to perceive. All, in it, that is elaboration and disposition of ideas is regulated by intellection and is a *means* of intellection. (*BPT,* p. 33)

17. What is the cultural significance of idealism? It carries along with it a sort anthropocentric optimism of thought. Optimism, because thought is a god who unfolds himself, and because things either conform to it, or do not even exist apart from it. What drama could possibly occur? Either there is no being to set off against thought, or there is only being completely docile to thought. An optimism which is anthropocentric, because the thought in question is the thought of man; it is around human thought that objects revolve. All is well for that thought; and all will be better and better.

But this optimism is, if I may say so, committed to suicide; for it presupposes a rupture with being, and finally, in spite of Descartes' personal intentions and in spite of the efforts of his immediate successors, it supposes an eviction of the ontological. There we have the great, the primordial Cartesian break. Man shut up within himself is condemned to sterility, because his thought lives and is nourished only upon the things that God has made. Man the centre of an intelligible universe which he has created in his own image, himself loses his centre of gravity and his own consistence, for his consistence is to be the image of God. He is in the middle of a desert. (*DD,* pp. 171–72)

18. The mind knows that its first duty is not to sin against the light. It must subject to the most careful verification its conceptual equipment, but it cannot prevent itself from rushing toward being. No matter what the price. It is required of the mind not to fall into error, but first of all, it is required of the mind that it *see*. (***RT*, p. 61**)

19. What, then, is a fact? It is a well-established existential truth. A certain connection in the objects of our concepts exists in the real. That very fact implies that this existence confronts a mind which can grasp therein those objects. A fact engaging human knowledge is not created by the human mind. A fact is given. But it is given to someone. And if it is given, it is received. A stone is not given to a stone. A fact is given to a mind. That is to say, it is discerned and judged. To conceive it as a pure and simple copy of the external real, devoid of any discrimination, is a deceptive simplification due to the unconscious materialism of the imagination. (***DK*, p. 51; CW 7, p. 55**)

20. The fact remains that, if the distinctions are made that should be made ... between the nature of philosophy and its status in the subject, we have to affirm that of itself philosophy is at once a purely rational knowledge and intrinsically depends only upon principles belonging to the natural order, and that it can only find the human conditions required for its full development in truth if it grows up under the heaven of faith. (***DK*, p. 287; CW 7, p. 306**)

CHAPTER THIRTY-ONE

POETRY AND THE POET

1. A true sense of the common good understands that Art and Poetry, though or rather *because* they deal with an object independent in itself of the rules and standards of human life and the human community, play an essential and indispensable part in the existence of mankind. Man cannot live a genuine human life except by participating to some extent in the supra-human life of the spirit, or of what is eternal in him. He needs all the more desperately poets and poetry as they keep aloof from the sad business and standards of the rational animal's maintenance and guidance, and give testimony to the freedom of the spirit. It is precisely to the extent to which poetry is useless and *disengaged* that poetry is necessary, because it brings to men a vision of reality-beyond-reality, an experience of the secret meanings of things, an obscure insight into the universe of beauty, without which men could neither live nor live morally. For, as St. Thomas put it, "nobody can do without delectation for long. That is why he who is deprived of spiritual delectations goes over to the carnal." And St. Theresa of Avila used to say that even for contemplatives, if there were no poetry life would not be tolerable. Leave, then, the artist to his art: he serves the community better than the engineer or the tradesman. (*RA,* **pp. 85–86**)

2. Nothing is more real, and more necessary to poetry, and to any great work, than inspiration. And nothing is more natural, and more *internal.* (*CI,* p. 243)

3. Great as the poetry of the Theatre and the poetry of the Novel may be, the poetry of the Poem or the Song is by nature and will always remain the prime and most spiritual type of poetry, and the dearest to the human soul, because it is closest to creative intuition. (*CI,* p. 399)

4. It is quite true that things are better in the mind than in themselves, that they take on their full proportions only when they have been uttered by a mind, and that they themselves crave to be taken up into the heaven of thought—metaphysics or poetry—where they proceed to live above time, and with a life that is universal. What would have become of the Trojan War without Homer? Unfortunate are the adventures which are not told. (*AS,* p. 127)

5. Just as the saint completes in himself the work of the Passion, even so the poet completes the work of creation; he co-operates in divine balancings, he moves mysteries about; he is in natural sympathy with the secret powers that play about in the universe.

Poetry, in its pure spiritual essence, transcends all technique, transcends art itself; one can be a poet and still produce nothing, just as a child baptized has sanctifying grace without yet acting morally. Metaphysical ratio: poetry is to art what grace is to the moral life. (*AF,* p. 90)

6. Creation forms at different levels in the spiritual substance of the soul, everyone by this very fact confesses what he is; the more the poet grows, the deeper the level of creative intuition descends into the density of his soul. Where formerly he could be moved to song, he can do nothing now, he is obliged to dig down deeper. One would say that the shock of suffering and vision break down, one after another, the living sensitive partitions behind which his identity is hiding. He is harassed, he is tracked down, he is destroyed pitilessly. Woe to him if in retiring into himself he finds a heaven devastated, inaccessible; he can do nothing then but sink into his hell. But if at the end of ends the poet turns silent, it is not that there is ever achieved the growth of which we speak, it is not that of itself the song does not still ask to be more deeply born in him, less distant from the creative uncreated spirituality, archtype of all creative life, it is that the last partition of the heart has been attained, and the human substance consumed.

I have spoken of the poet, but of the one that every artist should be, and not only of the one who versifies. And here, again, it is the composer who in truth offers to the speculations of the philosopher a privileged experience. Less bound to the universe of human ideas and human values than he who creates with the vocables of the language of men, less bound than the painter and the sculptor to the forms and images of things, less bound than the architect to the conditions for the use of the thing to be created, it is in the composer that are versified in the clearest fashion the metaphysical exigencies of poetry. So that when *he* falls short of them, the gap is most apparent. None other than the maker of operas could instruct a Nietzsche by so perfectly decisive a disappointment. (*AP,* pp. 91–92)

7. If modern poetry must become more ontological, get into closer contact with being, with human and terrestrial reality (and perhaps also with divine reality), it is not by cares foreign to its nature and well-intentional zeal that it will accomplish this, but only through that lyric element which is almost as hidden as grace, hidden in the deepest of creative sources. (*SO,* p. 64)

8. How essential to poetry is the subjectivity of the poet. I do not mean the inexhaustible flux of superficial feelings in which the sentimental reader recognizes his own cheap longings . . . I mean subjectivity in its deepest ontologic sense, that is, the substantial totality of the human person, a universe unto itself, which the spirituality of the soul makes capable of containing itself through its own immanent acts, and which, at the center of all the subjects that it knows as objects, grasps only itself as subject. In a way similar to that in which divine creation presupposes the knowledge God has of His own essence, poetic creation presupposes, as a primary requirement, a grasping, by the poet, of his own subjectivity, in order to create. The poet's aim is not to know himself. He is not a guru. To attain, through the void, an intuitive experience of the existence of the Self, of the Atman, in its pure and full actuality, is the specific aim of natural mysticism. It is not the aim of

poetry. The essential need of the poet is to create; but he cannot do so without passing through the door of the knowing, as obscure as it may be, of his own subjectivity. For poetry means first of all an intellective act which by its essence is creative, and forms something into being instead of being formed by things: and what can such an intellective act possibly express and manifest in producing the work if not the very being and substance of the one who creates? Thus it is that the works of painting or sculpture or music or poetry the closer they come to the sources of poetry the more they reveal, one way or another, the subjectivity of the author. (***CI*, pp. 113–14**)

9. It is true that poetry, as Aristotle said, is more philosophic than history. Not, surely, with respect to its mode or manner of knowing, for this mode is altogether existential, and the thing grasped is grasped as nonconceptualizable. But with respect to the very thing grasped, which is not a contingent thing in the mere fact of its existence, but in its infinite openness to the riches of being, and as a sign of it. For poetic intuition makes things which it grasps diaphanous and alive, and populated with infinite horizons. As grasped by poetic knowledge, things abound in significance, and swarm with meanings. (***CI*, pp. 126–27**)

10. The revelation of the Self is a blessing inasmuch as it takes place in the genuine line of poetry. It becomes a curse when it shifts from the line of poetry, and of the creative Self in the line of spiritual communication, to the line of man's material individuality, and of the self-centered ego, busy with self-interest and power. The egoism of man enters the sphere of the poetic act, and feeds on this very act. And being there in an unnatural state, it grows boundlessly. (***CI*, p. 145**)

11. Great poets and thinkers are the foster-fathers of intelligence. Cut off from them, we are simply barbarous. (***EM*, p. 85**)

12. The activity of man in the present order is divided into "poetic" activity, or activity concerned with the making of things (which has for its object what the Schoolmen call the *factibile*, the thing to be made or produced); and ethical or moral activity which has for its object what the Schoolmen call the *agibile*, or acts to be done. (***FMW*, p. 196; *CW* 11, p. 102**)

13. The simple-minded idolatry that the majority of artists bestow on their work, which becomes triply sacred once they have produced it, is proof of man's essential creative weakness. God does not adore His works. Nevertheless He knows they are good. He does not cling to them, He lets them be spoiled by man; even the gratuitous marvels of the supernatural order, charismata, prophecies, miracles, the purest gambols of His poetry, are as fires too beautiful wasted in the night. But there is one good to which He clings; souls, the pasture of His love. Do you think that He weighs man's greatest masterpiece against the smallest amount of charity in a soul? Neither art nor poetry justifies any want of sensitivity towards Him. (**AS, pp. 145–46**)

14. Creative innocence is in no way moral innocence. It is . . . of an ontologic, not a moral nature. It has essentially to do with the intuition of the poet, not with his loves. And of the two things which alone make life worth living, love is more valuable than intuition when it transforms us into something better than we are, but intuition is not liable to all kinds of illusion and moral defilement, as love is: because intuition deals with knowledge (creative knowledge in the case of the poet) and, *qua* intuition, never misses the mark. (**CI, p. 374**)

15. The inspiration of the poet, the love of the mystic . . . are, in Freud's opinion, only transformations and masks of animal instinct, the diverted path by which a sensuality, inhibited in its normal exercise, satisfies itself in an insidious and veiled manner: all human exhilaration is specifically sensual. (**SP, p. 129**)

CHAPTER THIRTY-TWO

POLITICS, SOCIETY, AND THE STATE

1. The aim of political society, as of all human society, implies a certain work to be done in common. Here is one property bound up with the rational and human character of society in its true sense: this work to be done is the objective reason for association and for consent (implicit or explicit) to the common life. Men assemble for a reason, for an object, for a task to be done.

In the bourgeois-individualist type of society there is no common work to do, nor is there any form of communion. Each one asks only that the State protect his individual freedom of profit against the possible encroachments of other men's freedoms. (*RM*, **p. 39**)

2. In reality men can only find communion in an object. That is why supreme communion is fulfilled for them in the knowledge and love of Someone, Who is the Truth itself and Love subsisting. And that is why, on the earthly plane of our rational nature, the political community is realized by virtue of an object, which is a task to be done in common. (*RM*, **p. 41**)

3. Political philosophy, being thus directed not toward pure and simple freedom of choice, nor toward the realization of Freedom of power and

dominion over the external order of nature and history, but toward the realization and progress of the spiritual freedom of individual persons, will make of justice and friendship the true foundations of social life. (***FMW,*** **p. 45; CW 11, p. 26**)

4. A political philosophy based on reality must struggle against two opposing errors: on the one hand against an optimistic pseudo-idealism that extends from Rousseau to Lenin, that feeds men with false hopes, and that, while pretending to hasten it, distorts the emancipation to which they aspire; and on the other hand, against a pessimistic pseudo-realism that extends from Machiavelli to Hitler and that bends man under violence, retaining only the animality which enslaves him. (***RM,*** **p. 58**)

5. [Man] is a political animal because he is a reasonable animal, because his reason seeks to develop with the help of education, through the teaching and the co-operation of other men, and because society is thus required to accomplish human dignity. (***SP,*** **p. 55**)

6. In the eyes of a sound political philosophy there is no sovereignty, that is, no natural and inalienable right to *transcendent* or *separate* supreme power in political society. Neither the Prince nor the King nor the Emperor were really sovereign, though they bore the sword and the attributes of sovereignty. Nor is the State sovereign; nor are even the people sovereign. God alone is sovereign. (***MS,*** **p. 24**)

7. Machiavelli never negates the values of morality, he knows them and recognizes them as they have been established by ancient wisdom, he occasionally praises virtuous leaders (that is, those whose virtues were made successful by circumstances). He knows that cruelty and faithlessness are shameful, he never calls evil good or good evil. He simply denies to moral values—and this is largely sufficient to corrupt politics—any application in the political field. He teaches his prince to be cruel and faithless, according to the case, that is, to be evil according to the case, and when he writes that the prince must learn how not to be good, he is perfectly aware that not to be good is to be bad. Hence his difference from many of his disciples, and the special savour, the special power of intellectual stimulation of his cynicism. But hence also his special sophistry, and the mantle of civilized intelligence with which he unintentionally covered and veiled for a time the deepest meaning, the wild meaning, of his message. (*RR,* **p. 139**)

8. In the sphere of private life we are called upon to exercise the natural and the supernatural virtues of Christian life. But in the sphere of social and political life, we are also called upon to exercise the natural virtues (guided and elevated by the supernatural ones) which properly have to do with that sphere, and by means of which the rules of Christian justice and charity may be introduced into it. (*SP,* **p. 185**)

9. Only in the Kingdom of God has the devil no part. In the world, and in every nation of the world, he has his part. The question, for a given nation, is whether it likes or dislikes the fact, and whether it strives to turn evil to account or to get clear of it. (*RON,* **pp. 63–64**)

10. What makes the study of Machiavelli extremely instructive for a philosopher, is the fact that nowhere is it possible to find a more purely artistic conception of politics. And here is his chief philosophical fault, if it is true that politics belongs to the field of the "praktikon" (to do), not of the "poietikon" (to make), and is by essence a branch—the principal branch, according to Aristotle—of ethics. Politics is distinct from individual ethics as one branch from another branch on the same tree. It is a special and specific part of ethics, and it carries within itself an enormous amount of art and technique, for the role played by the physical elements to be known and utilized, the forces and resistances to be calculated, the role played by the *making*, or by the work to perform successfully, the role played by the moulding intelligence and imagination is much greater in political than in individual or even familial ethics. But all this amount of art and technique is organically, vitally and intrinsically subordinated to the ethical energies which constitute politics, that is to say, art is there in no manner autonomous, art is there embodied in, and encompassed with, and lifted up by ethics, as the physico-chemical activities in our body are integrated in our living substance and superelevated by our vital energies. When these merely physico-chemical activities are liberated and become autonomous, there is no longer a living organism, but a corpse. Thus, merely artistic

politics, liberated from ethics, that is, from the practical knowledge of man, from the science of human acts, from truly human finalities and truly human doings, is a corpse of political wisdom and political prudence. (*RR,* pp. 139–40)

11. State and politics, when truly separated from ethics, are the realm of those demoniacal principalities of which St. Paul spoke; the Pagan Empire is the Empire of Man making himself God: the diametrical opposite of the kingdom of Redemptive Incarnation. (*RR,* p. 146)

12. May I repeat that a certain hypermoralism, causing Political Ethics to be something impracticable and merely ideal, is as contrary to this very Ethics as Machiavellianism is, and finally plays the game of Machiavellianism, as conscientious objectors play the game of the conquerors. The purity of means consists in not using means morally bad in themselves; it does not consist in refusing pharisaically any exterior contact with the mud of human life, and it does not consist in waiting for a morally aseptic world before consenting to work in the world, nor does it consist in waiting, before saving one's neighbor, who is drowning, to become a saint, so as to escape any risk of false pride in such a generous act. (*RR,* p. 161)

13. But things go entirely bad when at moments of profound trouble the political parties of the Right and the Left cease to form a more or less spirited team held in check by a firm political reason and become nothing but exasperated passionate complexes carried along by their political ideal myth with political reason henceforth nothing but a service of passion. To be neither of the Right nor of the Left then signifies that one knows how to keep his reason. (*LI,* p. 132)

14. Force is necessary in civil communities because of men who are violent and inclined to vice but it has a pedagogic office and ought to lead in the direction of freedom. It is only a substitute for those creations of freedom that we call virtues. The good man like the Prince has no contact with the bloody hand of the law; he knows only its kind eyes, for he fulfills the law not out of compulsion but out of love and of his own free will, *voluntarius non coactus.* (*FMW,* p. 79; CW 11, p. 43)

15. The whole order of human life is not ready-made in nature and in things; it is an order of freedom; it has not just to be discovered and accepted: it has also to be made. (***FMW*, p. 80; CW 11, p. 43**)

16. Because social life, while postulated by nature, is the work of reason and virtue and implies, however opposed it may be, a movement of progressive conquest of man over nature and over himself, social equality is not something ready-made; it implies in itself a certain dynamism. Like liberty, it is itself an end to struggle for, and with difficulty, and at the price of a constant tension of the energies of the spirit. If, by postulates of nature, it is, in its most general forms, basic and primary, social equality is yet only a seed which must develop and which works in the direction of fruition. It requires not only the exercise of distributive justice in the temporal community; it requires as wide a measure as possible of free participation by all in the necessary good things, material and spiritual, and that redistribution to persons of the common good. . . . It requires the progress of social justice; the organic development of institutions of law; the participation, in more and more extensive degrees, of persons as such in political life; the transition to conditions which would really offer to each an equal opportunity (equal in the proportional sense) to bring his gifts to fruit, and which would permit the formation of an aristocracy born of personal work, that pays back the good effects of its labour for common use; the sharing more and more by all in the benefits of culture and the mind, and in that inner liberty which is given by mastery over self and knowledge of the truth. (***RT*, p. 29**)

17. Yet we must not say that the aim of society is the individual good (or the mere collection of individual goods) of each person who constitutes it! This formula would dissolve society *as such* for the benefit of its parts, and would lead to the 'anarchy of atoms'. It would mean either a frankly anarchic conception or the old disguised anarchic conception of individualistic liberalism—according to which the entire duty of society consists in seeing that the freedom of each should be respected, though this permit the strong freely to oppress the feeble.

The end of society is its *common good*, the good of the body politic. But if one fails to grasp the fact that the good of the body politic is a common good of *human persons*—as the social body itself is a whole made up of human persons—this formula may lead in its turn to other errors of the collectivist or totalitarian type. The common good of society is neither a simple collection of private goods, nor a good belonging to a whole which (as in the case of the species in relation to its individual members) draws the parts to itself, as if they were pure means to serve itself alone. The common good is the *good human* life of the multitude, of a multitude of *persons*; it is their communion in the good life; it is therefore common *to the whole and to the parts*, on whom it flows back and who must all benefit from it. (*SP,* pp. 55–56)

18. The end of the state is the common good, which is not only a collection of advantages and utilities, but also rectitude of life, an end good in itself, which the old philosophers called *bonum honestum,* the intrinsically worthy good. For, on one hand, it is a thing good in itself to insure the existence of the multitude. And, on the other hand, it is the just and morally good existence of the community which may thus be insured. It is only on this condition, of being in accordance with justice and with moral good, that the common good is what it is: the good of a people, the good of a city, and not the 'good' of an association of gangsters or of murderers. That is why perfidy, the contempt of treaties and of sworn faith, political murder or unjust war—all these can be *useful* to a government, and procure, if only for a time, *advantages* to the peoples who have recourse to them; but they debase and destroy, as far as in them lies, the *common good* of these peoples.

The common good is a thing ethically good. And this common good itself includes, as an essential element, the greatest possible development of human persons, of those persons who form the multitude, united, in order to constitute a community, according to relations not only of power, but also of justice. Historical conditions, and the present inferior state of humanity's development, make it difficult for social life fully to attain its end. But the end toward which it tends . . . is to procure to the multitude the common good in such a fashion that the concrete person gains a real independence regarding nature, which is insured through the economic guarantees of labour and of property, through political rights, the civil virtues, and culture of the mind. (*SP,* pp. 56–57)

19. The liberty of the individual must be protected; man must work at subjugating material nature by his industry; the community must be strong and must defend itself effectively against disintegrating forces and against its possible enemies. All these things are necessary, but they do not define the essential and primordial aim of political association. *The political task towards which all this must tend is the good human life of the multitude, the betterment of the conditions of human life itself,* the internal improvement and the progress—material, of course, but also and principally moral and spiritual—thanks to which man's attributes are to be realized and made manifest in history. (*RM,* **p. 43**)

20. Thus, materialistic conceptions of life and of the world—philosophies which do not recognize in man the eternal, the spiritual element—are incapable of guiding man in the building up of a society, because these philosophies are incapable of respecting the exigencies of the person, and this means that they cannot understand the nature of society.

If this spiritual, this eternal element, is recognized, then one also recognizes the aspiration immanent in the person to surpass, by reason of what is highest in it, both the life and the conditions of temporal societies. But then, and at the same time, temporal society can be built up according to the proper order of its being. Its nature as a society of persons is understood, and the natural tendency of the person towards society, and the fact of its belonging morally and legally to the society of which it is part, are equally understood. (*SP,* **p. 65**)

21. A vitally Christian social renewal will be a work of sanctity or it will be nothing: a sanctity, that is, turned toward the temporal, the secular, the profane. Has not the world known leaders of the people who were saints? If a new Christendom arises in history, it will be the work of such a kind of sanctity. (***IH,* p. 122; CW 11, p. 229**)

22. It is important to stress the fact that even in the natural order itself the human person transcends the State, to the extent that man has a destiny superior to time, and sets in motion or ventures anything whatsoever which is connected in him with his destiny. (*RM,* **pp. 74–75**)

23. Politics deal with matters and interests of the world and they depend upon passions natural to man and upon reason.... Without goodness, love and charity, all that is best in us—even divine faith, but passions and reason much more so—turns in our hands to an unhappy use. The point is that right political experience cannot develop in people unless passions and reason are oriented by a solid basis of collective virtues, by faith and honor and thirst for justice. The point is that without the evangelical instinct and the spiritual potential of a living Christianity, political judgement and political experience are ill protected against the illusions of selfishness and fear; without courage, compassion for mankind, and the spirit of sacrifice the ever-thwarted advance toward an historical ideal of generosity and fraternity is not conceivable. (*CD,* pp. 63–64)

24. Because good life on earth is not the absolute ultimate end of man, and because the human person has a destiny superior to time, political common good involves an intrinsic though indirect reference to the absolutely ultimate end of the human members of society, which is eternal life, in such a way that the political community should temporally, and from below, help each human person in his human task of conquering his final freedom and fulfilling his destiny. (*RR,* p. 143)

25. Societies are like ever-growing organisms, immense and long-living trees, or coral-flowers, which would lead at the same time a moral and human life. And in the order to which they belong, which is that of Time and Becoming, death is natural; human communities, nations, states and civilizations naturally die, and die for all time, as would these morally-living coral-flowers of which I just spoke. Their birth, growth and decay, their health, their diseases, their death, depend on basic physical conditions, in which the specific qualities of moral behavior are intermingled and play and essential part, but which are more primitive than these qualities. Similarly, imprudence or intemperance may hasten the death of a man, self-control may defer this death, yet in any case this man will die. (*RR,* pp. 153–54)

26. The distinction between the things that are Caesar's and the things which are God's is fundamental for the Catholic conscience. This distinction guarantees the freedom of the spiritual with regard to the temporal,

and the freedom of the Church with regard to the State. Yet this distinction is not a separation: divine things should operate in common with human things. From this point of view it should be remembered that the sudden appearance of the gospel in history did not simplify human affairs. But it did accelerate the movement of history and gave it its direction. (**RT, p. 199**)

27. The *intrinsic morality* of the common good ... is not merely a set of advantages and conveniences, but essentially integrity of life, the good and righteous human life of the multitude. Justice and moral righteousness are thus essential to the common good. That is why the common good requires the development of the virtues in the mass of citizens, and that is why every unjust and immoral political act is in itself harmful to the common good and politically bad. Thereby we see what is the root-error of Machiavellianism. We also see how, because of the very fact that the common good is the basis of authority; authority, when it is unjust, betrays its own political essence. An unjust law is not a law. (***RM*, pp. 10–11**)

28. All authority, in so far as it concerns social life, demands to be completed (under some mode or other, which need not be juridical) by power, without which it threatens to become useless and inefficacious among men. All power which is not the expression of authority is iniquitous. Practically, it is normal that the word authority should imply power, and that the word power should imply authority. In so far as it has power, authority descends into the physical order; in so far as it has authority, power is raised to the moral and legal order. To separate power and authority is to separate force and justice. (***SP*, p. 74**)

29. Thus it is true that politics being something intrinsically moral, the first political condition of good politics is that it be just. And it is true at the same time that justice and virtue do not, as a rule, lead us to success in this world. But the antinomy is solved, because on the one hand success in politics is not material power nor material wealth nor world-domination, but the achievement of the common good, with the conditions of material prosperity which it involves. And because, on the other hand, these very conditions of material prosperity, terrible as the ordeals may be which the requirements of justice impose on a people, are not and cannot be put in jeopardy or destroyed by the use of justice itself, if historical duration is taken into account and if the specific effect of this use of justice is considered in itself, apart from the effect of the other factors at play. (**RR, p. 150**)

30. And an even profounder law requires that all men, in so far as they are co-heirs of the common good, should freely have a part in the elementary goods, both material and spiritual, of civilization, to the extent that the community and its organic groups can give their use *free of charge* to human persons who make up this civilization, helping them in this manner to free themselves from the necessities of matter and go forward in the life of reason and virtue. (**RM, p. 109**)

31. The objective spirit of capitalism is a spirit of exaltation of the active and inventive powers, of the dynamism of man and of the initiatives of the individual, but it is a spirit of hatred of poverty and of scorn of the poor man; the poor man exists only as an instrument of a production that yields profits, not as a person. The rich man, on the other hand, exists only as a consumer (for the benefit of the capital that this same production serves), not as a person; and the tragedy of such a world is that, in order to maintain and develop the monster of a usurious economy, it will inevitably be necessary to tend to make of all men consumers, or rich men; but then, if there are no longer any poor men, or instruments, this whole economy stops and dies. (**IH, p. 115; CW 11, p. 224**)

32. Both community and society are ethico-social and truly human, not mere biological realities. But a community is more of a work of nature and more nearly related to the biological; a society is more of a work of reason, and more nearly related to the intellectual and spiritual properties of man. Their inner social essences and their characteristics, as well as their spheres of realization, do not coincide. (**MS, p. 2**)

33. *Living together* does not mean occupying the same place in space. It does not mean, either, being subjected to the same physical or external conditions or pressures or to the same pattern of life; it does not mean *Zusammenmarschieren*. Living together means sharing as men, not as beasts, that

is, with basic free acceptance, in certain common sufferings and in a certain common task.

The reason for which men will to live together is a positive, creative reason. It is not because they fear some danger that men will to live together. Fear of war is not and never has been the reason for which men have wanted to form a political society. Men want to live together and form a political society for a given task to be undertaken in common. When men will have a will to live together in a world-wide society, it will be because they will have a will to achieve a world-wide common task. What task indeed? The conquest of freedom. The point is to have men become aware of that task, and of the fact that it is worthy of self-sacrifice.

Given the human condition, the most significant synonym of *living together* is *suffering together*. When men form a political society, they do not want to share in common suffering out of love for each other. They want to accept common suffering out of love for the common task and the common good. The will to achieve a world-wide common task must therefore be strong enough to entail a will to share in certain common sufferings made inevitable by that task, and by the common good of a world-wide society. What sufferings indeed? Sufferings due to solidarity. (***MS*, p. 207**)

34. For there exists a genuine temporal community of mankind—a deep intersolidarity, from generation to generation, linking together the peoples of the earth—a common heritage and a common fate, which do not concern the building of a particular *civil society,* but of the *civilization,* not the prince, but the culture, not the perfect *civitas* in the Aristotelian sense, but that kind of *civitas,* in the Augustinian sense, which is imperfect and incomplete, made up of a fluid network of human communications, and more existential than formally organized, but all the more real and living and basically important. To ignore this non-political *civitas humani generis* is to break up the basis of political reality, to fail in the very roots of political philosophy, as well as to disregard the progressive trend which naturally tends toward a more organic and unified international structure of peoples. (***RR*, p. 159**)

CHAPTER THIRTY-THREE

PRAYER AND CONTEMPLATION

1. Action is subject to time in which it takes place and disappears and the law which governs action is rapidity. Our Lord preached for three years. But whether one be as inactive as the hermits or as active as the doctors and the apostles, action triumphs over time only so far as it descends from contemplation, which unites the spirit to eternity. Three years in the life of Our Lord inserted into the flux of our continuance the infinite efficiency of His blessed contemplation and so occupy the whole of time to the last day. (*NC,* **p. 110**)

2. Christian contemplation, which is supernatural and the fruit of virtues which directly unite the soul to the inmost life of the Divinity, is a very different thing from contemplation as Aristotle saw it: yet, in fact, grace does no more than reduplicate, lifted to its own level, a relation already given in the natural order: in other words, it is still *by the object* that man is raised above himself and placed in the way of perfection. (*TS,* **p. 20**)

3. Christian contemplation is the fruit of the gift of Wisdom; and this gift, although a *habitus* of the intelligence (thus maintaining its intellectual char-

acter in the order of being, attributed by S. Thomas to the contemplative life), depends essentially on charity, and consequently on sanctifying grace, and causes us to know God by a sort of connaturality—in an affective, experimental and obscure manner, because superior to every concept and image. (**PI, pp. 22–23**)

4. Contemplation is a winged and supernatural thing, free with the freedom of the Spirit of God, more burning than the African sun and more refreshing than the waters of a rushing stream, lighter than birds' down, unseizable, escaping any human measure and disconcerting every human notion, happy to depose the mighty and exalt the lowly, capable of all disguises, of all daring and all timidity, chaste, fearless, luminous and nocturnal, sweeter than honey and more barren than rock, crucifying and beatifying (crucifying above all), and sometimes all the more exalted the less conspicuous it is. (**TP, p. 229**)

5. To wish paradise on earth is stark naïveté. But it is surely better than not to wish any paradise at all. To aspire to paradise is man's grandeur; and how should I aspire to paradise except by beginning to realize paradise here below? The question is to know what paradise is. Paradise consists, as St. Augustine says, in the joy of the Truth. Contemplation is paradise on earth, a crucified paradise. (**SP, p. 153**)

6. If one does not pray one will be able to gain empires and gain much money, but that with regard to that which matters most to man one will not be able to bring anything to consummation. If one does not pray one will be able indeed to be a great painter and a great musician, but there will be something dead in this grandeur. If one does not pray one can be a great philosopher, but one will betray philosophy and will pass by the side of truth—one can be a remarkably erudite and more or less daft expert in theology and in exegesis, one cannot be a great theologian or a great exegete. If one does not pray one cannot advance in the Christian life or receive all the good things, true fraternal charity, interior peace and interior joy, and the dunghill of Job and its vermin, through which one enters here on earth into eternal life.

    ... I would say that for a singularly greater part than we believe, the intentions of Heaven with regard to the earth and its goodness for us are frustrated or paralyzed by our neglect to pray, and especially to pray to the saints of the Church triumphant—exemplary saints and unapparent saints—and especially to pray *for the intentions* of these saints and for the purpose of the Church of Heaven. (**NB, pp. 282–83**)

7. It is *by virtue of the work accomplished in common* in the liturgical celebration, and the sanctification that flows back from it to each of those who have truly participated, that Christians who endeavor to advance toward sanctity are made better able to move forward. What they *have done* during the celebration, they have done as *members* of the whole. What they *receive*, they receive ultimately as *persons*. (***TP,* pp. 218–19**)

8. Purity! There is no purity where the flesh is not crucified, no liberty where there is no love. Man is called to supernatural contemplation: to offer him another night is to rob him of his proper possession. A revolution which does not change the heart is a mere turning over of whitened sepulchres. (***AS,* p. 134**)

9. It is absolutely necessary to shun as the most pernicious of vices the reflex action of the mind, the tendency to come back on ourselves. This evil is very frequent among moderns who are born with a taste for analysis and psychological curiosity. If we look at ourselves instead of looking at God, if we tighten our heart in order to scrutinise the state of our soul and take stock of our petty progress, if we leave our prayer in order to find out if it is good, or abandon our " quietude to see if it is really quiet," as S. Francis de Sales says . . . and agreeing with the descriptions of spiritual writers we lose the whole fruit of our spiritual life, we wander disquieted instead of entering into peace, we take the risk of numberless illusions. We must indeed examine ourselves, but under the eye of God and in order to bewail our faults before him, not to give ourselves the fallacious pleasure of thinking that we securely possess all the ranges of our being and are building by ourselves the edifice of our own perfection. Here, if ever, is where we should say: *he who loses his soul*—i.e. who commits it wholly into the hands of God— *shall save it*. What is demanded of us is, as S. Catherine of Siena taught us, to act manfully, to hate ourselves and to desire God without measure. (***PI,* pp. 26–27**)

10. To be anxious about one's perfection (according to the spirit of Christianity, let us understand) implies no egoist seeking of self, for it is for the love of God, not one's self, that the Christian aspires to become perfect. It is clear besides that one could not advance in the love of God if he were not constantly attentive to conquering himself and to purifying himself of all that which within him constitutes an obstacle to charity. There comes however a moment—when the soul has progressed rather far in the way of the spirit—when, through the effect of the contemplative union itself, concern for one's own perfection, as necessary as it may remain, passes into the background. Then the soul no longer thinks of anything but loving. With those who have reached this stage, holy preoccupation—centered in God, not in self—with one's own perfection ceases to attract the attention of conscious thought. (***LC*, pp. 67–68**)

11. The pure essence of the spiritual is to be found in wholly immanent activity, in contemplation, whose peculiar efficacy in touching the heart of God disturbs no single atom on earth. The closer one gets to the pure essence of the spiritual, the lighter and less palpable, the more spontaneously tapering become the temporal means employed in its service. And that is the condition of their efficacy. Too tenuous to be stopped by any obstacle, they pierce where the most powerful equipment is powerless to pierce. *Propter suam munditiam.* Because of their purity they traverse the world from end to end. Not being ordered to tangible success, involving in their essence no internal need of temporal success, they participate, for the spiritual results to be secured, in the efficacy of the spirit. (***PH*, p. 71**)

12. Without contemplation, every philosophical and theological doctrine, even true, becomes sectarian; all forms of even honourable zeal mere rivalries. Because it makes man one single spirit with God, it really makes unity in man and among men. It proceeds from the gift of wisdom and the beatitude of the peace-makers is the privilege of such a gift. (***NC*, p. 115**)

13. Contemplation is not work, but being of supreme benefit to the community it possesses in an eminent degree the utility that gives work its value. Contemplation is not work, it is fruition, and under one form or another, in a diffuse or in a concentrated state (for words being of specialists, its range is much wider than the word *contemplation* would appear to indicate), it will be found to be bound up with the achievement by the person of its freedom of autonomy. For this reason the wisdom of love that goes with contemplation, whose beginnings are in lowly places but whose peaks are known only to the saints, is rightfully entitled to the highest place in our scale of values. If it is proper for some to devote themselves to it in a special way, all have nonetheless a spiritual call to it in greater or lesser measure even as all have a social call to work; and all have the right to be allowed to share in some way the goods that wisdom dispenses. The week of human toil should issue in the rest of God. It is not the leisure of a few lovers of plain chant but the life of the mass of the people and the whole range of social action and the common works of men that should be crowned with fetes and liturgies and hymns and canticles. (***FMW,*** **pp. 59–60; CW 11, p. 34**)

14. Aristotle was right in sensing that contemplation is in itself better than action and more fitted to what is the most spiritual in man, but Aristotelian contemplation was purely intellectual and theoretical, while Christian contemplation, being rooted in love, superabounds in action. (***EM,*** **p. 54**)

15. Many things are excellent in the emphasis on action and "praxis," for life consists of action. But action and praxis aim at an object, a determining end without which they lose direction and vitality. And life consists, too, for an end which makes it worthy of being lived. Contemplation and self-perfection, in which human life aspires to flower forth, escape the purview of the pragmatic mind. (***EC,*** **p. 12**)

16. If contemplative souls invite silence, it is not because they put pure and simple silence above the spoken word. It is because in silence unbroken by any human word, they hear in their innermost selves the living Word which bestows being upon all that is. (***BPT,*** **p. 162**)

17. The contemplation of the saints is not the line of metaphysics; it is the line of religion. This supreme wisdom does not depend on the intellect's effort in search of the perfection of knowing but on man's gift of his entire self in search of a perfect rectitude in respect to his End. It has nothing to do with the "stultification" which Pascal advised the proud to cultivate (if it is there, it is because pride has already fallen). Rather, it knows so well that it no longer dreams of knowing. This highest kind of knowing supposes that knowing has been forgone.

The saints do not contemplate to know, but to love. They do not love for the sake of loving but for the love of Him whom they love. It is for the love of their first beloved, God, that they aspire to that very union with God that love demands whilst they love themselves only for Him. For them, the end of ends is not to bring exultation to their intellect and nature and thus stop at themselves. It is to do the will of Another, to contribute to the good of the Good. They do not seek their own soul. They lose it; they no longer possess it. If in entering into the mystery of Divine filiation and becoming something of God, they gain a transcendent personality, an independence and a liberty which nothing in the world approaches, it is by forgetting all else so that they do not live, but the Beloved lives in them. (*DK,* p. 10; CW 7, pp. 10–11)

18. The highest natural contemplation of God, angelic or human, cannot be made final happiness except by the love which makes the contemplated object the supreme joy and delight of the one contemplating, just because it is loved above all.

If, furthermore, (always in the hypothesis of pure nature), that final happiness is inadmissible, it is because the intelligent creature is fixed forever in the act of love for God above all. His liberty would have produced that act either in the instant in which his soul was separated from the body or in that in which the pure spirit made his choice. (*SA,* pp. 17–18)

19. The contemplation of the saints does not issue from the spirit of man. It issues from infused grace. (*DK,* p. 11; CW 7, p. 11)

20. Contemplation, being the highest degree of the life of the soul, can not be an instrument of the moral virtues and the operations of active life, but the end to which those things have to be directed as means and dispositions. (*SP,* p. 144)

21. The contemplation of the 'active' souls will be *masked* and inapparent, but they will have contemplative graces; perhaps they will be capable only

of saying rosaries, and mental prayer will bring them only headache or sleep. Mysterious contemplation will not be in their way of praying but in the grace of their behaviour, in their sweet-minded hands, perhaps, or in their way of walking perhaps, or in their way of looking at a poor man or at suffering. (*SP,* p. 148)

22. By the active life, the Ancients understood two distinct things, which yet go together: exterior activity in the midst of men and the effort to attain perfection in the virtues. This moral effort, from which we are never exempt, is ordered to contemplation and union with God to which it disposes the individual; the exterior activity ought—according to the perfected order of human life—to proceed from contemplation and union with God. To the extent that the order of charity still falls short of perfection in man, to that extent exterior activity, not proceeding as it ought from adhesion to God, runs the risk of squandering the substance of man in accordance with the rhythm of matter and impeding the progress by which, under the impulse of God, man builds himself; but at the same time moral effort, combined with that activity, is a necessary means of such progress. So that the active life is useful or harmful, may assist progress or compel retreat, according as one or other of these two aspects is predominant. Things then only go as they ought, if man, while steadily increasing the exercise of the virtues, simplifies his exterior activity, restricts it to what the order of charity requires, rids it of that sort of pertness and presumption, that "vagabond, disorderly and childish manner" which is an illusion of life. (*NC,* p. 111)

23. Contemplative activity is the highest of human activities. It binds man to things divine. It is better than life on the human scale. In supernatural contemplation it takes place according to a mode which is itself superhuman, through the connaturality of love with God and the action of the gifts of the Holy Spirit. It makes of the transfigured soul one spirit with God. It is supreme and active repose, activity essentially theological—received in its entirety from God, an imperfect and crucified beginning of beatitude. To it are ordained the moral virtues, which are at the service of wisdom as the valet is at the service of the king. It is from it, when the soul is perfect, that the works of the active life must overflow, at least as to the mode of their accomplishment. And if a man be called to abandon his contemplation to come to the aid of his brothers or to serve the good of the community, the reason for this call is not at all because the good of the practical order is of itself superior to his solitary contemplation. He must accept it only because the order of charity can require that an urgent necessity of a less elevated good, in the circumstances, be given priority. In truth, such a man if he has entered upon the pathways of the perfect life, would be abandoning rather the conditions and leisure of contemplation than contemplation itself, which would remain, in the recesses of the soul, the source from which his practical activity would descend into human affairs. (*PG,* pp. 26–27)

24. But if the contemplation of the saints be placed upon the summit of human life, must it not then be said that all the activities of man, and civilisation itself, are ordered thereto as to their end? It would appear to be so, says St. Thomas Aquinas (with a note of irony, perhaps). For what is the object of servile work and trade unless to provide the body with the necessaries of life so that it may be in a fit state for contemplation? What end do the moral virtues and prudence serve, if not to appease the turbulence of the passions and secure the interior tranquillity which contemplation needs? What end does the whole government of civil life serve but to assure the exterior tranquillity necessary to contemplation? (*RC,* p. 22)

25. Christian contemplation springs forth from that Spirit which bloweth where it listeth, and one hears His voice and one knows whence He comes or whither He goes. It means that Christian contemplation is not the affair of *specialists* or *technicians*. The active ways through which the soul disposes itself to it are not techniques, but only fallible preparations to receive a free gift, fallible preparations which this gift always transcends. (*SP,* p. 149)

26. It is true that contemplation itself is in fact not work, not a thing of utility. It is a fruit. It is not ordinary leisure; it is a leisure coinciding with the very highest activity of the human substance. According to the profound views of St. Thomas Aquinas, following Aristotle, those who go beyond the socio-temporal life achieve in themselves the supra-social good to which the social tends as to a transcendent term, and by that very act are free from the law of labour. There remains no more for them but Thee and I, Him whom they love, and themselves.

But in virtue of that generosity which is inherent in immanent activity at its highest degrees, loving contemplation overflows as a protection and a benediction to society. And though not itself a useful service or a work, even in the widest meaning of the word, that which is beyond usefulness superabounds thus in a usefulness, in which the notion of work is still realized at the extreme limit of refinement.

Thus, it will be understood . . . that all activities, from manual labour to the gratuitously added utility of contemplative leisure, are fraternal activities, in which the notion of work can be found at very different degrees of analogy. (*SP,* pp. 140–41)

27. It must be remarked that there are in the spirit many activities, discursive activity and activity of desire, which are neither repose nor contemplation.

But while being a labour, this labour of the intelligence and of the heart tends toward contemplation and prepares for it, and in this measure participates in the end to which it is directed. It follows that there is a vast region of life of the spirit, where contemplation is prepared, even outlined, not being, for all that, disengaged from active life and laborious activity. In this wider sense, the philosopher and the poet can be said to be already contemplative on the plane of natural activities.

This should help us to resolve a rather difficult problem. In the order of the Kingdom of God and eternal life, many are surprised by the theological teaching that action is directed to contemplation. In the order of temporal life and terrestrial civilization, the philosopher has to acknowledge that same law of work being directed in the end to contemplation and to the activities of repose. But what activity of repose and what contemplation? The contemplation of the Saints is not a proper and direct end of the political life. It would be more than a paradox to give as a direct end to the life of men, as members of a terrestrial community and as part of the temporal universe of civilization, the transcendent and superterrestrial end which is their absolutely ultimate end as consorts with the Saints, and souls redeemed at a great price; in other words, to solve the question of the workmen's leisure by saying that work has for its end, on the ethico-social plane, mystical union, preluding the ultimate end. And yet, even in the ethico-social order, work is not its own end; its end is rest. Is it then directed to leisure and holidays, understood as a mere cessation of work, a pleasure, or honest pastime, a family party, winter sports, or the movies? If so, it would then be directed to something less noble and less generous than itself. We are far from looking with scorn on rest and relaxation which recreates the worn out human substance. But that rest is but a preparation to a renewed labour, just as sleep prepares for the toils of the day.

In reality, human work, even on the plane of social terrestrial life, must be accomplished with a view to an active and self-sufficient rest, to a terminal activity of an immanent and spiritual order, already participating in some measure in contemplation's supertemporality and generosity. For all that, such active rest is not yet the rest of contemplation properly speaking; it has not yet attained to contemplation. Let us say it is the active rest of the culture of the mind and the heart, the joy of knowing, the spiritual delectations which art and beauty offer us, the generous enthusiasm supplied by disinterested love, compassion and communion, zeal for justice, devotion to the commonwealth and to mankind. The very law of work to which every member of the commonwealth has to submit, demands that all should have access to that leisure. There is nothing here that is contemplation, properly speaking. But if in this kind of leisure, instead of shutting up human concerns in themselves, man remains open to what is higher than himself, and is borne by the natural movement which draws the human soul to the infinite, all this would be contemplation in an inchoate state or in preparation. (*SP,* pp. 142–44)

CHAPTER THIRTY-FOUR

REASON AND REASONING

1. Of course "pure reasoning" is worth nothing without common sense; but common sense is not "quite a different thing" from reasoning, it is only the healthiness of reason, the lively perception of first principles and of the intelligible realities drawn from experience—it is the very life of logic. (*BPT,* p. 108)

2. Reason does not only consist of its conscious logical tools and manifestations, nor does the will consist only of its deliberate conscious determinations. Far beneath the sunlit surface thronged with explicit concepts and judgments, words and expressed resolutions or movements of the will, are the sources of knowledge and creativity, of love and supra-sensuous desires, hidden in the primordial translucid night of the intimate vitality of the soul. Thus it is that we must recognize the existence of an unconscious or preconscious which pertains to the spiritual powers of the human soul and to the inner abyss of personal freedom, and of the personal thirst and striving for knowing and seeing, grasping and expressing: a spiritual or musical unconscious which is specifically different from the automatic or deaf unconscious. (*CI,* **p. 94**)

3. Reason has this peculiar property: it can introduce the infinite everywhere, establish as absolute ends those things which in themselves are only means, and the ends which the reason sets itself escape control in us by any other ends, to the extent that the reason itself has not acknowledged the latter. Reason face to face with being is solitary; it is not, like nature, bound to a fixed limit; there lies hidden in its structure no submerged regulator capable of re-establishing, *in spite of reason,* order within reason. A boundless liberty is the reason's terrifying privilege.

To refuse everything predetermined and ready-made with which nature (which is itself descended from divine reason) supplies us and to abandon the safety of the human family to the play of its fallible reason alone is to make men run an unknown risk. It is to unchain by that very act what Saint Thomas calls "non-natural concupiscences," infinite in scope and of unlimited peril. (*RT,* **p. 45**)

4. If modern times feel at a loss in the face of metaphysical knowledge, I fancy that it is not metaphysical knowledge which is to blame, but rather modern times and the weakening of reason they have experienced. (*RR,* **p. 60**)

5. The cultural significance of rationalism thus becomes clearly apparent to us. It implies an anthropocentric naturalism of wisdom; and what optimism! It is a doctrine of necessary progress, of salvation by science and by reason; I mean, temporal and worldly salvation of humanity by reason alone, which, thanks to the principles of Descartes, will lead man to felicity, to "that highest degree of wisdom in which the sovereign good of human life consists" (he wrote it himself in the preface to the French translation of the *Principles*)—in giving man full mastery over nature and over his nature; and, as the Hegelians were to add two centuries later, over his history. As if reason by itself alone was capable of making men act reasonably and of securing the good of peoples! There is no worse delusion.

On the balance-sheet we should inscribe: rupture of the impulse which was directing all the labor of human science towards the eternal, toward conversation with the three divine Persons—upsetting of the élan of knowledge. Knowledge does not aspire to do more than give man the means of domesticating matter. The sole retreat remaining for the spiritual will be science's reflection upon itself. And doubtless, that is indeed something of spiritual but of an autophagous spiritual. To delude oneself with the thought that the idealistic ruminating of physics and mathematics is enough to force the gates to the kingdom of God, to introduce man to wisdom and to freedom, to transform him into a fire of love burning for all eternity, is psychological childishness and metaphysical humbug. Man becomes spiritualized only by joining with a spiritual and eternal living One. There is only one spiritual life which does not mislead—that which the Holy Spirit bestows. Rationalism is the death of spirituality.

Then it is through the experience of sin, of suffering and despair that in the nineteenth century we will see spirituality reawaken in the wilderness: through a Baudelaire, a Rimbaud. An ambiguous spirituality, good for heaven if grace takes hold of it, good for hell if pride interferes. Many of our contemporaries will seek nourishment for their souls in anti-reason, and below reason, nourishment which should be sought only above reason. And to have led so many reasoning animals around to a hatred of reason is another of rationalism's misdeeds. (***DD*, pp. 178–79**)

6. Instead of an *open* human nature and an *open* reason, which are real nature and real reason, people pretend that there exists a nature and a reason isolated by themselves and *shut up* in themselves, excluding everything which is not themselves.

Instead of a development of man and reason in continuity with the Gospel, people demand such a development from pure reason apart from the Gospel. And for human life, for the concrete movement of history, this means real and serious amputations.

Prayer, divine love, supra-rational truths, the idea of sin and of grace, the evangelical beatitudes, the necessity of asceticism, of contemplation, of the way of the Cross—all this is either put in parenthesis or is once for all denied. In the concrete government of human life, reason is isolated from the supra-rational.

It is isolated also from all that is irrational in man, or it denies this— always in virtue of the very sophism that whatever is not reducible to reason itself, must be anti-rational or incompatible with reason. On the one hand, the life proper to the sphere of will is ignored; and the non-rational in the very world of knowledge is equally ignored. On the other hand, the whole world of the infra-rational, of instincts, of obscure tendencies, of the unconscious, along with that which it includes of malicious and, indeed, of demonic, but also of fecund reserves, is put in parenthesis and religiously forgotten.

Thus, little by little, will spring up the man conformable to the pattern of bourgeois pharisaism, this respectable conventional Man in whom the nineteenth century so long believed, and in whose unmasking Marx, Nietzsche and Freud will glory. They really have unmasked him, but in the same act they have disfigured man himself.

At the same time, enormous promises have been made to man, ever since the day of Descartes, in the prediction that progressive enlightenment will automatically bring about a complete felicity of release and repose, an earthly beatitude.

This has not happened, as the unfolding of the story—of the history—has shown. Having given up God so as to be self-sufficient, man has lost track of his soul. He looks in vain for himself; he turns the universe upside-down trying to find himself; he finds masks, and behind the masks, death.

And then we witness the spectacle of a tidal wave of irrationality. Then comes the awakening of a tragic opposition between life and intelligence. (*SP*, pp. 2–3)

7. It is always dangerous to be half Christian. The impact of Christianity quickens reason (without rendering it infallible) when reason nourishes itself on the substance of Christianity. When reason fattens itself on the leftovers of Christianity, the impact of Christianity warps it. The sacralization of the moral life becomes a dangerous blessing when we cease to understand what that sacralization means. Then what was a supernatural reinforcement and a sacred promulgation of the moral law, becomes a hardening and an arrogance against nature in an ethics which only retains the imprint of the Tables of the Law in order to make of them the Tables of Pure Reason. (*MP*, p. 90)

CHAPTER THIRTY-FIVE

SCIENCE

1. Let us say that whereas science, or phenomenal knowledge, offers us, with wonderful richness paid for by revolutionary changes, coded maps of what matter and nature are as to the multifarious observable and measurable interactions which occur in them, philosophy makes us grasp, with greater stability paid for by limitation to essentials, what things are in the intrinsic reality of their being. Though carrying common sense and the natural language to an essentially higher level, philosophy is in continuity with them, and is based on the perceptive (not only constructive) power of the intellect as well as on sense experience. In other words, being is the primary object of philosophy, as it is of human reason; and all notions worked out by philosophy are intelligible in terms of being, not of observation and measurement. (*UP,* pp. 57–58)

2. A science is said to be subalternated to another when it derives *its principles* from this other science, which is called the subalternant. The subalternate science does not by itself resolve its conclusions into the first principles of reason, into self-evident principles but the subalternant science resolves its own conclusions into first principles and these conclusions of the subalternant serve as principles for the subalternate science. (*PN,* p. 103)

3. The sciences, according to the ancients, were the laborious work of an intellect that drew its ideas of things through the senses, immaterializing by abstraction the objects it attracted to itself, and by that very fact subject to discursive movement, to all the difficulties and all the precautions of logic; the work of an intellect which was to begin *tabula rasa,* and which received from tangible realities everything except its nature and its spiritual light. Science thus conceived built itself up on strict dependence upon things, and could regulate its exigencies only upon those of the object. Cartesian Science, on the contrary, is the work of an intellect which finds within itself, innate, all the ideas it needs, and which as a result is directly dependent upon, and receives everything from, God Who created it and not from the things it knows; the clear view of *simple natures* and of their connections, the notion of which is imprinted by God upon the soul from birth, is the instrument of our reason, more intuitive than discursive to the philosopher's taste. Science thus conceived is constructed within the mind without suffering the contact and domination of things, with which doubtless it is finally in agreement, but only by reason of the play of exigencies of the mind itself, and thanks to the veracity of Him Who made both things and mind.

That idea of science, only too flattering to our tendency to delight in our acquired knowledge, and to domineer over the real, will take on singular developments in the philosophers' speculations as well as in the use made of science at certain times. Finally, human thought will appear as a sort of demi-god fabricating the cognoscible world with its concepts; and it is not reality which will require science to be true, it is Science that will require reality to be "scientific," and to produce its credentials. (***DD,* pp. 49–50**)

4. A completely abstract epistemology too often forgets or neglects, on behalf of rational discourse, those aspects of the constitution of a science which depend on the intuitivity of the mind. An existential epistemology owes it to itself to give both intuitivity and reason their due. In addition we can say that both intuitivity and reason play an essential role in *established* science (when that science is a *habitus* that is truly exercised and lived in act and capable of making progress) just as they do in science *when it is in the process of being established;* but that the role of intuitivity is more apparent in this latter form of science, and the role of reason more apparent in established science. (***UA,* p. 315**)

5. I would like to recall a general principle in Thomist philosophy: it is *in* the singular, *in* the individual that science terminates. Not only does science begin with or start from the individual, but it terminates in the individual, completing therein the circle of its intelligible motion. This is why we have need of the senses, not only to draw from them our ideas of things, but also for the resolution of the judgment, which at least analogically must take place in the senses. (**PH, p. 11**)

6. In order to measure the importance of this evolution of the intellect in the direction of naturalism since the Cartesian reform, one has only to think of the astonishing change undergone in a few centuries by the meaning of the word science. For the Christian doctors, the science *par excellence* was the science which is at the same time wisdom—*sapientia per modum cognitionis,* that is to say metaphysics, the supreme fruit of purely human speculation, and far above it, theology, which is a kind of impression within us of the holy science that God has of Himself—and higher even than that, science no longer of the discursive mode, but of the mystic mode, *sapientia per modum inclinationis,* the wisdom of the saints. For Descartes science is all human learning taken in its unity, and fructifying in Medicine, Mechanics, and Ethics. For the moderns, science, speaking absolutely, is the putting of observable phenomena into mathematical or tangible formulas, "positive" science, which is akin to opinion as well as to knowledge, which teaches us nothing about the substance and causes of the physical world considered in their very being, and whose task it is simply to spread over the physical world, for the purpose of subjecting it to our practical needs, to our industry, to our desire for well-being, an immense network of quantitative relations and of theories which save sensible appearances. Although we put it to a use of perdition, this science is good in itself; but what is extraordinary, and what gives some idea of the lowering of intellectual values during the last two centuries, is the fact that it had reabsorbed into itself the whole meaning of the great it and terrible word Science. (**DD, pp. 100–101**)

7. Modern science has progressively "freed" or separated itself from philosophy (more specifically from the philosophy of nature) thanks to mathematics—that is to say by becoming a particular type of knowledge whose data are facts drawn by our senses or instruments from the world of nature, but whose intelligibility is mathematical intelligibility. As a result, the primary characteristic of the approach to reality peculiar to science may therefore be described in the following way: that which can be observed and measured, and the ways through which observation and measurement are to be achieved, and the more or less unified mathematical reconstruction of such data—these things alone have a meaning for the scientist as such.

The field of knowledge particular to science is therefore limited to experience (as Kant understood the word). And when the basic notions that science uses derive from concepts traditionally used by common sense and philosophy, such as the notions of nature, matter, or causality, these basic notions are recast and restricted by science, so as to apply only to the field of experience and observable phenomena, understood and expressed in a certain set of mathematical signs. Thus it is that physicists may construct the concept of antimatter, for example, which has a meaning for them, but not for the layman or for the philosopher. (*UP,* pp. 45–46)

8. To sweep away the certitudes of common sense in the name of science is just about as reasonable as to abandon the use of one's eyes because one has a telescope. From this point of view, a good many philosophical systems seem like the frenzy of savants. (*BPT,* p. 296)

9. The truth is, that science—science in the modern sense of the word—is *not* a philosophy, and consequently claims, if I dare use this barbarism, to *deontologize* completely its notional lexicon. (*SP,* p. 25)

10. Modern science of phenomena has its feet on earth and uses its hands to gather not only correctly observed and measured facts, but also a great many notions and explanations which offer our minds real entities; yet it has its head in a mathematical heaven, populated with various crowds of signs and merely ideal, even not intuitively thinkable entities.

These ideal entities constructed by the mind are symbols which enable science to manipulate the world, while knowing it as unknown, for then, in those higher regions where creative imagination is more at work than classical induction, science is intent only on translating the multifarious observable aspects of the world into coherent systems of signs.

The fact remains that the prime incentive of the scientist is the urge to know reality. Belief in the existence of the mysterious reality of the universe precedes scientific inquiry in the scientist's mind, and a longing (possibly more or less repressed) to attain this reality in its inner depths is naturally latent in him.

But as a scientist his knowledge is limited to a mathematical (or quasi-mathematical) understanding and reconstruction of the observable and measurable aspects of nature taken in their inexhaustible detail. (*UP,* pp. 48–49)

11. Like certain most general tenets of science, evolution is less a demonstrated conclusion than a kind of primary concept which has such power in making phenomena decipherable that once expressed it becomes almost impossible for the scientific mind to do without it. Now if it is true that in opposition to the immobile archetypes and ever-recurrent cycles of pagan antiquity, Christianity taught men to conceive history both as irreversible and as running in a definite direction, that it may be said that by integrating in science the dimension of time and history, the idea of evolution has given to our knowledge of nature a certain affinity with what the Christian view of things is on a quite different plane. In any case, the genesis of elements and the various phases of the history of the heavens, and, in the realm of life, the historical development of an immense diversity of evolutive branches ("phyla"), all this, if it is understood in the proper philosophical perspective, presupposes the transcendent God as the prime cause of evolution—preserving in existence created things and the impetus present in them, moving them from above so that superior forms may emerge from inferior ones, and, when man is to appear at the peak of the series of vertebrates, intervening in a special way and creating *ex nihilo* the spiritual and immortal soul of the first man and of every individual of the new species. Thus evolution correctly understood offers us a spectacle whose greatness and universality make the activating omnipresence of God only more tellingly sensed by our minds.

I do not believe, moreover, that science fosters a particularly optimistic view of nature. Every progress in evolution is dearly paid for: miscarried attempts, merciless struggle everywhere. The more detailed our knowledge of nature becomes, the more we see, together with the element of generosity and progression which radiates from being, the law of degradation the powers of destruction and death, the implacable voracity which are also inherent in the world of matter. And when it comes to man, surrounded and invaded as he is by a host of warping forces, psychology and anthropology are but an account of the fact that, while being essentially superior to all of them, he is the most unfortunate of animals. So it is that when its vision of the world is enlightened by science, the intellect which religious faith perfects realizes still better that nature, however good in its own order, does not suffice, and that if the deepest hopes of mankind are not destined to turn to mockery, it is because a God-given energy better than nature is at work in us. (*UP,* pp. 69–71)

12. Looking upon our world wherein all is in motion, more so in the invisible atom than in the visible stars, and wherein motion is the universal mediator of interaction, the philosopher sees it to be wholly pervaded and, as it were, animated by the sort of participation of the spirit in matter which we call intentionality.

Its hierarchy has been reversed: the atomic world and not the celestial spheres is now the basis of time. The center of the physical world is no longer the sublunary globe surrounded by eternally rotating bodies that are both incorruptible and divine; rather is it the human soul, living its corporeal life on a tiny precarious planet, which is the immaterial and spiritual center of this physical world. (*PN,* p. 154)

13. And if we say that science is inferior to wisdom, it is inferior in the sense in which one perfection is inferior to another perfection, one virtue to another virtue; inferior in the sense in which one world of mystery and beauty is inferior to another world of intelligence and mystery. (*SW,* pp. 5–6)

14. And this world is a world of contingence, of risk, adventure, irreversibility; it has a history and a direction in time. Bit by bit the giant stars grow smaller, are consumed and burn themselves out; for billions of years an enormous, original capital of dynamism and of energy has been tending toward equilibrium, using itself up, spending itself lavishly, bringing forth marvels in its rush toward death. The principle of entropy has been much

abused by philosophers, but we nevertheless have the right to note this deep meaning which agrees so well with Aristotle's philosophical, not astronomical, notion of time: *quia tempus per se magis est causa corruptionis quam generationis.* And we have also the right to point out how the natural exception which the least of living organisms makes to the law of the degradation of energy, (which applies, however, to the whole material universe) marks most significatively the threshold where something weightless, endowed with a singular metaphysical destiny and called the soul, empierces matter and opens up within it a new world.

In its way and with admirable precisions, science confirms that great idea by which the Thomistic philosophy of nature sees, in the universe of living and nonliving bodies, an inspiration and an ascent from one ontological degree to another toward forms of increasingly complex unity and individuality, and of increasing interiority and communicability at the same time; an ascent towards that which is no longer just a part in this vast universe but is itself a whole, a stable universe open to others through intelligence and love—the person which, as St. Thomas says, is the most perfect thing in all of nature. (*PN*, pp. 154–55)

15. The progressive escape from servitude among men depends, on the one hand, on technical progress, notably on the services rendered by the machine, and on certain transformations and transferences in the regime of property; but it necessarily demands also, on the other hand, a progressive spiritualization of humanity caused by the forces of the soul and of liberty, and the gospel leaven at work in human history. (*SP,* **p. 111**)

16. It is certainly remarkable that only in the world of sensible Nature do we find our knowledge shared by a philosophy and an experimental science related to each other as the soul to the body. No such duality is found in the other universes of intelligibility. Mathematics has no ontological soul; it has only an abstract and ideal body. Metaphysics has no empiriological body; it is only spirit. (***DK*, p. 184; CW 7, pp. 195–96**)

CHAPTER THIRTY-SIX

THEOLOGY AND THE THEOLOGIAN

1. If philosophy and theology are entirely distinct, they are not therefore unrelated, and although philosophy is of all the human sciences pre-eminently the free science, in the sense that it proceeds by means of premises and laws which depend on no science superior to itself, its freedom—that is, its freedom to err—is limited in so far as it is subject to theology, which controls it externally. (*IP,* pp. 95–96)

2. The theologian . . . makes use at every turn of philosophic propositions to prove his own conclusions. Therefore a system of theology could not possibly be true if the metaphysics which it employs is false. It is indeed an absolute necessity that the theologian should have at his disposal a true philosophy in conformity with the common sense of mankind. (*IP,* p. 97)

3. Let us not forget that metaphysics is a difficult thing for our minds and that the gods are jealous of our joy in it. There is only one way to stabilize it within us, and that is to order it to sacred science, which, in making use of it, elevates it. Oriented then toward those summits of supernatural truth

accessible to theology alone, metaphysics reaches with more strength and more security toward the heights of the natural truth where it has its domain. If not, it will tend to descend. (***DD*, p. 87**)

4. St. Thomas distinguished in order to unite, wherefore he distinguished only the more clearly and powerfully. At a moment in the history of culture when Christian thought, dominated by the Augustinian tradition, felt loth to make way for purely rational disciplines, one of the principal objects of his work was to distinguish philosophy from theology in an irrefutable fashion and thus to establish the autonomy of philosophy. He did succeed in establishing this autonomy in principle. After him, that autonomy was never truly established in fact and is not yet so established. The nominalism of the Scholastics who came after St. Thomas could not but jeopardise that autonomy when they dispossessed metaphysics of its certitudes and allotted them exclusively to the supra-rational domain of faith. The philosophical imperialism of the great thinkers who came after Descartes jeopardised it in another and contrary fashion by dispossessing theological wisdom in order to burden metaphysics and moral philosophy . . . with the major offices and supreme responsibilities which theology had had in its keeping. Philosophy thereafter took these offices and responsibilities upon itself, at first with vainglorious optimism but afterwards with the black pessimism of all great disillusions. The system of Malebranche is a theophilosophy. The monadism of Leibnitz is a metaphysical transposition of the treatise on the Angels. The morality of Kant is a philosophical transposition of the Decalogue. The positivism of Auguste Comte opened out into the religion of Humanity. The panlogism of Hegel was the supreme effort of modern philosophy to absorb all the realms of the spirit into the absolutism of reason. After that came the despair of reason, but it was a reason still held, still wounded by the theological obsession which had now become an anti-theological obsession. When Feuerbach declared that God was the creation and the alienation of man; when Nietzsche proclaimed the death of God, they were the theologians of our contemporary atheistic philosophies. Why are these philosophies so charged with bitterness, unless it is because they feel themselves chained in spite of themselves to a transcendence and to a past they constantly have to kill, and in the negation of which their own roots are planted? (***EE*, pp. 136–37**)

5. I know very well that every science is obliged to have its own technical vocabulary and that it would be simply absurd to ask theologians to speak like everyone else, under pretext of adapting the divine mystery to the mental capacities of the general Christian community and making easy what is difficult by its very nature. The Christian community has need of theology—and what a need!—but of a theology that is science and wisdom, and this requires a mental effort on the part of everyone. (*UA*, p. 251)

6. Philosophy will never truly free itself from all deforming servitude to the theological or the anti-theological heritage, will never be truly autonomous, unless it recognise the existence and value proper to theology, and thereby preserve its own autonomy (which is not supreme) by the free and normal avowal of its infravalence in comparison with the wisdoms that are higher than it. St. Thomas established philosophy in its own domain. He distinguished it from theology with a clarity and a firmness that cannot be broken. But he did so only by ensuring cohesion in difference and by affirming the intrinsic superiority of theological wisdom over metaphysical wisdom, and of mystical wisdom over theological wisdom. There is nothing to be done about this order, because it does not depend upon us. Only on the condition that we respect it can we preserve, at every degree, the autonomy of each and all the forms of knowing.

Yet these considerations, which concern essences or quiddities, are still not sufficient. The conditions or requirements of the existential order must also be taken into account. Thomist principles not only carry distinction and unity into the ordering of knowledge. They also disclose the quickening and strengthening which each degree receives from the others in the existential context and concrete reality of the life of the spirit. They oblige us to realise how, at the immaterial node of the soul's energies, mystical wisdom and theological wisdom vivify and fortify metaphysical wisdom just as the latter itself vivifies and fortifies philosophical activities of a lower rank. (*EE*, pp. 139–40)

7. Now this God of faith, Deity as such, not seen, but believed, or attained to in the testimony of first Truth and by means of dogmatic definitions, is also the object of theology. Theology envisages it from the point of view of "virtual revelation," as it is called; in other words, from the point of view of the consequences that reason, when enlightened by faith, can draw from formally revealed principles.

This is not the place to go into any lengthy development concerning the nature of theological wisdom. All that needs to be noted is that theology is quite a different thing from a simple application of philosophy to matters of revelation: that would truly be a monstrous conception; it would submit revealed data to a purely human light and subordinate theological wisdom to philosophy. There exists no genuine science or wisdom unless within the soul there be a genuine intellectual virtue proportioning the light of discrimination and judgment to the proper level of the object. To an object which is the depths of revealed divinity, insofar as it can be exploited by reason, there must necessarily correspond, as its light in the soul, not the light of philosophy, but a proportionate light, the light of supernatural faith taking up and directing the natural movement of reason and its natural way of knowing. Thus, theology is not a simple application of natural reason and of philosophy to revealed data: it is an elucidation of revealed data by faith vitally linked with reason, advancing in step with reason and arming itself with philosophy. That is why philosophy, far from subordinating theology to itself, is properly the "servant" of theology in the immanent use theology makes of it. Theology is free as regards philosophical doctrines. It is theology that chooses among these doctrines the one that will in its hands be the best instrument of truth. And, let a theologian lose theological faith; he still can keep the whole machinery and conceptual organization of his science, but he keeps it as something dead in his mind; he has lost his proper light. He is no longer a theologian except in the way that a corpse is a man. To sum up, Deity itself as seen or known quidditatively is the object of the knowledge of the blessed. Deity itself as believed and formally revealed is the object of faith. Deity itself as believed and virtually revealed is the object of theology. (*DK*, pp. 252–53; *CW* 7, pp. 268–69)

8. The Christian, because he is not of the world, will always be a foreigner in the world—I mean, in the world as separating itself from the Kingdom of God and shutting itself up in itself; he is incomprehensible to the world and inspires it with uneasiness and distrust. The world cannot make sense of the theological virtues. Theological faith, the world sees as a challenge, an in-

sult, and a threat; it is by reason of their faith that it dislikes Christians, it is through their faith that they vanquish it; faith is enough to divide them from the world. Theological hope, the world does not see at all; it is simply blind to it. Theological charity, the world sees the wrong way; it misapprehends it, is mistaken about it. It confuses it with any kind of quixotic devotion to whatever human cause it may profit by. And thus does the world tolerate charity, even admire it—insofar as it is not charity, but something else. (And so is charity the secret weapon of Christianity.) (***PH*, p. 148**)

9. Prayer, particularly in the case of intellectuals, can only preserve a perfectly right direction and escape the dangers which threaten it, on condition of being supported and fed by Theology.

Knowledge of the Sacred Doctrine has a peculiar tendency of its own to shorten and render safer the spiritual journey. It saves the soul from a number of errors, illusions and blind alleys. In relation to the purgative life, it possesses an ascetic virtue which succeeds in detaching the soul from the degradations and trivialities of self-love. As for those living the illuminative life, the purification that it brings simplifies the gaze of the soul and turns it from the human self to God alone. And finally, in relation to the unitive life, a knowledge of Theology plants the roots of the soul deep in Faith and the divine Truth, a predisposition essentially required for the life of union with God. (***PI*, pp. 6–7**)

10. I am not unaware that it is often dangerous for a philosopher to reply to the objections of a theologian, because these objections risk leading him onto a terrain which is not his and into a problematic which is not his.

In principle one does good intellectual work only by strictly limiting oneself (it is a discipline very manifest in Saint Thomas) to saying *only* that which one has really *seen* or grasped by the operation of one's reason. But if a theologian asks me to reply to one of his questions—a question which does not belong to my own problematic, and which comes to me from without like a ready-made picture frame which I must fill—I run the risk of replying to him by a construction of concepts whereby I adjust as best I can to what he sees, without having really *seen* myself; in which case I run the risk of talking nonsense. (***GE*, pp. 42–43**)

11. An act of faith or of love of a little child goes infinitely farther and is something incomparably more precious, more full of vigor and more effective than the most brilliant natural act of the highest of the angels. Pascal's famous phrase about the three orders expresses an elementary truth of Christianity. *Bonum gratiae unius majus est, quam bonum naturae totius universi.*

. . . . Grace orders us to the vision of the Divine Essence, or Deity itself which is beyond being, whereas, by nature, we are ordered only to a knowledge of being in general and, in the first instance, of the being of sensible things.

It is obvious what danger lies in the slightest confusion between two formal objects. It would be to risk confusing the intellectuality we have by nature with the intellectuality we have by grace. (**DK, p. 256; CW 7, pp. 272–73**)

CHAPTER THIRTY-SEVEN

ST. THOMAS AND THOMISM

1. Saint Thomas is properly and before everything else *the apostle of the intelligence*: this is the first reason why we must regard him as *the apostle of modern times.* (***TA*, p. 98**)

2. In reality, if the renaissance of Thomistic philosophy has any meaning, it is that this philosophy is not a philosophy of the vestry but a philosophy of the open air; it draws all its strength from what is most natural in man: sense and reason, and the Church recommends it so insistently only because, having among us the deposit of the divine Truth, she considers the health of our reason to be worth the most careful supervision. (***BPT*, p. 21**)

3. It is precisely because Thomism has been formed as a science with well-defined systematic equipment, which is also (but in another sense) incomplete, that it is capable of endless progression and growth. Far from telling us that since St. Thomas everything has been done, it says that as long as history shall last and bring new problems to light, so long will more still have to be done than has as yet been accomplished. (***DK*, p. 307; CW 7, pp. 326–27**)

4. If the ethics of St. Thomas is an ethics of beatitude, it is nevertheless something entirely different from an interested eudemonism, because it is also an ethics of love; and, when we act rightly, that in which our happiness consists (which is to say, God, the transcendent whole), is loved by us for Himself, not for ourselves, and He is loved above all else, loved more than ourselves; it is by virtue of our love for him that we ourselves want to be happy. (*SP*, p. 99)

5. It could easily be shown that all the other great specifically Thomist theses also possess meaning only for a mind turned in the first instance towards existence. This is why there will always be disputed by every philosophy that is not centered upon the primacy of the act of exisiting. (*EE*, p. 37)

6. [Thomism] welcomes all being, because it is absolutely docile to being. Its structure being as hard as steel, it is as extensible as may be; its discipline being the strictest possible, it enjoys the utmost freedom. (*NC*, p. 104)

7. Incomparably coherent, closely knit together in all parts, Thomism is, nevertheless, not what is called a "system." When it is said that Thomism is distinguished from all other philosophical doctrines by its universalism, that should not be understood as a mere difference of extent but, on the contrary, as a difference of nature. The word "system" evokes the idea of a mechanical linking-up, or, at the very least, of a quasi-spatial assemblage of parts and, consequently, of a personal, if not arbitrary, choice of elements, as is the case in all artistic constructions. A system unfolds or travels along bit by bit, starting with its initial elements. On the contrary, it is essential to Thomism that it require whatever has to do with its construction or its "machinery" to be rigorously subordinated to what belongs to the immanent activity and the vital movement of intellection: it is not a system, an artifact; it is a spiritual organism. (*DK*, p. xiii; CW 7, p. xiii)

8. I dislike the term "Neo-Scholasticism" or "Neo-Thomism." It involves the risk of pulling us down from the higher plane of wisdom to the lower plane of the problematic sciences and thereby leading us logically to demand for Thomism also a progress by substitution in which the *Neo* would devour the Thomism. (*PM*, p. 13)

9. One is a Thomist because one has repudiated every attempt to find philosophical truth in any system fabricated by an individual (even though that individual be called *ego*) and because one wants to seek out what is true—for oneself, indeed, and by one's own reason—by allowing oneself to be taught by the whole range of human thought, in order not to neglect anything of that which is. Aristotle and St. Thomas occupy a privileged place for us only because, thanks to their supreme docility to the lessons of the real, we find in them the principles and the scale of values through which the total effort of this universal thought can be preserved without running the risk of eclecticism and confusion. (***DK*, pp. xiii–xiv; CW 7, pp. xiii–xiv**)

10. Between Aristotle as viewed in himself and Aristotle viewed in the writings of St. Thomas is the difference which exists between a city seen by the flare of a torchlight procession and the same city bathed in the light of the morning sun.

For this reason, though St. Thomas is first and foremost a theologian, we may appropriately, if not with greater propriety, call his philosophy Thomist rather than Aristotelian. (***IP*, p. 74**)

11. Intellectualism, anti-intellectualism—to be absolutely exact one should use these words only to designate two opposing errors. It is improperly and through reaction against the contemporary anti-intellectualist current that the thought of Saint Thomas has sometimes been called intellectualist (it has been done in the present work); others in so designating it tended to displace its centre of gravity and in a way to transfer it into conditions of intellect in the pure state. The best way of designating it, in reality, would be rather as critical realism. Intellectualism which realizes abstractions or scorns experience or makes of the real a pure object which human intellect completely exhausts is no better than anti-intellectualism. (***BPT*, p. 43**)

12. We have seen how the existentialism of Thomas Aquinas differs from modern existentialism, both because it is rational in type and because, being founded upon the intuitiveness of the senses and the intellect, it associates and identifies being and intelligibility at every point. Descartes and the whole rationalist philosophy born of the Cartesian revolution raised a wall of insuperable enmity between intellect and mystery, and this is doubtless the deepest source of the fundamental inhumanity of every civilization based upon rationalism. St. Thomas reconciles intellect and mystery at the core of being, at the core of existence. He thereby liberates our intellect, restores it to its nature by restoring it to its object. Thereby, also, he makes it possible for us to effect unity within ourselves, and, without having to repudiate reason and philosophy, to win liberty and peace, though in regions which transcend philosophy and which are not to be reached by any path of philosophy.

We are here in the presence of the most significant privilege of that great zeal for being which animates Thomist thought and renders it so desperately necessary while at the same time so foreign and intolerable to the emptied, exasperated, ailing reason of our time. Thomist thought is a creator of unity; we cherish dispersion. It is a creator of liberty; we go in quest of any sort of collective yoke. It is a creator of peace; and violence is our preference. The ills that rend us are what we love most in the world. We do not want to be set free. (*EE*, p. 142)

13. Thomist peace and unity bear no relation to the facile balancings and the dialectical conciliations practiced by a reason installed in the security of an apparatus of ready-made answers that come forth at the click of every imaginable question. They call for never-ending triumphs over ceaselessly recurring conflicts. They require involvement in the thick of new questions in order to bring forth a fresh intuition of new truths, or cause old truths newly penetrated to gush forth from the rock of acquired knowing. They demand communion with all the strivings of research and discovery to release into the light that truth which those strivings ordinarily attain only with the help of the ferments of error, or in ill-fated conceptualisations. They exact from man a tension and an extension which, in truth, are possible only in the anguish of the Cross. For what St. Paul said is true also in the order of the things of the spirit: there is no redemption without the shedding of blood. The reconciliation of the supreme energies of intelligence and of life which, like every appetite for the absolute, are naturally ferocious, each claiming everything for itself, is a false reconciliation if it is not also a redemption; and it cannot be accomplished except at the price of an ordeal of suffering of which the spirit itself is the locus. (*EE*, pp. 144–45)

14. As much as Karl Marx, St. Thomas is cognizant of the humiliation inflicted on man by what Marx calls the alienation of work for the profit of another, and which St. Thomas called more simply servitude. As much as Marx, he renders intelligible this desire which possesses us, this nostalgia for a state where human work would be liberated and all servitude abolished.

But, in contra-distinction to Marx, he makes us understand that if the progress of human societies is to proceed in the direction of this liberation, it would be fully attained—that is, every form and modality of servitude, of service to another for the peculiar or private good of another, would be abolished for all men—only at the termination of the movement of human history. This will not be accomplished by a quick change and a messianic revolution abolishing private property, but by better and more human arrangements of private property. This progressive escape from servitude among men depends, on the one hand, on technical progress, notably on the services rendered by the machine, and on certain transformations and transferences in the regime of property; but it necessarily demands also, on the other hand, a progressive spiritualization of humanity caused by the forces of the soul and of liberty, and the gospel leaven at work in human history. (*SP,* **p. 111**)

15. There is no unity or integration without a stable hierarchy of values. Now in the true hierarchy of values, according to Thomist philosophy, knowledge and love of what is above time are superior to, and embrace and quicken, knowledge and love of what is within time. Charity, which loves God and embraces all men in this very love, is the supreme virtue. In the intellectual realm, wisdom, which knows things eternal and creates order and unity in the mind, is superior to science or to knowledge through particular causes; and the speculative intellect which knows for the sake of knowing, comes before the practical intellect which knows for the sake of action. In such a hierarchy of values, what is infravalent is not sacrificed to, but kept alive by, what is supravalent, because everything is appendant to faith in truth. (*EM,* **pp. 53–54**)

16. If his [St. Thomas] sanctity was the sanctity of the intelligence, this is because in him the life of the intelligence was fortified and completely transilluminated by the fire of infused contemplation and the gifts of the Holy Spirit.... He prayed without ceasing, wept, fasted, yearned. Each of his syllogisms is as a concretion of his prayer and his tears; the kind of grace of lucid calm which his words bring to us springs doubtless from the fact that the least of his texts retains invisible the impregnation of his longing and of the pure strength of the most vehement love. (*TA,* **p. 47**)

17. Saint Thomas in his probing the intimate nature of knowledge and the peculiar life of the intellect, establishes better than any other thinker—against positivism, but respecting the full role played by experience, and against idealism, but respecting the full role played by the immanent and constructive activity of the mind—the objectivity of knowledge, the rights and the value of the science of being. But he establishes also—against the false systems of metaphysics which threaten to assail us, against the pantheistic immanentism which some would impose on us in the name of the Orient, against the pragmatism of the West, against the Hegelian divinization of becoming, and against the diverse forms of radical atheism which have sprung up in the world since Feuerbach, Auguste Comte, and Karl Marx—he establishes, I say, the transcendence of Him Whom we know through His creatures but Who is without common measure with them; Who is being, intelligence, goodness, life, beatitude, but Who overflows and surpasses infinitely our ideas of being, goodness and all the other perfections: in short, Whom our concepts attain through analogy but do not circumscribe.

Thus metaphysics rises in his hands above agnosticism and rationalism; it starts with experience and mounts right up to Uncreated Being, and thus re-establishes in the human spirit the proper hierarchy of speculative values, and initiates in us the order of wisdom. (*TA,* **pp. 64–65**)

18. What constitutes the nobility of philosophers, of modern philosophers in particular, is that in spite of their erring ways they love the intellect, even when they ruin it. But for the most part they have loved it more than they have loved God. Saint Thomas loves God more than the intellect, but he loves the intellect more than all the philosophers have loved it. That is why he can restore it, reminding it of its duties. He shames it out of its cowardice, gives it again the courage to face the supreme truths. He shames it out of its vainglory, bends it to measure itself against things and to listen to a tradition. He teaches it again simultaneously the two complementary virtues it had lost together, magnanimity and humility. (***TA, p. 103***)

19. [The Thomists'] task has grown singularly difficult in a world whose whole mind is set upon a science immediately practical in its bearing, aiming at an exhaustive cataloguing of phenomena and the individual—and binding the mind in servitude to the flux of time. (***TS, p. 59***)

20. We see abolished that distinction—the *specifically hierarchized* distinction between Metaphysics, Mathematics and the knowledge of Nature—which played a principal part in Thomist wisdom, because it was drawn from the essential diversity of objects to be known (*orders of abstraction*)—and which witnessed the domination of the object over our minds. (***DD, p. 48***)

21. The marvel of Thomistic wisdom, the metaphysics of being and of causes, theology as a science, is that, being set at the peak of human reason, recognizing itself inferior to the knowledge of infused wisdom but superior to every other knowledge, and distinguishing only to unite, such a wisdom establishes within the human soul an enduring coherence and living solidarity between those spiritual activities that reach up to heaven and those that reach down to touch the earth. And it does so without in the least lessening or changing them, and always with objective exactness. (***DK, p. 302; CW 7, p. 321***)

22. Ambiguity is not a philosophical instrument and the conciliation of Thomism with certain modern systems would be too dearly paid for were it to be bought at the price of equivocal language. (***DK, p. 429; CW 7, p. 453***)

23. If his [St. Thomas Aquinas's] spirit and his doctrine tend to create unity in man it is always by virtue of the same secret—which is to understand all things in the light and the generosity of being. (***EE, p. 143***)

CHAPTER THIRTY-EIGHT

TRUTH

1. The great truths without which man's moral life is impossible—for example, knowledge of God's existence, the freedom of the will, etc.—belong to this domain of common sense, as consequences immediately deducible (proximate conclusions) from primary data apprehended by observation and first principles apprehended by the intellect. All men, unless spoiled by a faulty education or by some intellectual vice, possess a natural certainty of these truths. But those whose understanding has never been cultivated are not able to give any account or at least any satisfactory account of their convictions; that is to say, they cannot explain why they possess them.

These certainties of common sense, conclusions of an implicit reasoning, are as well founded as the certainties of science. But their possessor has no knowledge, or an imperfect knowledge, of the grounds on which he bases them. They are therefore imperfect not in their value as truth but in the *mode* or condition under which they exist in the mind. (*IP,* p. 101)

2. If a metaphysic is true, all complementary aspects of truth, however diverse and heterogeneous, must, of necessity, be logically reconcilable with its principles; and an intellect sufficiently penetrating, and sufficiently open to

the real, must be able to discern these complementary aspects of truth without the incidental assistance of the teachers of error. To hold the contrary would be to conclude that there is a radical inequality between the intellect and being, to admit that reality is illogical fundamentally—that necessities for thought are not necessities for being—in short, one way or another to yield to the Kantian or post-Kantian blandishments and ruin intellectual knowledge. (*TS,* **p. 177**)

3. To have the artless integrity to prefer truth to all intellectual opportunism and to all trickery, whether in philosophy, theology, art, or politics, to have such artlessness demands a purification more radical than one might think. Every philosopher loves truth, but with what admixtures? The super-ego of the philosopher is there to intrude into that love all sorts of monsters in disguise. If you analyze the philosophical systems from that point of view, you will find that a number of them embrace not only a sincere search for the truth but at the same time a shrewd desire to discover the most advantageous intellectual standpoints or to connive with the times, or the passion to rule tyrannically over a fictitious universe in order to compensate for various secret frustrations. If our love of the truth were purified by the flame of faith, no doubt we would not all share in the same philosophy, but we would be set free from an appreciable number of parasitical motives that cause division among us. (*RR,* **p. 212**)

4. The school of *Aristotle and St. Thomas* teaches that truth is neither impossible nor easy, but difficult for man to attain.

It is thus radically opposed alike to scepticism and to rationalism. It sees in the multitude of errors put forward by men and particularly by philosophers a sign indeed of the weakness of the human understanding, but a reason to prize the intellect the more dearly and to embrace truth the more ardently, and an instrument for the advancement of knowledge by the refutations and explanations which these errors call forth. And, on the other hand, it recognises that reason is our sole natural means of attaining truth, but only when formed and disciplined, in the first place and pre-eminently by reality itself (for our mind is not the measure of things, but things the measure of our mind), secondly by teachers (for science is a collective, not an individual, achievement, and can be built up only by a continuous living tradition), and finally by God, if he should please to instruct mankind and bestow upon philosophers the negative rule of faith and theology. (*IP*, pp. 137–38)

5. The more he [man] grasps truth, through science, philosophy, or faith, the more he feels what immensity remains to be grasped within this very truth. The more he knows God, either by reason or by faith, the more he understands that our concepts attain (through analogy) but do not circumscribe Him, and that His thoughts are not like our thoughts: for "who hath known the mind of the Lord, or who hath become His counselor?" The more strong and deep faith becomes, the more man kneels down, not before his own alleged ignorance of truth, but before the inscrutable mystery of divine truth, and before the hidden ways in which God goes to meet those who search Him. (*UP*, p. 22)

6. [As Pascal said:] "Justice and truth are two points so fine that our instruments are too blunt exactly to touch them. If they do arrive at them, they totally hide the point and rest on what lies around it—and more on the false than on the true." The only remedy is that man should learn the art of making right distinctions. That is one reason why philosophical studies, even when they do nothing but teach us this art, are of so vital a utility for the general government of our opinions! Yet it would be a good thing that we should seek to imitate in our knowledge, according to our imperfect mode, the marvellous precision with which the divine action permeates the created thing without sharing its deficiencies—running through the most tenuous fibres, nerves, ducts, veinules of being. (*TS*, p. 174)

7. Well, if it were true that whoever knows or claims to know truth or justice cannot admit the possibility of a view different from his own, and is bound to impose his true view on other people by violence, the rational animal would be the most dangerous of beasts. In reality, it is through rational means, that is, through persuasion, not coercion, that man is bound by his very nature to try to induce others to share in what he knows or claims to know as true and just. Be it a question of science, metaphysics, or religion, the man who says "What is truth?", as Pilate did, is not a tolerant man, but a betrayer of the human race. There is, in other words, real and genuine tolerance only when a man is firmly and absolutely convinced of a truth, or of what he holds to be a truth, and when, at the same time, he recognizes the right of those who deny this truth to exist, and to contradict him, and to speak their own mind, not because they are free from truth but because they seek truth in their own way, and because he respects in them human nature and human dignity, and those very resources and living springs of the intellect and of conscience which make them potentially capable of attaining the truth he loves, if some day they happen to see it. (***RON,*** **pp. 78–79**)

8. The first duty of a teacher is to develop within himself, for the sake of truth, deep-rooted convictions, and frankly to manifest them, while taking pleasure, of course, in having the student develop, possibly against them, his own personal convictions. (***EM,*** **p. 138**)

9. The sole philosophy open to those who doubt the possibility of truth is absolute silence—even mental. That is to say, as Aristotle points out, such men must make themselves vegetables. No doubt reason often errs, especially in the highest matters, and, as Cicero said long ago, there is no nonsense in the world which has not found some philosopher to maintain it, so difficult is it to attain truth. But it is the error of cowards to mistake a difficulty for an impossibility. (***IP,*** **pp. 135–36**)

10. Nothing is superior to truth. But on the level of action there are practical truths toward which viewpoints mutually opposed on the level of speculative truth can converge. That is why . . . there can be agreement and cooperation in regard to action and purely practical principles, between men who are divided in their deepest convictions. (***TP,*** **p. 71**)

CHAPTER THIRTY-NINE

VARIA

1. Of course it is true enough that outside the world of grace and of supernatural life, man's spirituality never transcends what is biological except in a more or less imperfect fashion. (*BPT,* **p. 329**)

2. It is not religion that helps to divide men and sharpen their conflicts; it is the distress of our human condition and the interior strife in our hearts. And without religion we should certainly be far worse than we are. We see today how, when man rejects the sacred traditions of humanity and aspires either to free himself from religion by atheism, or to pervert religion by deifying his own sinful blood through a kind of racist pseudo-theism or paratheism, the darkest forms of fanaticism then spread throughout the world. Only by a deeper and purer religious life, only by charity, is it possible to surmount the state of conflict and opposition produced by the impact of religion upon human weakness. To bring to an end all fanaticism and all pharisaism will require, I believe, the whole of human history. But it is the task of the religious conscience itself to overcome these evils. It alone is capable of doing so. It is the religious conscience which, by spiritualizing itself in suffering, must gradually rid itself and the world of the leaven of the pharisees and the fanaticism of the sectarians. (*RT,* **p. 129**)

3. Life . . . does not essentially involve change and becoming—far from it! Becoming, change, is only a consequence of the imperfection of all created life, and especially of all material life. What constitutes life is immanent activity, the activity whose beginning is in the acting subject, and whose term is still in the acting subject. And the higher one goes in the scale of the living, the more this immanence of the vital activity increases. So that what is most living in the world is intelligence, which by its own activity perfects itself from what it knows. (***BPT*, p. 202**)

4. Work, which is a fundamental necessity of our existence, is not an end in itself. We work in order to improve human life. But will this very improvement, in ourselves and in others, only consist in working again and working more? Or will it also consist in the attainment of some superior possession, in which we shall rest? There are many kinds of rest. Laziness is sin. Amusement is good, but less good than work. Certain kinds of repose, in which the mind is supremely active, and reaches, however imperfectly, some fruition of immortality through its contact with truth, or with Eternal Love, are better than work.

Higher forms of leisure are no longer leisure but act come to completion. And the highest form is contemplative activity. *Be still, and know that I am God.* (***RON*, p. 158**)

5. Gratitude is the most exquisite form of courtesy. (***RON*, p. 153**)

6. Friendship requires a great waste of time, and much idleness; creative thinking requires a great deal of idleness. (***RON*, p. 156**)

7. Charity does not exist here below without faith and hope. But of the three theological virtues, which are given us by grace together with gratuitous justification, it is charity which is the greatest and which deserves life eternal. (***LT*, p. 90**)

8. Nothing is more stupid than to imagine that in order to be true and profound friendship requires identity of thought. There are many Catholics who are far from being my friends; there are non-Catholics who are for me blessed friends. The truest and most fraternal friendship can exist between

men who think differently on essential matters. It includes doubtless, then, an element of suffering, but one which renders the friend more dear still. One prays for him, but far from bringing pressure to bear on him in order to convert him to one's own faith, one loves him such as he is, and one esteems, one respects, one strives to know better and to understand better that which he believes and that by which he lives. (***CC,* p. 111**)

9. It is always by an *impression* overwhelming reason that the devil seeks to entice the mind into error. Sentimentality of the atheists. (***NB,* p. 66**)

10. From *Moby Dick* and *The Scarlet Letter* to *Look Homeward, Angel* and *Requiem for a Nun*—from Edgar Allan Poe and Emily Dickinson to Hart Crane, Allen Tate and T. S. Eliot (who has remained an American in spite of himself)—American literature, in its most objectively careful scrutinies, has been preoccupied with the beyond and the nameless which haunt our blood. Man, as it sees him, is a restless being gropingly, sometimes miserably, at grips with his fleshly condition—whom obviously no kind of materialist paradise can ever satisfy. (***RON,* p. 42**)

11. What is important to consider first is that the intellect is above time, *intellectus supra tempus*: because the intellect is spiritual, and time, the perseverance of movement in being, or the continuity of perpetually vanishing existence proper to movement, is the proper duration of matter. (***AG,* pp. 76–77**)

CHAPTER FORTY

WISDOM

1. In the last resort, let us consider the spiritual man *par excellence.* What were the temporal means of Wisdom incarnate? He preached in villages. He wrote no books—that again was a means of action too heavily weighted with matter—He founded no newspapers or reviews. His sole weapon was the poverty of preaching. He prepared no speeches, gave no addresses; He opened his lips and the clamour of wisdom, the freshness of Heaven, passed over men's hearts. What liberty! If He had wanted to convert the world by the great means of power, by *rich temporal means* . . . what could have been easier? Did not somebody offer Him all the kingdoms of the earth? *Haec omnia tibi dabo.* What an opportunity for an apostolate! The like will never be seen again. He refused it. (*RC,* **p. 48**)

2. Christian wisdom, unlike that of the philosophers, is not merely speculative, but practical as well, and directive of human life, for this life is not regulated by human measures only, but by divine as well, and thus becomes the object of that very knowledge which contemplates God. More excellent than any purely intellectual wisdom, because it attains closer to God, being a wisdom of love and union, the act of the gift of wisdom is not a self-sufficing

contemplation, but one which, as St. Paul puts it, walks toward them that are without, redeeming time. (*SP,* **pp. 144–45**)

3. A philosopher is a man in search of wisdom. Wisdom does not indeed seem to be an exceedingly widespread commodity; there has never been overproduction in this field. The greater the scarcity of what the philosopher is supposed to be concerned with, the more we feel inclined to think that society needs the philosopher badly. (*UP,* **p. 3**)

4. Above philosophy, finally, the wisdom of the saints, which is supernatural, experiences divine things in the darkness of faith, in virtue of infused love which makes them one single spirit with God. All of this is what rationalism and a certain philosophical idolatry of learned notions fail to recognize. (*BPT,* **p. 37**)

5. A knowledge which is a wisdom, even though only in a certain respect, and in a given order (in the order of sensible nature), is a thing for "enjoyment," not for "use." And all wisdom must, in one way or another, pass through the eye of a needle. (*DK,* **p. 175; CW 7, p. 186**)

6. And if it is true that the human intellect is of its very nature so weak, and is further weakened by the heritage of original sin so that it cannot attain a complete philosophic wisdom without admixture of error except with the aid of grace, then metaphysics, one might feel, could in fact only keep itself pure among men if metaphysics were from time to time strengthened from on high by the experience of things divine. (*DK,* **p. 286; CW 7, p. 305**)

7. How could it be otherwise, given that metaphysics is, among all the sorts of knowledge within the reach of our natural reason, the one that is at the summit of intellectuality? That is why, considering in unity the first truth and the ultimate principles, it towers over all the inferior sciences precisely as *wisdom*—not wisdom by way of instinct or inclination like that Wisdom which is a gift of the Holy Ghost—but wisdom by way of knowledge—scientific wisdom. A striking sign of the depths to which the intellect has fallen in our day is the tendency of many fine minds to look upon philosophy as a sort of superior and cultured dreaming, in which every man, according to his own taste, expresses his individual personality and experience in certain views upon the world. The same fine minds usually proclaim the necessity of a return to philosophic culture; and they do not see that if philosophy is not a science, and in its nature the supreme science, it is nothing at all. (*TS,* **pp. 181–82**)

8. The wisdom of salvation is not open to our achievement. We do not carry the key that opens heaven. Heaven itself must open the gates. (*SW,* **p. 9**)

9. Aristotle could have been taken over by Christian wisdom, precisely because he succeeded, through a unique bit of luck and in spite of the errors of which he certainly was not free, in establishing the essential principles of metaphysics according to the demands of pure natural reason, and because Thomas Aquinas transfigured, strengthened and deepened that metaphysics in ordering it to the superior truth of theology. As for Descartes, eager to invent a more Christian and more spiritualistic philosophy, more simple and more angelic than that of St. Thomas, he allows preoccupations which come to him through his faith and even elements which derive from theology to filter into his philosophy itself, at the expense of its solidity. But that simplified and fragile philosophy he orders only to itself; philosophy is no longer to be strengthened and illumined by theology. And thus he shatters the foremost and highest of the hierarchical subordinations, the essential order which wills that in the vital economy of Christian intelligence, metaphysics, while keeping its autonomy as queen of human sciences, and depending intrinsically on rational evidence alone, should be placed under the superior light of theological wisdom and of supernatural truth. (*DD,* **p. 90**)

10. School and college education has indeed its own world, which essentially consists of the dignity and achievement of knowledge and the intellect, that is, of the human being's root faculty. And of this world itself that knowledge which is wisdom is the ultimate goal. (*EC,* **p. 28**)

11. The purpose of elementary and higher education is not to make of the youth a truly wise man, but to equip his mind with an ordered knowledge which will enable him to advance toward wisdom in his manhood. Its specific aim is to provide him with the foundations of real wisdom, and with a universal and articulate comprehension of human achievements in science and culture, before he enters upon the definite and limited tasks of adult life in the civil community, and even while he is preparing himself for these tasks through a specialized scientific, technical, or vocational training. (*EC,* p. 48)

12. A great deal of wisdom, a great deal of contemplation will be required in order to make the immense technological developments of our day truly human and liberating. At this point one should recall Henri Bergson's observations on the mutual need which "mystics" and "mechanics" have of each other, and on the *supplément d'âme,* the "increase in soul" that must vivify the body of our civilization, a body now become too large. Contemplative life, perhaps in new forms, and made available not only to the chosen few but to the common man if he actually believes in God, will be the prerequisite of that very activity which tries to make the leaven of the gospel penetrate every portion of the world. (*RR,* p. 101)

13. There is a curious analogy between the fine arts and wisdom. Like wisdom, they are ordered to an object, which transcends man and which is of value in itself, and whose amplitude is limitless, for beauty, like being, is infinite. They are disinterested, desired for themselves, truly noble because their work taken in itself is not made in order that one may use it as a means, but in order that one may enjoy it as an end, being a true *fruit, aliquid ultimum et delectabile.* Their whole value is spiritual, and their mode of being is contemplative. For if contemplation is not their act, as it is the act of wisdom, nevertheless they aim at producing an intellectual delight, that is to say, a kind of contemplation; and they also presuppose in the artist a kind of contemplation, from which the beauty of the work must overflow. That is why we may apply to them, with due allowance, what Saint Thomas says of wisdom when he compares it to play: "The contemplation of wisdom is rightly compared to play, because of two things that one finds in play. The first is that play is delightful, and the contemplation of wisdom has the greatest delight, according to what Wisdom says of itself in Ecclesiasticus: *my spirit is sweet above honey.* The second is that the movements of play are not ordered to anything else, but are sought for themselves. And it is the same with the delights of wisdom.... That is why divine Wisdom compares

its delight to play: *I was delighted every day, playing before him in the world."* (**AS, pp. 33–34**)

14. The truth is that it does not belong to science to regulate our lives, but to wisdom; the supreme work of civilization is not in the order of transitive activity, but of immanent activity: to really make the machine, industry, and technology serve man necessitates making them the servants of an ethics of the person, of love, and of freedom. It would be a serious error to repudiate the machine, industry, and technology, things good in themselves and, far from having to be repudiated, to be used for an economy of abundance. But it is the very illusion of rationalism not to see that we must choose between the idea of an essentially industrial civilization and the idea of an essentially human one, for which industry is really only an instrument and is therefore subjected to laws that are not its own. (***IH*, p. 194; CW 11, p. 275**)

15. The wisdom of the Old Testament cries out that our personality exists ultimately only in humility, and is only saved by the divine personality. For One is a personality which gives and the other only a personality that is given.

And here is the chief point I wish to make. This supernatural wisdom is a wisdom which gives itself, which descends from the Author of Being in a torrent of generosity. Then wisdom of salvation, the wisdom of holiness is not achieved by man but given by God. It proceeds essentially not from an ascending movement on the part of the creature but from a descent of the creative Spirit. And that is why it is essentially supraphilosophical, suprametaphysical, and really divine. . . . The wisdom of the sapiential books like the wisdom of the Gospel emanates from the depths of uncreated love, stretches from one shore to the other and descends into the deepest being of the creature. And that is why it cries out in public places, on the roofs, knocks at the doors and is freely given. What is essentially secret it proclaims: if anyone thirst, let him come and drink; a secret so hidden that it hides within itself him to whom it is made known. (***SW*, pp. 16–17**)

BIBLIOGRAPHY OF MARITAIN SOURCES

Works are listed separately by author or coauthors. *Freedom in the Modern World, Distinguish to Unite or The Degrees of Knowledge,* and *Integral Humanism* occur in two versions with minor differences in English translation. Page numbers are provided after quotations for both versions, using the abbreviations *FMW, DK,* and *IH* for the earlier editions and CW for the Collected Works editions. The anthology quotations follow the CW editions.

Works by Jacques Maritain

Approaches to God. Translated by Peter O'Reilly. New York: Harper & Brothers Publishers, 1954.
Antisemitism. London: Geoffrey Bles, The Centenary Press, 1939.
Art and Faith: Letters Between Jacques Maritain and Jean Cocteau. Translated by John Coleman. New York: Philosophical Library, 1948.
Art and Poetry. Translated by E. de P. Matthews. New York: Philosophical Library, 1943.
Art and Scholasticism and the Frontiers of Poetry. Translated by Joseph W. Evans. Notre Dame, IN, and London: University of Notre Dame Press, 1974.
Bergsonian Philosophy and Thomism. The Collected Works of Jacques Maritain, vol. 1. Translated by Mabelle L. Andison in collaboration with J. Gordon Andison. Presented by Ralph McInerny. Notre Dame, IN: University of Notre

Dame Press, 2007. (This volume contains an exact reprint of the original English edition: *Bergsonian Philosophy and Thomism.* New York: Philosophical Library, 1955. Page numbers of Maritain's text are identical to the 1955 edition.)

Challenges and Renewals: Selected Readings. Selected and edited by Joseph W. Evans and Leo R. Ward. Notre Dame, IN, and London: University of Notre Dame Press, 1968.

Christianity and Democracy. Translated by Doris C. Anson. New York: Charles Scribner's Sons, 1950.

Creative Intuition in Art and Poetry. Bollingen Series 35; A. W. Mellon Lectures in the Fine Arts 1. New York: Pantheon Books, 1953.

Distinguish to Unite or The Degrees of Knowledge. Translated by Gerald B. Phelan. New York: Charles Scribner's Sons, 1959.

Distinguish to Unite or the Degrees of Knowledge. The Collected Works of Jacques Maritain, vol. 7. Translated by Gerald B. Phelan. Presented by Ralph McInerny. Notre Dame, IN: University of Notre Dame Press, 1995.

The Dream of Descartes Together with Some Other Essays. Translated by Mabelle L. Andison. New York: Philosophical Library, 1944.

Education at the Crossroads. New Haven and London: Yale University Press, 1943.

The Education of Man: The Educational Philosophy of Jacques Maritain. Edited with an Introduction by Donald and Idella Gallagher. Westport, CT: Greenwood Press, 1976.

An Essay on Christian Philosophy. Translated by Edward H. Flannery. New York: Philosophical Library, 1955.

Existence and the Existent. English version by Lewis Galantiere and Gerald B. Phelan. New York: Pantheon Books, 1948.

France, My Country: Through the Disaster. New York and Toronto: Longmans, Green and Co., 1941.

Freedom in the Modern World. Translated by Richard O' Sullivan, K. C. New York: Gordian Press, 1971.

Freedom in the Modern World. The Collected Works of Jacques Maritain, vol. 11. Translated by Richard O' Sullivan, K. C. Revised by Otto Bird. Notre Dame, IN: University of Notre Dame Press, 1996.

God and the Permission of Evil. Translated by Joseph W. Evans. Milwaukee: Bruce Publishing Co., 1966.

Integral Humanism: Temporal and Spiritual Problems of a New Christendom. Translated by Joseph W. Evans. Notre Dame, IN: University of Notre Dame Press, 1973.

Integral Humanism: Temporal and Spiritual Problems of a New Christendom. The Collected Works of Jacques Maritain, vol. 11. Translated by Joseph W. Evans. Revised by Otto Bird. Notre Dame, IN: University of Notre Dame Press, 1996.

An Introduction to Logic. London: Sheed & Ward, 1937.

An Introduction to Philosophy. London: Sheed & Ward, 1981.

An Introduction to the Basic Problems of Moral Philosophy. Translated by Cornelia N. Borgerhoff. Albany, NY: Magi Books, 1990.

A Letter on Independence. The Collected Works of Jacques Maritain, vol. 11. Translated by Otto Bird. Notre Dame, IN: University of Notre Dame Press, 1996.

The Living Thoughts of Saint Paul. The Living Thoughts Library. Edited by Alfred O. Mendel. New York and Toronto: Longmans, Green and Co., 1943.

Man and the State. Chicago: University of Chicago Press, 1952.

Moral Philosophy: An Historical and Critical Survey of the Great Systems. London: Geoffrey Bles, 1964.

Notebooks. Translated by Joseph W. Evans. Albany, NY: Magi Books, 1984. (Copyright 1984 by University of Notre Dame Press.)

On the Church of Christ: The Person of the Church and Her Personnel. Translated by Joseph W. Evans. Notre Dame, IN, and London: University of Notre Dame Press, 1973.

On the Grace and Humanity of Jesus. Translated by Joseph W. Evans. New York: Herder and Herder, 1969.

On the Philosophy of History. Edited by Joseph W. Evans. New York: Charles Scribner's Sons, 1957.

On the Use of Philosophy: Three Essays. Princeton, NJ: Princeton University Press, 1961.

The Peasant of the Garonne: An Old Layman Questions Himself About the Present Time. Translated by Michael Cuddihy and Elizabeth Hughes. New York, Chicago, San Francisco: Holt, Rinehart and Winston, 1968.

The Person and the Common Good. Translated by John F. Fitzgerald. Notre Dame, IN: University of Notre Dame Press, 1972

Philosophy of Nature. To which is added Maritain's Philosophy of the Sciences by Yves R. Simon. Translated by Imelda C. Byrne. New York: Philosophical Library, 1951.

A Preface to Metaphysics: Seven Lectures on Being. London: Sheed & Ward, 1943.

The Range of Reason. New York: Charles Scribner's Sons, 1953.

Ransoming the Time. Translated by Harry Lorin Binsse. New York: Gordian Press, 1972.

Reflections on America. New York: Charles Scribner's Sons, 1958.

Religion and Culture. In *Essays in Order*, by Jacques Maritain, Peter Wust, and Christopher Dawson, with a general introduction by Christopher Dawson, pp. 1–61. General editors Christopher Dawson and T. F. Burns. New York: Sheed & Ward, 1939.

The Responsibility of the Artist. New York: Charles Scribner's Sons, 1960.

The Rights of Man and Natural Law. Translated by Doris C. Anson. New York: Charles Scribner's Sons, 1947.

Saint Thomas and the Problem of Evil. The Aquinas Lecture, 1942. Milwaukee: Marquette University Press, 1942.
St. Thomas Aquinas. New York: Meridian Books, 1958.
Scholasticism and Politics. Translation edited by Mortimer J. Adler. London: Geoffrey Bles, 1954.
Science and Wisdom. Translated by Bernard Wall. New York: Charles Scribner's Sons, 1940.
The Sin of the Angel. Translated by William J. Rossner, SJ. Westminster, MD: Newman Press, 1959.
The Social and Political Philosophy of Jacques Maritain: Selected Readings. By Joseph W. Evans and Leo R. Ward. New York: Charles Scribner's Sons, 1955.
Theonas: Conversations of a Sage. Translated by F. J. Sheed. London and New York: Sheed & Ward, 1933.
The Things that Are Not Caesar's. Translated by J. F. Scanlan. London: Sheed & Ward, 1939.
Three Reformers: Luther—Descartes—Rousseau. London: Sheed & Ward, 1950.
The Twilight of Civilization. Translated by Lionel Landry. New York: Sheed & Ward, 1943.
Untrammeled Approaches. The Collected Works of Jacques Maritain, vol. 20. Translated by Bernard Doering. Preface by Ernst R. Korn (Heinz R. Schmitz). Notre Dame, IN: University of Notre Dame Press, 1997.

Works by Jacques and Raïssa Maritain

Liturgy and Contemplation. Translated by Joseph W. Evans. New York: P. J. Kennedy & Sons, 1960.
Prayer and Intelligence. Translated by Algar Thorgold. New York: Sheed & Ward, 1929.
The Situation of Poetry: Four Essays on the Relations between Poetry, Mysticism, Magic, and Knowledge. New York: Philosophical Library, 1955.

INDEX

The reader should consult the table of contents for chapters devoted to particular thinkers and concepts, such as "Aristotle," "faith," or "poetry." In general, the index does not duplicate the pages for these chapters under the corresponding main entry. For example, references below under "poetry" include only those page numbers found outside of the chapter "Poetry and the Poet"; in addition, the reader should consult the chapter as a whole.

absolute, 25, 38, 45, 76, 107–8, 127–28, 131, 139–40, 150, 153, 161, 173, 178, 190, 195, 198, 207, 209–11, 214, 218, 232–33, 282
abstraction, 15, 20, 24, 36, 65, 79, 115, 141–43, 151, 154, 160–61, 171, 177, 180–81, 183, 224, 227, 234, 267, 272, 281, 285
act, 34, 37, 44, 55, 111, 148, 149, 183, 189, 192, 221, 280, 296
    evil, 97, 99, 101, 103, 249
    free, 97, 110, 118–19, 121, 130–31, 219, 257
    generative, 105
    intellect and, 148, 150, 169, 181, 239
    knowledge and, 127, 131, 152–53, 227
    loving, 156, 257, 278
    moral, 119
    pleasure and, 78
    poetic, 239
    potency and, 38, 224
    pure, 37, 121, 126, 153, 204
    subjectivity and, 206, 213
agnosticism, 74, 76, 78, 131, 233, 284
American literature, 292
analogy, 32, 183, 260, 268, 296
    being and, 36–38, 128–29, 131, 223, 229, 284, 288
    of faith, 114–15
    of God as cause, 130
    of intellection, 181
    person and, 204
    proportionality and, 39, 115
angel, 16, 20, 24, 26, 43–44, 53, 73, 79–80, 88, 95, 97, 98–99, 121, 138,

140, 159, 169, 178, 181–82, 204,
208–9, 223, 225, 231, 257, 274,
278, 295
animal, 20–21, 24, 25, 29, 67, 85, 107,
118–19, 121, 125, 150, 155–56,
163, 165, 168–69, 196, 199, 200,
212, 215–16, 219, 223, 228, 236,
240, 242, 264, 271, 288, 299
political, man as, 84, 214–15, 242
anti-Semitism. *See* racism
Aquinas. *See* Thomas Aquinas, Saint
Aristotle, 16, 150, 157, 173, 181, 214,
223, 224, 251, 272, 289, 295
abstraction and, 15
Aquinas and, 50–51, 111, 148, 160,
227, 259, 281, 287
contemplation and, 252, 256
Descartes and, 52–53, 76
ethics of, 17, 110, 243
liberty of intellect in, 156, 230
metaphysics of, 15–16, 160, 295
Plato and, 53, 224
poetry and, 239
"pure nature" in, 15
truth and, 39
art, 160, 232, 261, 287. *See also* atheism,
art of; beauty, art and; being, art
in; conscience, artistic; freedom,
art and; Greeks, art and; intellect,
art as activity in; morality, as
superior to art; science(s), art and;
truth(s), artistic
activities, 61
art for art's sake (motto), 19
beauty for beauty's sake, and, 29
contemplation of, 296
contemporary, 226
dealers of, 151
ethics and, 107, 184, 243
faith and, 31, 116
Greek, 222
habitus of, 18

human stamp in, 20
imitation in, 19
individuality of, 212–13, 222
intellectual order of, 31
Machiavelli's concept of politics and,
243
metaphysics and, 177
peculiar dignity in, 19
philosophers and artists, 226, 232,
288
philosophy of, 141
Picasso's, 64
poets and artists, 124, 161, 236–38,
240
science and, 42, 166
teacher as, 88, 91, 94–95, 124
virtuous, 30, 107
atheism, 132, 139, 143, 274, 284, 290,
292. *See also* human being,
reduced to atheism
absolute, 63
art of, 64
communist, 131, 166
democracy and, 70, 72
ethics of, 132
existentialist, 52
Marxist, 174
mirror of humanity and, 63–64
Augustine, Saint, 66, 89, 251, 253, 274
Averroës, 51

beatitude, 19, 40, 51, 53, 58, 63, 66, 107,
110, 153, 188, 191, 220, 239, 253,
255, 258, 265, 276, 280, 284, 291
beauty, 39–40, 93, 240. *See also* being,
beauty and
art and, 19, 21, 23, 25, 29
being and, 154
Catholicism and, 40, 42
freedom and, 124
God and, 131
humanities and, 85

beauty (*cont.*)
  humans and, 205, 213
  infinite, 296
  love and, 26, 42
  morality and, 18, 62, 92, 112
  music and, 27
  nature and, 29, 83, 236
  object of intelligence and, 24–26, 158, 180
  truth and, 86, 124
  work and, 261
being, 19, 23, 28, 79, 82, 94, 147, 149–53, 159–61, 168, 178, 209, 218, 234, 238, 256, 271, 288. *See also* analogy, being and; existence; individuality, rational being and; intellect, union of being with; ontology
  action as epiphany of, 48
  Aristotle and, 16, 181, 224
  art in, 19, 29, 296
  beauty and, 25–26, 27
  being as, 181, 183
  cosmic, 106
  divine, 53, 104, 153, 278
  evil (non-being) and, 96–104, 211, 227
  freedom of man and, 117–18, 122–23
  God as cause of, 121, 130, 200, 220, 297
  God's, 126, 128–29, 131, 133–34, 169, 204, 218
  the good and, 96, 101
  ideas and, 148
  infinite, 24–25, 103, 128, 296
  intuition of, 52
  mystery of, 176
  natural, 94
  as object of intellectual knowledge, 32–34, 107, 115–16, 148, 153–54, 223, 227, 235, 266, 268, 278, 292
  order of, 101, 144, 253
  Parmenides on, 227
  philosophy of, 53
  rational, 24, 96, 287
  spiritual, 88
  Thomism and, 280–82, 284–85
  transcendental, 231
Bergson, 32, 106–7, 149, 223, 296

capitalism, 63, 140
Catherine of Siena, Saint, 143, 254
Catholicism, 42, 44, 47, 55, 59, 116, 166, 176, 248, 291
cause, 23, 32, 46, 88–89, 97–98, 99, 121, 128, 130, 134, 140, 152, 200, 220, 270
charity, 62–63, 67, 98, 105, 123, 157, 167, 192, 240, 248, 253, 255, 258–59, 277, 283, 290–91. *See also* love
  divine, 170
  grace and, 57
  justice and, 47, 104, 243
  primacy of, 42
Chesterton, 83
church, 21, 31, 40, 71, 116, 136, 167, 198, 254, 279
  state and, 172, 249
Cicero, 289
civilization, 21, 30, 42, 56, 59, 81, 86, 88, 111, 139–40, 145–46, 169, 170, 176, 191, 216, 243, 248, 250–51, 259–60, 282, 296–97
  Greek, 17
  "to civilize is to spiritualize," 127
common good, 65, 108, 123–24, 145, 153, 171, 194, 199, 201–2, 207, 214–15, 236, 245–46, 248–51
communism, 124, 131, 166, 173, 175, 229
Comte, Auguste, 50, 139, 274, 284
connaturality, 25, 28, 109, 121, 154, 160, 169, 253, 258

conscience, 44, 64, 70, 94, 145, 185, 189, 191, 289
   artistic, 22–23
   Christian or religious, 46–48, 248, 290
   moral, 22–23, 184, 193
   objection and, 244
   political party and, 172
   secular, 71
contemplation, 16–17, 23, 29–30, 36, 45, 58, 76–77, 115, 122, 152, 178, 224, 284, 291, 294, 296. *See also* Aristotle, contemplation and; art, contemplation of; grace, contemplation and; theology, speculative (contemplative)
   eternal, 53–54
   grace-given, 124
   highest, 123
   metaphysics and, 180
   mystical, 195
   poetry and, 236
   truth and, 48
Cross, the, 40, 42–43, 46, 58–59, 75, 100, 128, 196–97, 224, 253–54, 258, 264, 282. *See also* suffering
   Easter and, 45
   Good Friday and, 45, 57
   Resurrection and, 41, 79, 136
culture, 26, 41, 70, 82–83, 88, 91, 145–46, 166, 185, 229, 245–46, 251, 261, 274, 294

Dante, 30, 39
Darwin, 167
democracy, 124, 164. *See also* atheism, democracy and; individuality, democracy and
   education and, 94
   society and, 85
Denis the Areopagite (Pseudo-Dionysus), 131

Descartes, 17, 50, 52–53, 73, 227, 234, 263, 295. *See also* Aristotle, Descartes and; metaphysician, Descartes as
   dualism of, 169
   error of, 60
   on existence of God, 133
   intellectual intuition and, 181, 223
   modernity of, 232–33, 265, 274, 281
   reform of, 168, 268
   science and, 267–68
   on the soul, 211
destiny, 18–19, 22, 70, 82, 129, 186, 199, 202, 206, 214, 229, 247–48. *See also* eternity, life and
devil, 26, 97, 122, 136–37, 243, 292
dignity, 19, 70, 77, 83–84, 94, 111, 117, 157, 163, 165, 170, 174, 196, 198–200, 207, 209–10, 214, 216, 218, 228, 242, 289, 295
Dostoievsky, 43

education, 67, 114, 123–25, 155, 190–91, 199, 214, 286, 295. *See also* democracy, education and; freedom, education and; human being, education of; modernity, education and; science(s), education and
epistemology, 15, 73, 267. *See also* knowledge; theology, truths of
Epicureanism, 21, 110–11
eternity, 59, 62, 103–4, 113, 121, 127, 135, 178, 182, 208, 210, 219–20, 228, 236, 247, 252, 263–64, 271. *See also* time
   bliss and, 207
   common good and, 108, 143
   contemplation of, 53
   instant and, 27, 102–3, 122
   intelligibility of, 133, 283
   Jerusalem and, 41

eternity (*cont.*)
  justice and, 100, 191
  the Law and, 118, 165
  life and, 56, 61–62, 71, 113, 146, 214, 215, 248, 253, 260, 291
  light and, 167
  Love and, 291
  order of, 143, 177
  plan of, 100, 102, 122, 200
  purposes of, 100
  truths of, 153, 183, 190
  the Word and, 52
ethics, 16, 61, 168, 178, 186–87, 189–91, 239, 244, 246, 250, 260, 265, 297. *See also* act, moral; Aristotle, ethics of; art, ethics and; atheism, ethics of; beauty, morality and; conscience, moral; human being, morality and; individuality, ethics and; knowledge, ethical; metaphysics, ethics and; morality; philosopher(s), moral; science, ethics and; truth(s), moral; virtue, moral
  Cartesian, 77, 268
  Kantian, 186
  Machiavellian, 243–44
  order of, 44, 61, 67
  Thomist, 280
evil, 26, 42–43, 46, 56–57, 67, 78, 110, 118, 122–23, 136, 138, 140, 143, 146, 163–64, 166, 170, 187, 196, 200–201, 205, 242–43, 254, 290
existence, 15, 27, 59, 63, 78, 85, 113, 160, 164, 221, 225, 280, 292
  conditions of, 51, 154, 214
  contingent, 34
  essence and, 32
  evil and, 170
  human, 194, 202, 204, 206, 213–14, 216, 219–20, 236, 291
  God's, 38, 74, 76, 89, 127, 129, 132–33, 134, 218, 270, 286
  levels of, 159
  love of, 126, 217
  secular/temporal, 56, 71, 114, 140, 170, 175, 183
  soul's, 209–10, 217, 262
  subjects and, 129, 133–34, 137, 206, 209–10, 217, 238
existentialism, 21, 52, 108, 134, 148, 233, 281

faith, 40–41, 43, 46–47, 53, 70–71, 73–75, 85, 124, 135, 156, 225, 231, 233, 235, 246, 275–78, 283, 288, 291–92, 294–95. *See also* analogy, of faith; art, faith and; freedom, religion and; metaphysics, faith and; theology, faith and
  divine, 248
  flame of, 287
  gift of, 200
  Incarnate Word as root of, 52
  mechanical, 57
  mystery and, 35, 195
  negative rule of, 288
  order of, 62
  religious, 67, 109, 191, 271
  supernatural, 79
  supra-rational, 274
  virtue of, 58
Feuerbach, 274
force, 89, 110–11, 120, 168, 170, 186, 192, 200, 242, 264, 282, 288
  adverse, 42, 59, 104–5, 247, 271
  angelic, 16
  belief in, 162
  Christianity and, 139–40
  creative, 137, 201, 226
  inner, 56
  living, 20
  preservation of state and, 145, 202, 244, 249
  racism and, 166

soul, 272, 283
universe's, 145–46, 198, 212, 243
foundations, 16, 53, 69–70, 86, 161–62, 171, 183–84, 242, 295
Francis de Sales, Saint, 254
Francis of Assisi, Saint, 26
freedom, 65, 84, 94, 108, 130–31, 134, 139, 144–45, 163, 165, 169, 173, 187, 199–200, 217, 236, 244, 245, 248, 251, 253, 264, 273, 280, 297. *See also* act, free; beauty, freedom and; being, freedom of man and; human being, freedom and; morality, freedom and
   Aristotle and, 16
   art and, 29
   choice (will) and, 22–23, 64, 97, 101, 106–9, 117–21, 130, 132, 139, 141, 166, 168, 171, 190, 202, 204, 219, 220–21, 227, 241–42, 244, 256–57, 262, 286
   church and, 249
   education and, 85–87
   as era of modern, 232
   God's children and, 48
   Gospel's, 45
   personal, 92, 194, 209, 212–13, 241
   religion and, 56, 64, 116, 186, 197
   youth and, 90
Freud, 92, 229, 240, 265

genius, 16, 18, 132
geometry, 22, 73, 78–79
Gilson, Etienne, 74
God. *See* absolute; analogy, of God as cause; beauty, God and; being, divine; being, God as cause of; being, God's; charity, divine; Descartes, on existence of God; existence, God's; freedom, God's children and; grace, divine; human being, God relates to; image, of God; individuality, divine; intellect, first principles and; knowledge, God and; science(s), God's; truth(s), theological (divine); wisdom, divine
Goethe, 228
good. *See* being, the good and; common good; individuality, good and; knowledge, of good and evil; morality; ontology, good and
Gospel, 17, 43–46, 48, 59, 70–71, 74, 114, 146, 172, 176, 192–93, 198, 200, 210, 229, 249, 264, 272, 283, 296–97
grace, 43, 48, 57–58, 62, 80, 98, 101, 111, 130, 144, 161, 169, 195, 238, 257–58, 264, 278, 284, 290–91. *See also* charity, grace and; contemplation, grace-given; reason, grace aided by
   of Adam, 193, 203
   of Christ, 65, 200
   contemplation and, 124, 257
   divine, 166
   faith and, 75
   freedom of, 163
   nature and, 41, 49, 83, 94–95, 177, 198, 220, 252, 294
   reason aided by, 168
   redemptive, 123, 237, 253
   state of, 15
Greeks, 53, 163. *See also* wisdom, Greek
   art and, 222
   civilization and, 17
   optimism and, 182
   reason and, 39, 191, 226
   Thomism coincides with, 199

habitus, 18, 24, 36, 252, 267
Hegel, 50, 66, 139, 172–74, 206, 223, 263, 274, 284
Heidegger, 219

heroism, 40, 42, 70–72, 83, 115, 124, 146, 213
history, 21, 41–42, 47, 49, 58–59, 66–67, 71–72, 111, 113, 120, 144–45, 160, 164, 172–75, 180, 190, 193, 199, 201, 219, 226, 228–29, 242, 247, 247, 263–65, 270–72, 274, 283
human being, 20, 44, 65, 110, 136, 138, 156, 157, 174, 178, 187, 201, 295
  as distinct from animals, 119, 223
  education of, 86–87, 95, 155
  freedom and, 122
  God relates to, 113
  morality and, 143, 190, 192
  purity of, 42, 204
  reduced to atheism, 63
  two principles of, 78, 164, 204, 212–13
humanism, 73, 172–74, 179, 200
humanities, 83, 85–86, 102, 124, 273, 295
human person(s), 64, 66, 70, 72, 78–79, 81, 84, 86, 92, 94, 137, 145, 167, 173–74, 199, 201–3, 207–10, 213–15, 217–18, 238, 246–48, 250
  personality and, 92, 216
human rights, 24, 64–65, 70, 72, 86–87, 89–90, 110, 169–70, 173, 178, 185–86, 194–95, 210, 216, 218, 234, 242, 246, 256, 272, 284, 289

ideal, the, 126, 147–48, 150, 158, 208, 232
  Platonic Idea (essence), 20, 149
idealism, 21, 52–53, 73, 77, 80, 106, 133, 227, 232, 234, 242, 264, 284
image, 27–28, 59, 71, 91–92, 138, 200, 238, 253
  of God, 20, 63, 200, 209, 210, 218, 234
imitation, 19, 44, 91, 288
immanent, 20, 53, 89, 124, 131, 139, 149, 153, 173, 179, 208, 223, 234, 238, 247, 255, 260–61, 276, 280, 284–85, 291, 297

individuality, 39, 49, 73, 76, 84, 129, 143, 148, 159, 165, 210, 219, 220–22, 239, 241–42, 250, 272, 285
  appropriation of, 24, 146
  democracy and, 71
  divine, 113
  ethics and, 108, 243
  free, 163, 199, 245, 247
  good and, 245, 246, 258
  humanism and, 72
  knowledge of, 154, 268, 270, 287–88
  originality of, 38
  person and, 94–95, 108–9, 173–74, 183, 193, 216–18, 295
  rational being and, 24, 89, 281
  reality and, 37, 161
  singular, 141
  of soul, 59
infinity, 222
  of being, 24–25, 103, 128
  of human experience, 30
  of matter, 141
intellect, 16, 17, 24, 25, 26, 39, 43, 78, 203, 268, 271, 280, 284, 287, 289, 295. *See also* act; analogy; Aristotle, liberty of intellect in; art, intellectual order of; beauty, object of intelligence and; Descartes, intellectual intuition and; eternity, intelligibility of; intelligence; knowledge, intellectual; truth(s), intellect and
  art as activity of, 29
  first principles and, 76, 89, 116, 127, 134, 149, 229, 286
  habit or metaphysical *habitus*, 36, 177, 179, 226, 252
  imagination and, 155
  intellectualism and, 109, 151, 153, 188, 281
  intuition and, 37, 76, 147–49, 150, 154, 181, 223, 227, 230, 281

man as maker of, 18, 194
mystery of, 148, 281–82
practical, 20, 22, 30, 149, 283
primacy of, 188
pure, 204
speculative, 22, 73, 149, 189, 283
spiritual, 150, 292
as truthful faculty, 34, 36, 51, 58, 70, 92–93, 160–61
union of being with, 35, 107, 148
virtues of, 42, 62–63, 83, 109, 189, 276
as weak by nature, 294
intelligence, 21, 24, 26–27, 29–33, 37, 42–43, 50–51, 58, 60, 74–75, 78, 84–85, 90–93, 103, 114–17, 119, 126, 129, 133, 164, 166–68, 171, 182, 201, 204, 206–7, 210, 213, 216–18, 226, 232, 239, 243, 252, 260, 265, 271–72, 279, 282–84, 291, 295

Jews
  anthropology of, 163, 199
  Jesus, Mary, apostles, and prophets as, 47–48
  Mosaic revelation for, 17
  murder of, 229
John of the Cross, Saint, 48, 126

Kant, 107, 152, 181, 186, 229, 233, 269, 274, 287
Kierkegaard, 206
knowledge, 21, 28, 30, 33–34, 52, 57, 63, 79–80, 115–16, 124, 178, 217, 227, 245, 264, 277, 288. *See also* act, knowledge and; epistemology; individuality, knowledge of; theology, truths of
  abstract, 143, 151, 154
  angelic, 79, 121
  Christian, 49
  common, 176
  composite, 127
  connatural, 109, 143
  ethical, 108–9, 189
  God and, 76, 89, 100, 127, 130–31, 133, 153, 206, 219, 220 (First Cause), 228, 238, 241, 276, 286, 293
  of good and evil, 42
  human, 16, 81, 87–88, 91–92, 208, 210, 213–14, 216, 223, 230, 235, 244, 295
  of infinite, 74
  intellectual, 32, 36, 90, 92–93, 177, 287
  metaphysical, 183, 185, 263, 278, 284, 294
  natural, 36, 67, 89, 135, 142, 178, 185, 193, 201, 285
  order of, 56, 275, 283, 295
  philosophical, 82, 141, 148, 184–86, 189, 234, 235
  poetic, 21, 29, 239–40
  progress in, 155, 287
  of the real, 231–32
  reflective, 185–86
  religious, 89
  as sense, 25–26, 155, 266–70, 272
  speculative, 22, 80, 106, 108–9, 149, 160, 184, 188–89, 283–84
  Spinoza, third genus, 223
  subjective, 29
  theory of, 73, 284 (Thomist)
  of transcendentals, 86
  of universal(s), 94, 109
  wisdom and, 148, 294–95

Leibnitz, 206–7, 274
life, Christian, 139, 195, 243, 253
logic, 16, 32, 38, 85, 92, 148, 155, 158, 180, 186, 228, 262, 267
  antinomy and, 74–75, 249
  contradiction in, 34, 70, 76, 138–39, 198, 227, 231, 233, 289

logic (*cont.*)
    copula and, 159
    paradox and, 50, 69, 94, 116, 140, 164, 222, 260
    tautology and, 36
love, 15, 17, 20, 23, 26, 31, 37, 39, 42–46, 48, 53–54, 57–58, 65–67, 70–72, 83, 87, 91–92, 94, 100–101, 105, 111, 122–24, 126, 129, 131–32, 139–40, 146, 153–56, 163–65, 168, 170–71, 188, 190–92, 199–201, 204, 207–10, 213, 216–18, 219–21, 229, 234, 240–41, 244, 251, 254–59, 261–62, 264, 272, 278, 280, 283–84, 291–94, 297

Machiavelli, 242–44, 249
Malebranche, 53, 274
man. *See* animal; art, human stamp in; atheism, mirror of humanity and; beauty, humans and; being, freedom of man and; existence, human; human being; humanism; human person(s); human rights; individuality, humanism and; infinity, of human experience; knowledge, human; metaphysics, man and; modernity, man and; soul, human; wisdom, human
marriage, 19, 110
Marx, 21, 139, 229, 265, 283–84
materialism, 21, 70, 72, 85, 124, 165–66, 169, 175, 190, 208, 233, 235, 247, 292
metaphysician, 36–37, 108, 185, 196
    Descartes as, 75–77
metaphysics, 38, 52, 77, 79, 128, 130, 157, 165, 210–11, 231–32, 237–38, 286, 288. *See also* art, metaphysics and; contemplation, metaphysics and; metaphysician; philosopher(s), metaphysician as; science(s), higher (metaphysics); truth(s), metaphysical; wisdom, metaphysics and
    Aristotle and, 15–16, 160, 295
    ethics and, 106–7, 112, 185, 188
    faith and, 116
    freedom and, 118, 273–74
    idealist, 234
    man and, 167, 169–71, 204, 208–9, 212, 217–21, 294
    Marx and, 173
    separation from science, 73, 232, 263, 268, 272
    Thomist, 32, 35–36, 109–10, 275, 284–85, 295
    unity of, 66, 287
Middle Ages, 30, 67
miracles, 18, 40, 240
modernity, 114, 140, 144, 161, 175, 232, 254, 263, 279. *See also* Descartes, modernity of; existentialism; freedom, as era of modern; ontology, direction of modern thought and; philosopher(s), modern
    education and, 90
    individualism and, 219
    man and, 72, 83, 170–71
    philosophy and, 73, 76, 106, 115, 179, 231, 274, 284–85
    poetry and, 238
    publicity and, 46
    science and, 70, 82, 164, 171, 268–69
    world and, 63, 65, 68–70, 83, 111, 143, 166
morality, 18, 21, 87, 184–87, 191, 194
    ascetic, 168
    Christian, 191
    freedom and, 119, 202
    intrinsic, 249
    Kantian, 274

Machiavellian, 242
order of, 101
philosophy and, 51, 106–7, 143, 274
as superior to art, 19
mystery, 35–37, 43, 45–46, 50, 75, 77, 81, 92–93, 95, 100, 103–4, 113, 115, 117, 119, 134, 139, 148–49, 152, 156, 164, 173, 176, 181, 209–10, 216–18, 222, 234, 237–38, 240, 257–58, 260, 268, 270–71, 275, 281–82, 288, 295
mysticism. *See* mystery

Napoleon, 124
natural law, 22, 41, 185, 193–94
neo-Thomism, 280
Nietzsche, 274

ontology, 52, 74, 78, 82, 182, 184, 234, 238, 240, 272
  argument of, 133
  deontology and, 269
  direction of modern thought and, 76
  evil and, 99
  fulfillment and, 101
  good and, 133, 186
  order (structure) of, 204, 218, 220
  subjectivity and, 238
  substance as root of, 38, 212
  unity and, 209, 221

pantheism, 32, 76, 127, 131, 153, 174, 284
paradise, 25, 42, 47, 71, 90, 253, 292
paradox. *See* logic, paradox and
Parmenides, 227
Pascal, 278, 288
Paul, Saint, 94, 100, 102, 123, 244, 282, 294
personality, 24, 56, 62–63, 70, 78, 92, 94–95, 121, 164, 168–69, 178, 204, 208–10, 212–15, 257, 295, 297

philosopher(s), 16, 75–76, 123–24, 135, 139, 142–43, 149–50, 161, 171, 181–82, 185, 196, 232–33, 238, 246, 253, 260, 267, 271–72, 277, 284, 287–89, 293–94
  Aristotle as, 15
  Christian, 77, 139, 198
  Descartes as, 52
  Greek, 17
  metaphysician as, 37
  modern, 36, 85, 114
  moral, 185, 204
Picasso, 64, 151
Plato, 37, 53, 79, 91, 180–81, 224, 228
poetry, 21–23, 28–30, 92–94, 124, 161, 177, 260
prayer, 21, 83, 264, 277, 284, 292
  for the deceased, 47
  Lord's, 140
psychology, 16, 28, 66, 82, 90, 109, 111, 118, 155, 178, 187, 193, 196, 205, 219–21, 264, 271

quiddity, 36, 128, 133, 142, 159–60, 275–76

racism, 45, 47–48, 66–67, 124, 132, 164–66, 229, 290
realism, 16, 21, 53, 73, 78, 154, 162, 199, 227, 242, 281
reason, 15, 24, 30, 37, 43, 49–50, 52, 55, 59–65, 74–75, 77–80, 83–84, 89–90, 92–93, 96, 99, 107, 110, 113–16, 117, 120, 123, 128, 133, 143, 145–46, 148, 159, 166, 170, 173–74, 180–81, 183, 185–86, 214, 225, 248, 250–51, 266, 267, 276–77, 288. *See also* faith, mystery and
  absolutism of, 274
  discursive, 154

reason (*cont.*)
 erring, 289
 faith against, 73
 grace aided by, 168
 Greek, 39
 integral, 178
 law of, 168
 moral, 186–87
 natural, 53, 135, 156, 163, 168–69, 187, 196, 199–202, 223, 242, 276, 285, 287, 294–95
 political, 244–45
 principles of, 53, 157, 266
 Thomas Aquinas and, 279, 281–82
Resurrection. *See* Cross, the
Rousseau, 43, 71, 98, 169, 173, 242

saints, 15, 39, 44, 51, 55, 59, 100–101, 111, 114, 124, 172, 206, 213, 219, 234, 247, 254, 256–57, 259–60, 268, 294
Scholasticism, 60, 74, 76, 127, 142, 280
 Schoolmen (Scholastics), 24, 26, 70, 76, 221, 239, 231, 274
Schopenhauer, 223
science(s), 15, 38, 67, 70, 73–74, 82–86, 90, 116, 141–43, 146, 148, 151, 158–61, 168, 171, 178–82, 184–86, 188–89, 193, 205, 230, 232–33, 244, 263–64, 273, 275–76, 279–80, 283
 art and, 42, 62, 166
 education and, 82
 ethics and, 108–9, 297
 God's, 102–3
 higher (metaphysics), 16, 176–77, 183, 284–87
 history as, 141
 lower, 196, 294
 philosophy and, 20, 35, 66, 76–80, 225, 295–96

"science of vision," 102, 133–34
 theology and, 60, 75, 102
 truth and, 63, 170, 288
sin, 22, 33, 45–46, 59, 82, 98, 100, 102–3, 105, 107, 113, 122–23, 137, 146, 151, 165, 191–93, 200, 203, 220, 227, 235, 264, 291, 294
slavery, 17, 18, 146, 168, 171, 180, 227, 229, 242
socialism, 173
Socrates, 112, 124
soul, 27, 59, 61, 80, 88–89, 104, 110, 115, 125, 127, 146, 157, 159, 167, 180, 190–92, 195–97, 211, 219, 225, 231, 240, 254, 256–57, 259–62, 264, 267, 272, 275–77, 283, 296
 Christian's, 30, 47–49, 57
 communication of, 39, 78
 human, 19–21, 70, 91–92, 104, 111–12, 150, 171, 202, 208–12, 214, 237, 261–62, 265, 271, 285
 immortal, 200, 214–15, 220, 270
 spiritual, 25, 43, 78–79, 150, 156, 195, 203–4, 212, 217, 237–38, 252, 255
 transfigured, 258
 and unity with body, 33, 78–79, 212, 221–22, 257
speculation, 16, 22, 25, 51, 61, 73, 76, 80, 106, 108–9, 116, 149, 160, 177–78, 184, 188–89, 226, 238, 268, 283–84, 289, 293
Spinoza, 32, 37, 57, 223
Stoicism, 23, 44, 110–11, 218
suffering, 28, 45–46, 51, 100–101, 104–5, 111, 115, 137, 163–64, 192, 200, 231, 237, 251, 258, 264, 267, 282, 290, 292

supernatural, 15, 26, 35, 43, 49–50, 52,
62, 67, 79–80, 82, 97, 114–15, 123,
166, 193, 198, 225, 243, 252–54,
258, 265, 273, 276, 290, 294–95, 297
  order of, 60, 77, 114, 128, 207, 225, 240

theologian(s), 110, 178, 193, 253, 281
theology, 53, 60, 70–71, 253
  faith and, 46, 58, 288
  order of, 77, 82
  speculative (contemplative), 80, 116,
    255, 260, 268
  system of, 60, 196
  truths of, 51, 60, 135, 197, 287, 295
  virtues of, 42, 45, 58, 291
  wisdom and, 50–51, 285, 295
Theresa of Avila, Saint, 236
Thomas Aquinas, Saint, 16, 22, 24, 32,
    35, 50–51, 54, 60, 75, 88, 98,
    102–3, 106–7, 109, 111, 118, 123,
    130–31, 134, 152, 154–55,
    167–68, 183, 188, 204–5, 211–12,
    236, 253, 259, 263, 272, 274–75,
    277, 287, 295–96
Thomism, 22, 33, 36, 51, 117, 120, 127,
    148, 152, 164, 199, 227, 268, 272,
    275, 285
time, 20, 27, 33, 41, 58–59, 62, 100,
    102–4, 121–22, 135–40, 153, 164,
    182–83, 190, 209–10, 214, 217,
    221, 231, 233, 237, 247–48, 252,
    270–72, 283, 285, 292
transcendence, 20, 25, 26–27, 29, 32,
    43–44, 62, 64, 66, 70, 84, 104, 108,
    116, 121, 123, 130, 145, 148, 151,
    170, 174, 181, 191, 195, 206,
    207–8, 214–15, 217, 220, 223, 237,
    242, 247, 259–60, 270, 274, 280,
    282, 284, 290, 296
transcendentals, 21, 25, 37–38, 85, 107,
    115, 129–30, 147, 154, 168–69,
    183, 224, 231, 257

truth(s), 62–64, 79, 91, 108, 119, 129, 133,
    135, 150–52, 154, 183–85, 192, 200,
    205, 209–10, 228–29, 282–83, 291
  artistic, 23
  basic, 47, 207, 275, 278, 294
  Christian, 47
  eternal, 153, 183, 190, 199
  existential, 148, 235
  factual, 63
  friendship and, 291
  geometric, 22, 75
  Greeks and, 17
  highest, 50, 94, 284, 295
  instrument of, 60, 276
  intellect and, 34
  love of, 44, 70
  metaphysical, 75, 179, 273
  moral, 191
  mysterious, 45
  philosophical, 52–53, 143, 273, 281
  revealed, 60
  rules of, 232
  source of, 89
  supra-rational (supernatural), 264,
    273–74, 295
  theological (divine), 45, 51, 60, 71,
    79, 277, 279
  Truth itself, 26, 39, 41–42, 44, 46,
    48, 51, 57–57, 63, 85–86, 97, 110,
    113, 116, 118, 124, 129–30, 138,
    148–49, 156–57, 165–70, 177, 179,
    186, 189, 224, 233, 241, 245, 253

Vatican II (Council), 156
virtue, 18, 20, 25, 29–30, 44, 61, 64, 71,
    83, 88, 107, 110, 118, 143, 167–69,
    185, 187, 194, 209, 214–15, 221,
    242–46, 248–50, 252, 271, 277,
    283, 285
  moral, 22–23, 42, 62, 81, 84, 109,
    189, 257–58
  theological, 31, 42, 58, 276, 291

Wilde, Oscar, 22
wisdom, 23, 44, 66, 70, 77, 100, 135,
　　141–42, 148, 181, 190, 223–24,
　　226, 230, 252, 255–56, 258, 280
　ancient, 242
　Christian, 67, 130, 207, 275
　creative, 200
　divine, 50–51, 89, 102–3, 123, 274–76
　Greek, 145
　human, 16, 48–50, 60, 86, 94,
　　114–15, 123, 146, 148, 151, 171
　metaphysics and, 36, 50, 180, 268,
　　275
　mystical, 195, 197
　political, 244
　practical, 59
　principles of, 16
　profane, 48, 80, 207, 263–64
　sovereign, 23
　superior, 53, 113, 185, 256, 271,
　　283–84
　Thomist, 285

MARIO O. D'SOUZA, C.S.B., is dean emeritus of the Faculty of Theology at the University of St. Michael's College, Toronto, where he holds the Basilian Fathers Chair in Religion and Education.

JONATHAN R. SEILING is an independent scholar affiliated with the University of Toronto.

www.ingramcontent.com/pod-product-compliance
Lightning Source LLC
Chambersburg PA
CBHW050430240426
43661CB00055B/2336